THE PSALMS OF SOLOMON

Society of Biblical Literature

Early Judaism and Its Literature

Rodney A. Werline, Editor

Editorial Board
Mark J. Boda
George J. Brooke
Esther Glickler Chazon
Steven D. Fraade
James S. McLaren

Number 40

THE PSALMS OF SOLOMON

LANGUAGE, HISTORY, THEOLOGY

Edited by
Eberhard Bons and Patrick Pouchelle

SBL Press
Atlanta

Copyright © 2015 by SBL Press

All rights reserved. No part of this work may be reproduced or transmitted in any form or by any means, electronic or mechanical, including photocopying and recording, or by means of any information storage or retrieval system, except as may be expressly permitted by the 1976 Copyright Act or in writing from the publisher. Requests for permission should be addressed in writing to the Rights and Permissions Office, SBL Press, 825 Houston Mill Road, Atlanta, GA 30329 USA.

Library of Congress Cataloging-in-Publication Data

The Psalms of Solomon : language, history, theology / edited by Eberhard Bons and Patrick Pouchelle.
    p. cm. — (Society of Biblical Literature. Early Judaism and its literature ; no. 40)
    Includes bibliographical references and index.
    Summary: "This volume includes revised essays originally presented at the First International Meeting on the Psalms of Solomon. Researchers whose work focuses on the Psalms of Solomon, experts on the Septuagint, and scholars of Jewish Hellenistic literature take a fresh look at debates surrounding the text. Authors engage linguistic, historical, and theological issues including the original language of the Psalms, their historical setting, and their theological intentions with the goal of expanding our understanding of first-century BCE Jewish theology"— Provided by publisher
    ISBN 978-1-62837-042-3 (paper binding : alk. paper) — ISBN 978-1-62837-043-0 (electronic format) — ISBN 978-1-62837-044-7 (hardcover binding : alk. paper)
    1. Psalms of Solomon—Criticism, interpretation, etc.—Congresses. I. Bons, Eberhard, editor. II. Pouchelle, Patrick, editor.
    BS1830.P73P73 2015
    229'.912—dc23
    2015006067

Printed on acid-free, recycled paper conforming to
ANSI/NISO Z39.48-1992 (R1997) and ISO 9706:1994
standards for paper permanence.

Contents

Abbreviations vii

Introduction
    Eberhard Bons and Patrick Pouchelle 1

The Psalms of Solomon as a Historical Source for the Late
    Hasmonean Period
    Benedikt Eckhardt..7

Reflections on the Original Language of the Psalms of Solomon
    Jan Joosten..31

Philosophical Vocabulary in the Psalms of Solomon: The Case
    of Ps. Sol. 9:4
    Eberhard Bons 49

Some Thoughts on and Implications from Genre Categorization in
    the Psalms of Solomon
    Brad Embry..59

Perceptions of the Temple Priests in the Psalms of Solomon
    Kenneth Atkinson 79

Die Rede vom Schlaf in den Psalmen Salomos und ihr traditions-
    geschichtlicher Hintergrund
    Sven Behnke...97

Prayers for Being Disciplined: Notes on παιδεύω and παιδεία in
    the Psalms of Solomon
    Patrick Pouchelle...115

The Formation of the Pious Person in the Psalms of Solomon
  Rodney A. Werline 133

What Would David Do? Messianic Expectation and Surprise in
  Ps. Sol. 17
  Joseph L. Trafton 155

Responses
  Kenneth Atkinson 175

Bibliography 193
Contributors 211
Index of Ancient Sources 215
Index of Modern Authors 225

Abbreviations

AB	Anchor Bible
ABD	*Anchor Bible Dictionary.* Edited by David Noel Freedman. 6 vols. New York: Doubleday, 1992.
ABRL	Anchor Bible Reference Library
AcBib	Academia Biblica
AGJU	Arbeiten zur Geschichte des antiken Judentums und des Urchristentums
A.J.	Josephus, *Antiquitates judaicae*
AJEC	Ancient Judaism and Early Christianity
AJP	*American Journal of Philology*
ALGHJ	Arbeiten zur Literatur und Geschichte des Hellenistischen Judentums
Am.	Ovid, *Amores*
AnBib	Analecta Biblica
ANRW	*Aufstieg und Niedergang der römischen Welt.* Edited by Hildegard Temporini and Wolfgang Haase. Berlin: de Gruyter, 1972–.
Ant. Rom.	Dionysus of Halicarnassus, *Antiquitates Romanae*
APOT	*The Apocrypha and Pseudepigrapha of the Old Testament in English.* Edited by Robert H. Charles. 2 vols. Oxford: Clarendon Press, 1913.
BDAG	Danker, Frederick W., Walter Bauer, William F. Arndt, and F. Wilbur Gingrich. *Greek-English Lexicon of the New Testament and Other Early Christian Literature.* 3rd ed. Chicago: University of Chicago Press, 2000.
Bibl.	Diodorus Siculus, *Bibliotheca historica*
B.J.	Josephus *Bellum judaicum*
BSGRT	Bibliotheca scriptorum Graecorum et Romanorum Teubneriana
BWANT	Beiträge zur Wissenschaft vom Alten und Neuen Testament

BZ	*Biblische Zeitschrift*
BZAW	Beihefte zur Zeitschrift für die alttestamentliche Wissenschaft
CBET	Contributions to Biblical Exegesis and Theology
CBQ	*Catholic Biblical Quarterly*
ConBNT	Coniectanea Biblica: New Testament Series
CQS	Companion to the Qumran Scrolls
CRINT	Compendia Rerum Iudaicarum ad Novum Testamentum
CSSCA	Cambridge Studies in Social and Cultural Anthropology
CurBR	*Currents in Biblical Research*
Cyr.	Xenophon, *Cyropaedia*
DBSup	*Supplément au Dictionnaire de la Bible*. Edited by Louis Pirot and André Robert. Paris: Letouzey et Ané, 1928–.
DCLY	Deuterocanonical and Cognate Literature Yearbook
DJD	Discoveries in the Judaean Desert
DNP	*Der neue Pauly: Enzyklopädie der Antike*. Edited by Hubert Cancik and Helmuth Schneider. Stuttgart: Metzler, 1996–.
DPA	*Dictionnaire des philosophes antiques*. Edited by R. Goulet. Paris: CNRS, 1989–.
DSD	*Dead Sea Discoveries*
Ecl.	Stobaeus, *Eclogae*
EKKNT	Evangelisch-katholischer Kommentar zum Neuen Testament
EJL	Early Judaism and its Literature
Elem. Apo.	Paulus Alexandrinus, *Elementa apotelesmatica*
Ep.	Nilus Ancyranus, *Epistulae*
Epict. diss	Arrian, *Epicteti disssertationes*
Epigr Graec.	G. Kaibel. *Epigrammata Graeca ex lapidibus conlecta*. Berlin: Reimer, 1878.
Evag.	Isocrates, *Evagores* (*Or.* 9)
FBBS	Facet Books Biblical Series
fr.	fragment
FGrHis	*Die Fragmente der griechischen Historiker*
FRLANT	Forschungen zur Religion und Literatur des Alten und Neuen Testaments
Geogr.	Strabo, *Geographica*
HBS	Herders Biblische Studien
Hist. Rom.	Cassius Dio, *Historia Romana*
Historia	*Historia: Zeitschrift für Alte Geschichte*
Il.	Homer, *Ilias*

Inst.	Quintilian, *Institutio oratoria*
JAJSup	Journal of Ancient Judaism Supplements
JBL	*Journal of Biblical Literature*
JCTC	Jewish and Christian Texts in Contexts and Related Studies
JSHRZ	Jüdische Schriften aus hellenistisch-römischer Zeit. Edited by Werner G. Kümmel. Gütersloh: Gerd Mohn, 1973–.
JSJ	*Journal for the Study of Judaism in the Persian, Hellenistic, and Roman Periods*
JSJSup	Supplements to the Journal for the Study of Judaism
JSNT	*Journal for the Study of the New Testament*
JSOTSup	Journal for the Study of the Old Testament: Supplement Series
JSP	*Journal for the Study of the Pseudepigrapha*
JSQ	*Jewish Studies Quarterly*
LAVTG	Fritzsche, Otto Fridolin, ed. *Libri Apocryphi Veteris Testamenti Graece*. Leipzig: Brockhaus, 1871.
LEH	Lust, Johan, Erik Eynikel, and Katrin Hauspie, eds. *Greek-English Lexicon of the Septuagint*. Rev. ed. Stuttgart: Deutsche Bibelgessellschaft, 2003.
LSTS	Library of Second Temple Studies
LUÅ	Lunds universitets årsskrift
Luc.	Plutarch, *Lucullus*
LSJ	Liddell, Henry George, Robert Scott, Henry Stuart Jones. *A Greek-English Lexicon*. 9th ed. with revised supplement. Oxford: Clarendon, 1996.
LXX	Septuagint
LXX.D	Karrer, Martin and Wolfgang Kraus, eds. *Septuaginta Deutsch: Das griechische Alte Testament in deutscher Übersetzung*. 2nd ed. Stuttgart: Deutsche Bibelgesellschaft, 2010.
LXX.D-E	Karrer, Martin and Wolfgang Kraus, eds. *Septuaginta Deutsch: Erläuterungen und Kommentare*. 2 vols. Stuttgart: Deutsche Bibelgesellschaft, 2011.
MAAR	Memoirs of the American Academy in Rome
MMT	Miqṣat Maʿaśê ha-Torah (4QMMT)
MS(S)	manuscript(s)
MSU	Mitteilungen des Septuaginta-Unternehmens
MT	Masoretic Text of the Hebrew Bible

NETS	*New English Translation of the Septuagint*. Edited by Albert Pietersma and Benjamin G. Wright. Oxford: Oxford University Press, 2007.
NovT	*Novum Testamentum*
NovTSup	Novum Testamentum Supplements
NTS	*New Testament Studies*
OLA	Orientalia Lovaniensia Analecta
OTP	*The Old Testament Pseudepigrapha*. Edited by James H. Charlesworth. 2 vols. New York: Doubleday, 1983, 1985.
OTS	Augsburg Old Testament Studies
PMTKA	Palingenesia: Monographien und Texte zur klassischen Altertumswissenschaft
PO	*Patrologia Orientalis*
Pomp.	Plutarch, *Pompeius*
Ps. Sol	Psalms of Solomon
PTSDSSP	The Princeton Theological Seminary Dead Sea Scrolls Project
PVTG	Studia in Veteris Testamenti Graece
QC	*Qumran Chronicle*
Rahlfs	Rahlfs, Alfred and Robert Hanhart, eds. *Septuaginta: Id est Vetus Testamentum graece iuxta LXX interpretes*. Rev. ed. Stuttgart: Deutsche Bibelgesellschaft, 2006.
RBL	*Review of Biblical Literature*
resp.	respectively
RevQ	*Revue de Qumran*
RRJ	*Review of Rabbinic Judaism*
SAM	Studies in Ancient Monarchies
SBEC	Studies in the Bible and Early Christianity
SCS	Septuagint and Cognate Studies
Sib. Or.	Sibylline Oracle
SJ	Studia Judaica
SJC	*Scripta Judaica Cracoviensia*
SJLA	Studies in Judaism in Late Antiquity
SJMT	Studies in Judaism in Modern Times
SOLZ	Sonderabzug aus der orientalischen Litteratur-Zeitung Jahrgang
SQAW	Schriften und Quellen der alten Welt
SR	*Studies in Religion*
STDJ	Studies on the Texts of the Desert of Judah

SUNVA	Skrifter utgitt av det norske videnskaps-akademi i Oslo. Historisk-filosofisk klasse
SVTG	Septuaginta: Vetus Testamentum Graecum Auctoritate Academiae Scientiarum Gottingensis editum
SVTP	Studia in Veteris Testamenti Pseudepigrapha
Sym	Symmachus
SymS	Symposium Series
T. Mos.	Testament of Moses
TDNT	*Theological Dictionary of the New Testament*. Edited by Gerhard Kittel and Gerhard Friedrich. Translated by Geoffrey W. Bromiley. 10 vols. Grand Rapids: Eerdmans, 1964–1976.
TSAJ	Texte und Studien zum antiken Judentum
TUGAL	Texte und Untersuchungen zur Geschichte der altchristlichen Literatur
Vit. philos.	Diogenes Laërtius, *Vitae philosophorum*
VT	*Vetus Testamentum*
VTSup	Supplements to Vetus Testamentum
WUNT	Wissenschaftliche Untersuchungen zum Neuen Testament
ZNW	*Zeitschrift für die neutestamentliche Wissenschaft und die Kunde der älteren Kirche*
ZPE	*Zeitschrift für Papyrologie und Epigraphik*
ZWT	*Zeitschrift für wissenschaftliche Theologie*

Introduction

Eberhard Bons and Patrick Pouchelle

The idea of organizing a conference on the Psalms of Solomon began in autumn, 2012, during a telephone conversation between two Old Testament scholars, Eberhard Bons (University of Strasbourg, France) and Markus Witte (Humboldt Universität, Berlin, Germany). Both of them had students who were working on the same neglected corpus of the Psalms of Solomon: Patrick Pouchelle, who had written a master's thesis on Ps. Sol. 13, and Sven Behnke, who was preparing a doctoral dissertation on Ps. Sol. 14. An initial contact between the two young scholars was soon accomplished. Patrick Pouchelle and Sven Behnke were convinced that the corpus of the Psalms of Solomon still does not receive as much attention as it deserves in the context of biblical studies. Hence, they decided to organize an international conference with a twofold aim: to take a fresh look at established views and to develop perspectives for future research. This First International Meeting on the Psalms of Solomon convened in Strasbourg, France, in June, 2013.

Indeed, when, in 1994,[1] Joseph L. Trafton presented the *status quaestionis* of the Psalms of Solomon, he defined a framework for future research. In particular, he formulated the following needs:

(1) A new critical edition.
(2) Fresh consideration of the authorship because the arguments in favor of Pharisaic authorship turn out to be invalid and no other identification has convinced the community of scholars.[2]

---

1. Joseph L. Trafton, "The *Psalms of Solomon* in Recent Research," *JSP* 12 (1994): 3–19.
2. Robert B. Wright ("The *Psalms of Solomon*: The Pharisees and the Essenes," in

(3) New methods to be used in order to analyze the Psalms of Solomon, for example, literary criticism.
(4) New monographs and new commentaries.

In the last twenty years, these objectives have been partly achieved. Surprisingly, whereas there is a degree of renewal in studies of the Pseudepigrapha as well as of the Septuagint, the corpus of the Psalms of Solomon remains the poor cousin of current research.

Indeed, the long-awaited critical edition by Robert B. Wright, published in 2007, has met with a mixed response.[3] That is why the Göttingen Unternehmen has decided to edit a new edition. During the 2013 colloquium in Strasbourg, Felix Albrecht explained the need for a new edition in an English translation of a previous contribution in German.[4]

The authorship of the Psalms of Solomon is still debated. Mikael Winninge argued that this collection is of Pharisaic origin, or that it is at least the "ultimate link between the Chasidim and the Pharisees."[5] On the other hand, Kenneth Atkinson contends that the authorship cannot be deter-

---

1972 Proceedings for the International Organization for Septuagint and Cognate Studies and the Society of Biblical Literature Pseudepigrapha Seminar, ed. Robert A. Kraft, SCS 2 [Missoula, MT: Society of Biblical Literature, 1972], 136–54) promoted the identification with the Essenes. However, this identification is also problematic; cf. Trafton, "The *Psalms of Solomon* in Recent Research," 12.

3. Cf., e.g., Joel Willitts, "Review of Robert. B. Wright, *The Psalms of Solomon: A Critical Edition of the Greek Text*," RBL (2009), http://www.bookreviews.org/pdf/6010_6722.pdf; Rodney A. Werline, "Review of Robert. B. Wright, *The Psalms of Solomon: A Critical Edition of the Greek Text*," RBL (2009), http://www.bookreviews.org/pdf/6010_6398.pdf; and Felix Albrecht, "Zur Notwendigkeit einer Neuedition der Psalmen Salomos," in *Die Septuaginta: Text, Wirkung, Rezeption: 4. Internationale Fachtagung veranstaltet von Septuaginta Deutsch (LXX. D), Wuppertal 19.–22. Juli 2012*, ed. Wolfgang Kraus and Siegfried Kreuzer, WUNT 1/325 (Tübingen: Mohr Siebeck, 2014), 110–23.

4. Albrecht, "Zur Notwendigkeit."

5. Mikael Winninge, *Sinners and the Righteous: A Comparative Study of the Psalms of Solomon and Paul's Letters*, ConBNT 26 (Stockholm: Almqvist & Wiksell, 1995), 180. But his conclusions have not been widely accepted, cf. Joseph, L Trafton, "Review of Mikael Winninge, *Sinners and the Righteous: A Comparative Study of the Psalms of Solomon and Paul's Letters*," RBL (2009), http://www.bookreviews.org/pdf/2815_1253.pdf. On the contrary, cf. Jens Schröter, "Gerechtigkeit und Barmherzigkeit: das Gottesbild der Psalmen Salomos in seinem Verhältnis zu Qumran und Paulus," NTS 44 (198): 557–77.

mined precisely.⁶ Several essays in this volume will refer to the full range of possibilities and problems related to this issue.

New methods have been applied to the Psalms of Solomon, mainly by Rodney A. Werline, who also noticed similarities between these texts and a genre he defined as "penitential prayer."⁷ However, one of the major desiderata still is a literary analysis.⁸

Finally, to the best of our knowledge, apart from the critical edition by Robert B. Wright, only two important monographs have been published, namely, by Mikael Winninge and Kenneth Atkinson.⁹ Atkinson's work made significant contributions to the task of relating the psalms to historical events of the era while avoiding the overly ambitious approaches of the old commentary by Ryle and James.¹⁰

These and other open questions were the major reasons for organizing the conference. Admittedly, it was not our intention to answer all the long-debated, open questions. On the contrary, our purpose was to focus scholarly attention on this corpus whose theological and literary importance is

---

6. Although Kenneth Atkinson (*I Cried to the Lord: A Study of the Psalms of Solomon's Historical Background and Social Setting*, JSJSup 84 [Leiden: Brill, 2004], 220–21) asserts that "the community of the *Psalms of Solomon* was theologically closer to the Pharisees than to the Sadduccees" and that there is "no evidence to connect these poems with this religious sect." As for the Essenes attribution, he noticed that "many of the Dead Sea scrolls were not written by the Essenes, but were composed by unknown authors who apparently did not belong to the Essenes." In a nutshell, the Psalms of Solomon cannot be attributed to any known Jewish religious sect.

7. Rodney. A Werline, *Penitential Prayer in Second Temple Judaism: The Development of a Religious Institution*, EJL 13 (Atlanta: Scholars Press, 1985); idem, "The Experience of God's *Paideia* in the *Psalms of Solomon*," in *Experientia, Volume 2: Linking Text and Experience*, ed. Colleen Shantz and Rodney A. Werline, EJL 35 (Atlanta: Society of Biblical Literature, 2012), 17–44. See also, e.g., Robert R. Hann, "The Community of the Pious: The Social Setting of the *Psalms of Solomon*," SR 17 (1988): 169–89.

8. Rollin J. Blackburn ("Hebrew Poetic Devices in the Greek Text of the *Psalms of Solomon*," [PhD diss., Temple University, 1995]) has done such research, but his dissertation is still unpublished.

9. Winninge, *Sinners and the Righteous*; Atkinson, *I Cried to the Lord*.

10. Atkinson, *I Cried to the Lord*. See also idem, "On the Herodian Origins of the Militant Davidic Messianism at Qumran: New Light from *Psalms of Solomon* 17," JBL 118 (1999): 435–60; Herbert E. Ryle and Montague R. James, ΨΑΛΜΟΙ ΣΟΛΟΜΩΝΤΟΣ: *Psalms of the Pharisees, commonly called The Psalms of Solomon* (Cambridge: Cambridge University Press, 1891).

beyond doubt. Therefore, we invited some of the most renowned experts on the Psalms of Solomon, asking them to take a fresh look at frequently held assumptions. Concretely, the articles collected in the present volume deal with the following subjects:

(1) The question of the date of the Psalms of Solomon and their importance as a historical source for the Hasmonean period is addressed afresh by Benedikt Eckhardt. He explains the bias of scholars who determined the date of composition of these psalms. Obviously, modern approaches to the Psalms of Solomon bear the traces of nineteenth century research, particularly negative statements about Jewish piety as well as those concerning putative oriental despotism. Needless to say, these approaches should be dismissed. For Eckhardt, the date of composition of the Psalms of Solomon is still an open question and modern scholars should be careful about using them as a historical source.

(2) The question of the original language of the Psalms of Solomon also needs fresh consideration. Eberhard Bons and Jan Joosten independently address this issue. In their view, the former consensus about a Hebrew *Vorlage* should be challenged. Jan Joosten provides an overview of words and expressions that would suggest a redaction of the Psalms of Solomon in Greek. He concludes by putting forward a new hypothesis concerning the provenance of these psalms. For him, the Psalms of Solomon display several points of contact with the Greek vocabulary of the revisions of the Septuagint. Eberhard Bons claims that the vocabulary of Ps. Sol. 9:4 is to be explained against the background of contemporary Greek Stoic philosophy. Therefore, the words in question could hardly be retranslated into Hebrew.

(3) Brad Embry offered a paper in which he addressed the issue of the genre of the Psalms of Solomon. For him, the genre has more in common with biblical prophecy and Deuteronomic thought than with psalmic prayer or biblical wisdom. The corpus focuses on a specific view of history, one which describes covenantal infidelity, God's judgment, and the restoration of Israel.

(4) As stated above, a crucial question concerns the community that lay behind the Psalms of Solomon. Of course, it is difficult to give clear-cut answers. However, by studying the corpus itself, one can arrive at a better understanding of this community. Kenneth Atkinson, who argues that the Psalms of Solomon were anti-Sadducean,[11] analyzed the way in which the

---

11. Atkinson, *I Cried to the Lord*, 221.

psalms perceive the temple priests. Such an analysis brings new insights into the community and the circumstances in which the Psalms of Solomon originated.

(5) Much work remains to be done on key terms and metaphors in the psalms; in fact, little has been accomplished in this area. Two more articles deal with specific topics of the Psalms of Solomon. Sven Behnke focuses on the imagery of sleep in the Psalms of Solomon, which has negative connotations. It is used to emphasize the difference between the righteous and the wicked. Patrick Pouchelle addresses the question of παιδεία in the Psalms of Solomon. He shows how the concept that lies behind this word is theological and less connected to historical events than expected.

(6) New methods may also offer fresh perspectives on the interpretation of these psalms. Rodney A. Werline analyzes the Psalms of Solomon using anthropological methods. He argues that the psalms belong to an emotional liturgy in which the community declares God's righteousness and the condemnation of the wicked. The aim of this liturgy is to invite the community to live a righteous life. Therefore, the psalms have an educational rather than a didactical goal.

(7) Last but not least, one of the main causes of interest in the Psalms of Solomon lies in the fact that it is an important witness of messianic expectation in the last century BCE. However, Joseph L. Trafton notices that this source, mainly Ps. Sol. 17, has been neglected in recent research. Furthermore, he states that the biblical texts alluded to by the authors of the Psalms of Solomon are completely different from those quoted by the Essenes. Hence, if the χριστός[12] described by Ps. Sol. 17 is a Davidic king, it is not clear why the author alludes sometimes to non-Davidic Scriptures. Trafton rounds off his contribution by raising many fundamental questions that should be taken into account by anyone wishing to study messianism in the Psalms of Solomon in particular and in the Judaism of the Second Temple in general.

At the conclusion of this colloquium, we were able to say that some long-held opinions had been challenged, particularly concerning the historical context, the original language, and messianic expectations. An analysis of content sheds some new light on the community, even if it appears too risky to draw definitive conclusions.

---

12. I.e., the Messiah.

Needless to say, some questions remain unaddressed. For example, research should be done on the Syriac version and its relationship to the Greek texts of the Psalms of Solomon. Moreover, the influence of this corpus on the New Testament, particularly on the theology of Paul, should receive further consideration. However, we hope that the present book will draw the attention of scholars to this important but neglected corpus. Our wish is that the articles will engender further discussions in biblical research on this unknown Jewish community behind the Psalms of Solomon.

In publishing the proceedings of the colloquium, we would like to express our gratitude to the EA 4377, "Équipe d'accueil en Théologie Catholique," of the University of Strasbourg, and to the GIS Monde Germanique "Groupement d'intérêts scientifiques," an organization of the French Research Agency that fosters academic cooperation between France and Germany. This has allowed Sven Behnke and Patrick Pouchelle to fullfill their dream of organizing a small but ambitious conference with the most eminent specialists of their beloved corpus. Our gratitude also goes to the MISHA (Maison Interuniversitaire des Sciences de l'Homme, Alsace), and particularly to Ms. Magali Vogt who provided the logistical support for this event. We are also grateful to the contributors who enthusiastically accepted the invitation.

Rodney A. Werline not only proofread some of the articles written by non-English-speaking authors but also made possible the publication of the proceedings in the Society of Biblical Literature series Early Judaism and Its Literature. The editors are particularly indebted to him for his invaluable advice.

The Psalms of Solomon as a Historical Source for the Late Hasmonean Period

Benedikt Eckhardt

1. Introduction

The Psalms of Solomon are an important historical source for the history of late Second Temple Judaism. While most scholars would probably agree with that statement, it is worth reconsidering what it actually means. Is it their content that marks the Psalms of Solomon as a historical source? Or, is it only their presumable date? For what sort of historical knowledge can they be regarded as a source? Or, in short, what do they prove? And, of primary importance, what is meant by "historical source"?

This is an old question that has found many different answers in the course of time. Nineteenth-century definitions of historical sources were quite rigid. For Droysen, sources were "oral or written transmissions with the aim of conveying historical knowledge."[1] The definition given by Bernheim is more complex: sources are "results of human activities that were either originally designed for the perception and the detection of historical facts, or are at least especially apt for that purpose due to their existence, their genesis and other circumstances."[2] Both definitions would probably rule out the Psalms of Solomon as a source, but such approaches can no

---

1. Droysen: "mündliche oder schriftliche Überlieferung zum Zweck, historische Kenntnis zu verschaffen." Cited by Ahasver von Brandt, *Werkzeug des Historikers: Eine Einführung in die Historischen Hilfswissenschaften*, 16th ed. (Stuttgart: Kohlhammer, 2003), 48. All translations from the German are mine.

2. Bernheim: "Resultate menschlicher Betätigungen, welche zur Erkenntnis und zum Nachweis geschichtlicher Tatsachen entweder ursprünglich bestimmt oder doch vermöge ihrer Existenz, Entstehung und sonstiger Verhältnisse vorzugsweise geeignet sind." Cited by von Brandt, *Werkzeug des Historikers*, 48.

longer be upheld; they have been demolished, inter alia, by the history of mentalities.[3] A well-known example is the study of Michel Vovelle on "piété baroque et déchristianisation," where he argues that the declining weight of funeral candles provided for in testaments indicates a change in religious mentalities.[4] So, if candles are historical sources, surely the Psalms of Solomon are, although they were hardly written to tell us what happened, but rather to explain the reasons for what has happened to those who had witnessed it.

However, the example of Vovelle's study is also a reminder of the truism that the definition of something as a historical source depends on the uses one intends to make of that source. For the historical agents involved and even for most historians, a candle presumably remains just a candle. This raises the question under what circumstances and with what interest in mind historians declare a prayer book like the Psalms of Solomon to be a source, and even a source of prime importance, for the late Hasmonean period.

In an article originally published in 1965, Joshua Efron expressed his view on this matter.[5] According to him, German scholars of the nineteenth century originally used the Psalms of Solomon as a historical source for rather sinister reasons. As a means to bolster their antisemitic readings of history, these scholars denied the existence of Jewish nationalism in antiquity. In order to make this claim, German theologians and historians developed a model that gave pride of place to a very special corpus of sources: pseudepigraphical literature. As mentioned, an important source for these German scholars was the Psalms of Solomon. Using these sources, German scholars went on to argue that Jewish pietism had always resisted attempts to erect a national state on Israelite soil. In order to refute their position, Efron argued that the books of the Maccabees and Rabbinic literature embodied the true tradition of Jewish pietism and that pseudepigraphical books were of dubious quality.[6] He maintained that these books were Christian texts of uncertain date and origin, and, thus, should not

---

3. "Tout est source pour l'historien des mentalités," is a programmatic statement by Jacques Le Goff, "Les mentalités: Une histoire ambiguë," in *Nouveaux objets*, vol. 3 of *Faire de l'histoire*, ed. Jacques Le Goff and Pierre Nora (Paris: Gallimard, 1974), 85.

4. Michel Vovelle, *Piété baroque et déchristianisation en Provence au XVIIIe siècle: Les attitudes devant la mort d'après les clauses des testaments* (Paris: Plon, 1973).

5. Joshua Efron, *Studies on the Hasmonean Period* (Leiden: Brill, 1987), 219–86.

6. See the fierce polemic in ibid., 1–32.

be treated as Jewish sources from the Hasmonean era. Efron then makes rather sweeping claims about more recent interpreters that place almost every scholar of early Judaism, including someone like Elias Bickerman, within the Wellhausen mold.

If Efron were correct that pseudepigrphical books are merely later Christian productions, then none of the historical claims that have been based on the Psalms of Solomon could be accepted. However, several reasons have led more recent scholars to disregard Efron's work. In fact, John Collins has labeled it as "a work of apologetics rather than of history," and continues his critique by saying that Efron's "emotional rhetoric undermines his credibility" and that "the work is too blatantly prejudiced to merit further discussion."[7] Collins also criticizes Efron for casually dismisssing the Dead Sea Scrolls. However, while one cannot follow Efron in his ideological and methodological positions, he has still raised a number of important points that have been too rashly neglected.

I will argue in this paper that the value of the Psalms of Solomon as a historical source is still severely overrated, and that in large parts of (especially German) scholarship, the historical arguments supported by them have not actually changed since the days of Julius Wellhausen and Eduard Meyer.[8] In order to demonstrate this, I will first highlight the place and function of the psalms in historical reconstructions. I will then test the validity of historical claims that are based on the psalms. Finally, I will return to the problem raised by Efron and offer some explanatory tools that lead beyond his rather one-sided polemics. I will not only point to the anti-Semitism in nineteenth-century German scholarship, but also highlight those scholars' interest in theoretical political discourse about different types of states.

2. The Psalms of Solomon in Historical Scholarship

Let me begin with a history of Second Temple Judaism that has largely fallen into oblivion, one reason certainly being its author's anti-Semitism:

---

7. John J. Collins, review of *Studies on the Hasmonean Period* by Joshua Efron, *CBQ* 52 (1990): 372.

8. "Historical" is meant not in the narrow sense of an academic discipline, but as the designation for a way of writing that tells the reader what happened at a certain time and why; such accounts are of course produced by historians, theologians and scholars of religion alike. Following the lead of Efron, the German scholarly tradition is given pride of place.

The second volume of *Ursprung und Anfänge des Christentums* by Eduard Meyer.⁹ For the period from 63 to 40 BCE, Meyer draws heavily on the Psalms of Solomon, following Wellhausen's interpretation of the text against what is called by Meyer "the lack of historical sense and historical knowledge that is so often to be found in this area (i.e., of scholarship)."¹⁰ Meyer's treatment of the Psalms of Solomon is determined by his complex assessment of Hasmonean rule that has been laid out in the preceding pages of his work. While he does note the brutality, the fanaticism, and the opposition to culture that supposedly characterized the Hasmoneans, and while that leads him to a very positive assessment of Pompey as the one who made an end to the "Jewish robber state,"¹¹ Meyer also presents his position on the difficulties of ruling the Jewish people in very clear-cut remarks. For him, the decisive factor in the course of events is "that the law does not know and does not tolerate an independent Jewish state";¹² "the theocracy demanded by the law is not compatible with the existence of an earthly state."¹³ This is what causes problems for the Hasmonean rulers once an independent state has, in fact, emerged as a result of the declining Seleucid empire. They are political rulers, but Jewish law is inimical to political considerations. Therefore, he argues, the Hasmonean period gives rise to a religious opposition against both the rulers and the Jewish state as a whole, as well as to the religious strife between Pharisees and Sadducees.

---

9. Eduard Meyer, *Die Entwicklung des Judentums und Jesus von Nazaret*, vol. 2 of *Ursprung und Anfänge des Christentums*, 4th and 5th ed. (Stuttgart: Cotta, 1925). On Meyer's anti-Semitism, which became more and more visible after 1919, see Christhard Hoffmann, *Juden und Judentum im Werk deutscher Althistoriker des 19. und 20. Jahrhunderts*, SJMT 9 (Leiden: Brill, 1988), 158–59, 184–85.

10. Meyer, *Die Entwicklung des Judentums*, 315 n. 3: "Daß trotz der ganz detaillierten Beschreibung der Taten und Schicksale des Pompejus in Ps. 3 [sic] u. 8 die Erkenntnis der richtigen Datierung dieser Psalmen sich erst so spät und so langsam durchgesetzt hat, ist bezeichnend für den Mangel an historischem Sinn und historischem Wissen, der auf diesem Gebiet so vielfach hervortritt." His positive point of reference is Julius Wellhausen, *Die Pharisäer und die Sadducäer: Eine Untersuchung zur inneren jüdischen Geschichte* (Greifswald: Bamberg, 1874).

11. Especially Meyer, *Die Entwicklung des Judentums*, 280–81, ending on 281 with a praise for Rome: "Diese Tatsachen muß man sich klar machen, um richtig zu würdigen, welchen Segen die Aufrichtung der römischen Herrschaft und die Beseitigung des jüdischen Raubstaats durch Pompejus gebracht hat."

12. Ibid., 305.

13. Ibid., 306.

Although Meyer sees Pompey's conquest of Jerusalem as a victory of culture and civilization, he acknowledges that this might not be the perspective of the conquered people themselves. At this point, he introduces the Psalms of Solomon as a representative text of the period (because he believes it is Pharisaic, and the Pharisees are supported by the majority). According to Meyer, the reader would expect to find anger, resistance, or at least lamentations in the text. But nothing of the sort can be detected. Meyer is literally disgusted by the observation that "the national significance of the catastrophe" is not felt at all in the Psalms of Solomon; on the contrary: "Party politics with their totally one-sided and narrow-minded doctrinairism have choked down any salutary national feeling"—as happened in Greece before Chaironea, and, according to Meyer, in a "devastating manner" in his own lifetime.[14] So, the Psalms of Solomon exhibit a general absence of Jewish nationalism, to Meyer a deplorable fact. Adherence to a national cause would have allowed for compassion towards fellow members of the *ethnos*, for support for its political leaders, and, more fundamentally, for some insight into the necessities of governing according to rational principles. Meyer believes that the Psalms of Solomon show that the Jews were lacking all these qualities.

The last point mentioned is important because it is here that the Psalms of Solomon as a historical source are most useful for Meyer. His narrative continues with the rise of the Idumeans and Herod's reign. This section is also introduced with the Psalms of Solomon, again because Meyer presumes that they represent the widespread views of the Pharisees. He believes Antipater to be the villain mentioned in Ps. Sol. 4, "who sits in the congregation of the pious."[15] His son Herod is, for Meyer, a capable, energetic figure who well understood that governing requires tough decisions in order for rule to be effective. Nevertheless, Herod, Meyer maintains, was bound to fail:

---

14. Ibid., 316: "Von der tiefen Empfindung für die nationale Bedeutung der Katastrophe ... findet sich in diesen Gedichten nichts: die Parteipolitik mit ihrem ganz einseitigen und enghergzigen religiösen Doktrinarismus hat jedes gesunde Nationalgefühl hier in derselben Weise erstickt, wie etwa in der Griechenwelt bei den Politikern der Demosthenischen Zeit im Gegensatz zu Isokrates oder wie in so furchtbar verheerender Weise in unserer Gegenwart."

15. Ps. Sol. 4:1: Ἵνα τί σύ, βέβηλε, κάθησαι ἐν συνεδρίῳ ὁσίων καὶ ἡ καρδία σου μακρὰν ἀφέστηκεν ἀπὸ τοῦ κυρίου ἐν παρανομίαις παροργίζων τὸν θεὸν Ισραηλ; see Meyer, *Die Entwicklung des Judentums*, 320.

The task of ruling a Jewish kingdom to the satisfaction of its subjects was exasperating and, in fact, unachievable. A ruler who would not degrade himself to the point of being a weak-willed instrument (like Hyrcanus) was especially forced into endless conflicts. The inflexible doctrinairism that had become the whole people's second nature was simply incompatible with the considerations and requirements of any political rule.[16]

Again, doctrinairism is Meyer's main explanatory principle, which he had deduced from the Psalms of Solomon a few pages earlier. He again opposes it to an interest in the national cause and to the acknowledgment of political necessities, and he now explicitly attributes it to the Jewish people as a whole.

As stated above, many of these arguments were not really new. Meyer based his interpretation of the Psalms of Solomon on Wellhausen, who had used them as additional evidence for his general reconstruction of Pharisaism in the Hasmonean and Herodian periods. For both authors, the Psalms of Solomon were important not because they provided new information (be it on historical events or mentalities), but because they enhanced the plausibility of a scenario that had been developed on the basis of other sources.[17] Wellhausen had formulated his views on the Pharisees—and on their adherents, that is, the great majority of the Jewish people—in hardly less radical terms than Meyer. The Pharisees, in his view, are theoreticians concerned with upholding the theocracy,[18] they do not get involved into politics, and they have no loyalty at all to the idea of

---

16. Ibid., 323: "Aber die Aufgabe, ein jüdisches Reich zur Befriedigung der Untertanen zu regieren, war verzweifelt und in Wirklichkeit unlösbar; vollends mußte sie eine Herrschernatur, die sich nicht wie Hyrkanos zum willenlosen Werkzeug erniedrigen konnte, fortwährend in Konflikte führen. Der starre, dem gesamten Volk in Fleisch und Blut übergegangene Doktrinarismus verträgt sich eben nicht mit irgendwelchem politischen Regiment und den Rücksichten, die dies erforderte."

17. It should be stressed that this point is made much more explicit in Wellhausen's work than in Meyer's. While Meyer discusses the period from 63 to 40 BCE almost solely on the basis of the Psalms of Solomon, Wellhausen introduces them only after his narrative has reached 70 CE, with the comment that, due to the lack of consensus regarding the date of the collection, he had judged it imprudent "es von vornherein als Quelle für die geschichtliche Darstellung des Wesens der Parteien zu verwerthen" (Wellhausen, *Die Pharisäer und die Sadducäer*, 112).

18. Ibid., 39: "Wie hätten für diese [sc. politische] Aufgabe Schriftgelehrte gepasst, Theoretiker, die mit der Wirklichkeit noch ungleich geringere Fühlung hatten, als event. die Philosophen der platonischen Republik!"

a Jewish state. If faced with an alternative between loyalty to the state and devotion to God, they would happily choose treason.[19] This antinationalist, theocratic perspective pervades the whole people and precludes political rule: "When the Hasmoneans tried to form a nation out of the Palestinian community…, they acted against the 'idea' of Judaism, for this idea was not the earthly fatherland, but God and the law."[20] The Psalms of Solomon, although treated by Wellhausen in a more sympathetic way than by Meyer, serve to bolster this image of Pharisaism, and, in fact, Judaism. It should not be overlooked that while the nature of the Pharisees was still debated at that time, the general claim that a majority of Jews in the Second Temple period was uninterested in politics and national causes as long as religious laws stayed intact was generally accepted in German scholarship. Wellhausen's "Theokratie" does not significantly differ, for example, from Heinrich Leo's "Hierarchie," which was also conceptualized in a Hegelian manner as the "idea" that determined the history of Israel.[21]

Leo, Wellhausen, or Meyer is unlikely to be read by many students of the Second Temple period anymore. However, a look at more recent works on the period and their uses of the Psalms of Solomon as a historical source does not result in a different impression. According to Martin Hengel, the Hasmoneans's constant neglect of the law led to opposition from the "pious ones." His basis for this statement is, again, Ps. Sol. 4, although the villain has become Alexander Jannaeus.[22] Viktor Burr notes that at the beginning of Roman rule, "the invasion of Pompey in Judea was predominantly seen from a religious angle by the inhabitants, and

---

19. Ibid., 97: "die Consequenz, die zur Ehre Gottes den Landesverrath nicht scheute."

20. Ibid., 95: "Als die Hasmonäer aus der palästinischen Gemeinde … eine Nation zu bilden versuchten, da handelten sie der 'Idee' des Judenthums zuwider. Denn diese Idee war nicht das irdische Vaterland, sondern Gott und das Gesetz."

21. Heinrich Leo, *Vorlesungen über die Geschichte des jüdischen Staates* (Berlin: Duncker & Humblot, 1828). Leo interchangeably uses the terms "Hierarchie" and "Theokratie." See on his model Hoffmann, *Juden und Judentum*, 42–73.

22. Martin Hengel, *Die Zeloten: Untersuchungen zur jüdischen Freiheitsbewegung in der Zeit von Herodes I. bis 70 n. Chr.*, AGJU 1, 2nd ed. (Leiden: Brill, 1976), 193 (see also 323 n. 3 on the "Kritik der Frommen" that was directed against the Hasmoneans, based on the Psalms of Solomon and the Testament of Moses). That the villain in Ps. Sol. 4 is Jannaeus (which would call for a date in the 80s BCE) had already been suggested by Wellhausen, *Die Pharisäer und die Sadducäer*, 146–47.

felt by many to be a just punishment for preceding sins."²³ He supports the statement with Ps. Sol. 8. Only when the Jews surprisingly found out that Pompey was "now acting as a foreign conqueror in Jerusalem," the "happiness about the fall of the dynasty and the slaughter or captivity of the political opponents" was supplemented by hatred towards the sinner Pompey. A quotation from Ps. Sol. 17 further documents this shift in the assertion that Pompey sinned "by looking at" the holiest of holies, thus violating Jewish religious sensibilities.²⁴ In the New Schürer, we read that in 63 BCE, "there was little trace left of that spirit which a hundred years earlier had led the nation into battle."²⁵ This is a faithful translation of the original Schürer, but a new footnote now lists a number of texts which "shed indirect but valuable light on Palestinian society and its [sic] attitude towards Rome at the time of the conquest of Jerusalem by Pompey." The Psalms of Solomon takes pride of place. In Bringmann's history of the Jews in antiquity, Ps. Sol. 2 is strategically placed at the end of the chapter entitled "The End of Independence." The text is used to demonstrate that "the pious inhabitants of the country interpreted the extraordinary happenings…as God's punishment for the sins of the rulers and the people."²⁶ In an article by Trampedach on the Hasmoneans and their problems with the Jewish theocracy (a title that calls to mind the treatments of Leo, Wellhausen, and Meyer), only the Psalms of Solomon support the statement that "the break between the ruling dynasty and the beneficiaries of their

---

23. All quotations from Viktor Burr, "Rom und Judäa im 1. Jahrhundert v. Chr. (Pompeius und die Juden)," *ANRW* 1:881.

24. Ps. Sol. 17:13: ἐν ἀλλοτριότητι ὁ ἐχθρὸς ἐποίησεν ὑπερηφανίαν. Burr gives no indication about the textual basis of his translation ("durch Anschauen"). It can in fact be traced back to a suggestion made by Karl Georg Kuhn, *Die älteste Textgestalt der Psalmen Salomos: Insbesondere auf Grund der syrischen Übersetzung neu untersucht*, BWANT 73 (Stuttgart: Kohlhammer, 1937), 61–62, who connected ἐν ἀλλοτριότητι via the Syriac ܒܢܘܟܪܝܘܬܐ not with נכר (1) "being alien" but with נכר (2) "to look at," which would make the Greek a mistranslation.

25. Emil Schürer, *The History of the Jewish People in the Age of Jesus Christ (175 BC–AD 135)*, rev. and ed. Géza Vermès and Fergus Millar, 2 vols. (Edinburgh: T&T Clark, 1973), 1:241. For the original, see idem, *Geschichte des jüdischen Volkes im Zeitalter Jesu Christi*, 3rd and 4th ed. (Leipzig: Hinrich, 1901), 1:301.

26. Klaus Bringmann, *Geschichte der Juden im Altertum: Vom babylonischen Exil bis zur arabischen Eroberung* (Stuttgart: Klett-Cotta, 2005), 166.

regime, on the one hand, and the scholarly elites and a great portion of the population, on the other, proved to be irreparable."[27]

The list could of course be continued. However, to summarize, the Psalms of Solomon are generally used to support three historical claims about the late Hasmonean period: (1) The majority of Jews welcomed Pompey's conquest of Jerusalem because it made an end to Hasmonean rule; (2) Hasmonean rule was rejected because the Hasmoneans had neglected Jewish law (especially by combining kingship and high priesthood); and (3) The Hasmoneans could hardly have avoided this opposition, because the general problem any political ruler had to face was that the only acceptable model of state organization—theocracy—was incompatible with political governing as well as with any positive form of adherence to an independent Jewish state.

Is this use of the Psalms of Solomon as a historical source justified?

3. Testing Hypotheses

The first problem to be investigated is the tendency of scholars to use one single source for the reconstruction of a general Jewish attitude towards independence and foreign rule (especially evident in the quotation from the New Schürer). It is surprising that the Psalms of Solomon have so often been treated as representative of Jewish society as a whole, because this is exactly the impression that the psalms themselves eagerly strive to avoid. They heap accusations on the inhabitants of Jerusalem, from incest via adultery to the desecration of the sanctuary (Pss. Sol. 2:3–14; 8:8–13, 20–22; 17:14–15). These rather stereotypical accusations are not only raised against the priests, but quite explicitly against the whole population.[28] Due to the moral decline of the Jerusalemites, the difference in

---

27. Kai Trampedach, "Between Hellenistic Monarchy and Jewish Theocracy: The Contested Legitimacy of Hasmonean Rule," in *The Splendors and Miseries of Ruling Alone: Encounters with Monarchy from Archaic Greece to the Hellenistic Mediterranean*, ed. Nino Luraghi, SAM 1 (Stuttgart: Steiner, 2013), 247.

28. This emerges from the frequent use of designations like "the sons (and daughters) of Jerusalem," "the sons of the covenant," etc. A different view is presented by Kenneth Atkinson, *I Cried to the Lord: A Study of the Psalms of Solomon's Historical Background and Social Setting*, JSJSup 84 (Leiden: Brill, 2004), who generally seeks for very concrete referents. According to him (20–21, 37), "the sons of Jerusalem" in Ps. Sol. 2:3 who have profaned the sanctuary are the priests of Jerusalem. This forces him to argue that the "sons and daughters" in 2:6 are the family of Aristobulus II. Similarly,

behavior between Jews and gentiles has collapsed.²⁹ The Psalms of Solomon imagines a small group of pious Jews against the sinful behavior that has supposedly pervaded society and is justly punished by God. Such a positive image certainly has high potential for self-identification, and the Dead Sea Scrolls demonstrate similar attitudes.³⁰ However, these texts also come from a sectarian movement that may not have been as marginal as

---

Atkinson interprets the accusations in Ps. Sol. 8 as referring to offences committed by the (Hasmonean) priests against purity regulations (65–80). For similar views, but focused even more on the opposition against either the Hasmoneans in general or Aristobulus II, see Joseph Viteau, *Les Psaumes de Solomon: Introduction, texte grec et traduction, avec les principales variantes de la version syriaque par François Martin*, Documents pour l'étude de la Bible (Paris: Letouzey et Ané, 1911), 23–24, 257–58, 294–95; Otto Kaiser, *Gott, Mensch und Geschichte: Studien zum Verständnis des Menschen und seiner Geschichte in der klassischen, biblischen und nachbiblischen Literatur*, BZAW 413 (Berlin: de Gruyter, 2010), 93–96. Eyal Regev (*The Hasmoneans: Ideology, Archaeology, Identity*, JAJSup 10 [Göttingen: Vandenhoeck & Ruprecht, 2013], 94–95) correctly understands the accusations, e.g., concerning the defilement of sacrifices with menstrual blood (Ps. Sol. 8:12), in a rather metaphorical sense, but agrees on the fact that the polemics are directed against the Hasmonean priests. I do not think that this does justice to the frequent use of inclusive designations ("the sons and daughters" and the like). The assumption that only priests could profane the sanctuary seems unwarranted to me. The point rather seems to be that through their abhorrent behavior, the Jerusalemites had rendered the temple cult invalid. See, from a different angle, Nadav Sharon ("Setting the Stage: The Effects of the Roman Conquest and the Loss of Sovereignty," in *Was 70 CE a Watershed in Jewish History? On Jews and Judaism before and after the Destruction of the Second Temple*, ed. Daniel R. Schwartz and Zee Weiss, AJEC 78 [Leiden: Brill, 2012], 437–38) on the Psalms of Solomon's lack of interest in the temple.

29. This is explicitly said in Ps. Sol. 8:13: οὐ παρέλιπον ἁμαρτίαν, ἣν οὐκ ἐποίησαν ὑπὲρ τὰ ἔθνη. Again, I do not think that this refers only to priests. The same thought can perhaps be found in the part of Ps. Sol. 17 that is contemporary with Ps. Sol. 8, namely, in v. 14. The subject of the sentence πάντα, ὅσα ἐποίησεν ἐν Ιερουσαλημ, καθὼς καὶ τὰ ἔθνη ἐν ταῖς πόλεσι τοῦ σθένους αὐτῶν is ὁ ἐχθρός (i.e., Pompey) in the Greek, but the Syriac version may be correct in attributing these deeds to Jerusalem itself (through the verb ܥܒܕ). See Benedikt Eckhardt, "PsSal 17, die Hasmonäer und der Herodompeius," *JSJ* 40 (2009): 474–75.

30. On parallels between the DSS and the Psalms of Solomon, see Joseph L. Trafton, "The Bible, the *Psalms of Solomon*, and Qumran," *The Dead Sea Scrolls and the Qumran Community* in vol. 2 of *The Bible and the Dead Sea Scrolls: The Second Princeton Symposium on Judaism and Christian Origins*, ed. James H. Charlesworth (Waco: Baylor University Press, 2006), 427–46.

was earlier believed, but was certainly far from representing an average Jewish perspective.

The traditional interpretation was, of course, originally developed under the assumption that the Psalms of Solomon were Pharisaic. This idea has justly been abandoned. Kenneth Atkinson argues for an unknown Jewish sect behind the psalms, which is probably the best we can hope to achieve.[31] The recent attempt by Stefan Schreiber to enhance the text's potential for representing large parts of Jewish society by declaring it the product of a traditional Jewish group with an anti-Hellenistic stance, alienated not from Jewish society as such but only from the temple elite, is not convincing.[32] While one should expect exaggeration of differences in inner-Jewish polemics,[33] there is no reason to turn things around and regard the Psalms of Solomon as an expression of mainstream Judaism.

Do the Psalms of Solomon really contain references to historical events surrounding the conquest of Pompey? For Pss. Sol. 2 and 8, this still seems to be the most plausible explanation. Admittedly, Ps. Sol. 8 in itself does not contain any truly decisive element. The enemy's peaceful advent in Jerusalem (by invitation of the "rulers of the land"), as well as the ensuing massacre and the capture of many Jerusalemites, do not quite match our information about the events. One could at least take the "rulers of the land," ἄρχοντες τῆς γῆς, as a designation for Hyrcanus and Aristobulus and connect the phrase, as is often done, with Josephus's judgment: "Responsible for this calamity that befell Jerusalem was the strife between Hyrcanus and Aristobulus" (that had led them to ask Pompey for a decision) (Josephus, A.J. 14.77). Captivity is also mentioned in Pesher Nahum, which seems to refer to the events, so it may well be that Josephus's information is incomplete.[34] Pompey may have taken more Jerusalemites to Rome for his

---

31. Atkinson, *I Cried to the Lord*, 213–14.

32. Stefan Schreiber, "Can Wisdom be Prayer? Form and Function of the *Psalms of Solomon*," in *Literature or Liturgy? Early Christian Hymns and Prayers in their Literary and Liturgical Context in Antiquity*, ed. Clemens Leonhard and Hermut Löhr, WUNT 2/363 (Tübingen: Mohr Siebeck, 2014), 89–106. One should place stronger emphasis on the condemnation of the behavior of virtually all other Jews, and the catchword "anti-Hellenistic" has no explanatory value. Since nothing in the Psalms refers specifically to Hellenistic culture, the statement is based solely on the questionable assumption that "real" Judaism and Hellenism are incompatible.

33. See on this problem Günter Stemberger, "Was There a 'Mainstream Judaism' in the Late Second Temple Period?" *RRJ* 4 (2001): 205.

34. Ps. Sol. 8:21; cf. 2:6; 17:12. On 4Q169 fr. 3–4, II, 5, see Shani Berrin, "Pesher

triumph than just Aristobulus and his family, and a fragmentary text from Qumran seems to refer to people killed by Aemilius Scaurus, Pompey's representative in the region.[35] Ps. Sol. 2 is generally taken as clear evidence for a Pompeian background. The death of the dragon "on the mountains of Egypt" (2:26) can plausibly be explained as a reference to the death of Pompey, who was murdered in Egypt.[36] This part of the psalm could be a later addition, which would open the possibility that the first part did not originally refer to Pompey. But another indication may be seen in the beginning of the psalm, where the Syriac text has the enemy attack "on a feast day" (the siege of Jerusalem supposedly started on a Sabbath).[37]

Pss. Sol. 1, 4, and 7 do not contain references to identifiable historical events, although a number of suggestions and assumptions have been made concerning these texts as well. Ps. Sol. 17 is complicated. On the one hand, the captives are now explicitly said to have been led "to the West," which clearly points to a Roman conqueror, namely Pompey (Ps. Sol. 17:12). On the other hand, that part of the psalm seems to have been originally separate from the first part, which mentions a "man that is alien from our house" whose actions, namely the extinction of a group of sinners, are described with approval (Ps. Sol. 17:7). I take this designation to refer to Herod the Great, not to Pompey, not least because the circumstantial (and unparalleled) phrasing that stresses the genealogical distinction seems to be explicable in light of the controversies surrounding Herod's Jewish identity, but is difficult to explain when the reference is to Pompey, "the one from the end of the earth," whose foreign origin is by all means obvious.[38] This is one

---

Nahum, *Psalms of Solomon* and Pompey," in *Reworking the Bible: Apocryphal and Related Texts at Qumran*, ed. Esther G. Chazon, Devorah Dimant, and Ruth A. Clements, STDJ 58 (Leiden: Brill, 2005), 78. On Josephus and the Psalms of Solomon, see Viteau, *Les Psaumes de Salomon*, 20–22.

35. 4Q333, l. 4 and 8; see Kenneth Atkinson, "Representations of History in 4Q331 (4QpapHistorical Text C), 4Q332 (4QHistorical Text D), 4Q333 (4QHistorical Text E), and 4Q468e (4QHistorical Text F): An Annalistic Calendar Documenting Portentous Events?" *DSD* 14 (2007): 125–51; Hanan Eshel, *The Dead Sea Scrolls and the Hasmonean State* (Grand Rapids: Eerdmans, 2008), 138–42.

36. Albeit not on a mountain, but rather on the shores; the biblical background may perhaps explain that difference. For a possible parallel in 4Q386, see Eshel, *The Dead Sea Scrolls*, 151–61.

37. Most scholars nevertheless prefer the Greek version (not "on a feast day", but "with battering ram"). See Atkinson, *I Cried to the Lord*, 25–28.

38. Note also that the only Septuagint parallel for ἄνθρωπος ἀλλότριος is Deut

more example of a redactional combination of originally separate parts into one psalm,[39] and it has some consequences for historical interpretation.

Do the psalms condemn the Hasmoneans? This is often taken for granted. But Pss. Sol. 2 and 8 do not single out the ruling dynasty in any way. From the leaders to the women everyone has sinned. Even the ἄρχοντες τῆς γῆς who pave the way for Pompey and may be identified as Hyrcanus and Aristobulus are not specifically accused. Their action is explained immediately before by the claim that God has mixed a drink of confusion for the whole people, which naturally affects its leaders as well.[40] So the reason for inviting the enemy to Jerusalem is not Hasmonean wickedness, but the sinful behavior of all the inhabitants. The same impression, as may be noted in passing, emerges from the Qumran pesharim. They are certainly hostile to the Hasmoneans and to the society of Jerusalem, but the Hasmoneans are not singled out for having caused the Roman conquest. Where the commentaries on Nahum, Habakuk, and Isaiah do refer to the events, they usually either blame Jerusalem and its society as a whole[41] or

---

17:15, which would point to Jewish kingship as the background. For the argument that 17:1–10 are later than 11–20, see Eckhardt, "PsSal 17."

39. On redaction in the Psalms of Solomon, see Otto Kaiser, "Beobachtungen zur Komposition und Redaktion der Psalmen Salomos," in *Das Manna fällt auch heute noch: Beiträge zur Geschichte und Theologie des Alten, Ersten Testaments: Festschrift für Erich Zenger*, ed. Frank-Lothar Hossfeld and Ludger Schwienhorst-Schönberger, HBS 44 (Freiburg: Herder, 2004), 362–78.

40. Ps. Sol. 8:14: Διὰ τοῦτο ἐκέρασεν αὐτοῖς [i.e., the population of Jerusalem, see above] ὁ θεὸς πνεῦμα πλανήσεως.

41. 4Q162 (4QpIsa^b) col. II may refer to the famine of 65 BCE and (esp. II, 9) to the subsequent conquest by Pompey. It seems to blame אנשי הלצון אשר בירושלים, "the scoffing men who are in Jerusalem" (II, 6–7), also labeled עדת אנשי הלצון אשר בירושלים, "the congregation of the scoffing men who are in Jerusalem" (II, 10), for the events because these people have rejected the law of God (Isa 5:24). The group in question has often been identified as "the Pharisees, the supporters of Hyrcanus," as it is put by Hanan Eshel, *The Dead Sea Scrolls*, 147. Although the introduction in ii 1 (פשר הדבר לאחרית הימים) dates the events to the "last days," it is plausible to assume that this refers to the author's present, as is often the case in the DSS; see Annette Steudel, "אחרית הימים in the Texts from Qumran," *RevQ* 16 (1993): 225–46. But the "scoffing men" do not have to be interpreted as a specific (Pharisaic and/or Hasmonean) group. An עדה of scoffing men in Jerusalem could simply mean that Jerusalem has become a community of scoffers, as opposed to the holy congregation of Israel, i.e., the sect; see on the use of עדה as a self-designation Sarianna Metso, "Qumran Community Structure and Terminology as Theological Statement," *RevQ* 20 (2002): 432–34. A member of the sect, who did not live in Jerusalem, would understand this as an explanation for

abstain from any accusations and simply state that Jerusalem has been (or in prophetic speech: will be) conquered.[42]

The anonymous evildoers in Pss. Sol. 1 and 4 have no evidently Hasmonean characteristics. Ps. Sol. 1 is especially interesting in this regard, because it introduces the whole compilation, and some commentators have found an anti-Hasmonean stance in Jerusalem's (?) lamentation.[43] But the claim that "their" wealth has made "them" arrogant, that "their" sins were in secret and that "they" profaned the sanctuary of the Lord is not very specific; if Jerusalem is speaking, the accusations may well be directed against her τέκνα mentioned immediately before.[44] The whole population of Jerusalem has sinned, not just (or primarily) the Hasmoneans.[45] The anti-Hasmonean (rather than antisocietal) reading of the Psalms of Solomon can be based solely on a single passage. In the part of Ps. Sol. 17 that is Herodian at the earliest, it is stated that "they replaced their highness with kingship."[46] Those who introduced kingship in Judea

---

the catastrophe that befell the city, and as an illustration of Ps 1:1: "happy is the man who does not sit in the seat of scoffers" (אשרי־האיש אשר ... במושב לצים לא ישב).

42. 1QpHab IX, 4–7 comes closest to blaming the Hasmoneans. "The last priests of Jerusalem" (כוהני ירושלם האחרונים) will plunder the nations and amass wealth, but in the end (לאחרית הימים), everything will be given to the army of the Kittim, i.e., the Romans. Since this is a commentary on Hab 2:8 (NRSV: "Because you have plundered many nations, all that survive of the peoples shall plunder you"), one could infer from this that the Romans would not have come had the Hasmoneans not deviated from God's will. But this point is not made explicitly in the pesher. 4Q169 (4QpNah) certainly blames those who lead people astray, but the result is that "kings, leaders, priests, and the people, together with the *ger*," are in sin (fr. 3–4, ii, 9). For a similar, hierarchically organized list of sinners, see Ps. Sol. 8:20–22.

43. That the subject of ἐβόησα πρὸς κύριον is Jerusalem has often been suggested; e.g., by Kaiser, *Gott, Mensch und Geschichte*, 98.

44. Ps. Sol. 1:3: καὶ πολλὴν γενέσθαι ἐν τέκνοις. Grammatically, ὁ πλοῦτος αὐτῶν in 1:4 can only be the wealth of Jerusalem's (?) children.

45. For the opposite view, see Wellhausen, *Die Pharisäer und die Sadducäer*, 139–40. Robert B. Wright, *The Psalms of Solomon: A Critical Edition of the Greek Text*, JCTC 1 (New York: T&T Clark, 2007), 55 ad loc. cites 1 Macc. 10:4 (Demetrius I offering peace to Jonathan, who rejects that offer) and 2 Macc. 4:18–20 (the Jewish delegation sent by Jason to the Tyrian games) for the statement in Ps. Sol. 1:4 that "their wealth was spread over the whole earth." I am unable to see the connection.

46. Ps. Sol. 17:6: ἔθεντο βασίλειον ἀντὶ ὕψους αὐτῶν. This is a difficult verse. In my view and contrary to the Greek editions of the text, it does not begin with ἐν δόξῃ, because that is the ending of the preceding verse, as in the Syriac text (see Willem Baars, "Psalms of Solomon," part 4.6 of *The Old Testament in Syriac according to the*

were, of course, the Hasmoneans. If the "highness" replaced by kingship was the high priesthood, as seems plausible, the verse not only contains criticism of the Hasmoneans, but also the claim that kingship and high priesthood should not be combined.

So here we have a condemnation of the Hasmoneans based on a constitutional argument. But it was not, in my view, written before the days of Herod. This changes the basis for our understanding of the debates involved. Herod not only put many Hasmoneans to death, but also reduced the high priesthood to a mere cultic office without any political authority.[47] The Hasmonean combination of kingship and high priesthood is thus criticized at a time when both that combination and Hasmonean rule had been abolished. There is no indication in the sources that this issue had come up in any serious way at an earlier date. The complaint raised against Hyrcanus I at a banquet in the presence of Pharisees (but not necessarily by a Pharisee) does not concern the constitution, but the genealogical qualification of Hyrcanus: he is said to be the son of a woman who was a war captive under Antiochus IV (Josephus, *A.J.* 13.288–292).[48] The double messiah that is sometimes expected in the Dead Sea Scrolls has been explained as a response to the combination of royal and priestly authority,[49] and that may even be true, but it is far from evident that this was an issue of prime importance standing between the *yahad* and the Hasmonean

---

Peshiṭta Version [Leiden: Brill], 22): ܩܘܡܗܘܢ ܚܠܦ ܪܒܘܬܗܘܢ ܐܩܝܡܘ (Ps Sol. 17:6[7]). See Kuhn, *Die älteste Textgestalt*, 57. That βασίλειον means "kingship," although one would expect βασιλεία, is supported by the Syriac ܪܒܘܬܗܘܢ (so one should not translate "palace" or the like). Ἀντί with a genitive—as well as Syriac ܚܠܦ—describes an act of substitution. The very smooth recent translations by Atkinson in NETS ("They set up in glory a palace corresponding to their loftiness," but see Atkinson, *I Cried to the Lord*, 130, "They set up in glory a king because of their arrogance"), Wright, *The Psalms of Solomon*, 179 ("In their pride they flamboyantly set up their own royal house") and Kaiser, *Gott, Mensch und Geschichte,* 120 ("In Herrlichkeit errichteten sie ein Königtum aufgrund ihres Hochmuts") are therefore difficult to accept.

47. For an overview, see James C. VanderKam, *From Joshua to Caiaphas. High Priests after the Exile* (Minneapolis: Fortress, 2004), 394–417.

48. For a good treatment of this episode, see VanderKam, *From Joshua to Caiaphas,* 298–304.

49. E.g., Atkinson, *I Cried to the Lord,* 147; John J. Collins, "What Was Distinctive about Messianic Expectation at Qumran?" in *The Dead Sea Scrolls and the Qumran Community,* vol. 2 of *The Bible and the Dead Sea Scrolls: The Second Princeton Symposium on Judaism and Christian Origins,* ed. James H. Charlesworth (Waco, TX: Baylor University Press, 2006), 81.

state. Neither MMT nor the pesharim ever mention that problem. All in all, Ps. Sol. 17 is the first text known to us that raises the issue (if the interpretation of the "highness" is correct), and it does so at a time when such a statement could only be read as an affirmation of the present constitution. This does not mean that the psalm is a propaganda text for Herod,[50] for in that case, he would not have been called a foreigner. But it fits the way Jewish texts generally reacted to constitutional changes, by reconfiguring traditions and testing alternatives (as in the Temple Scroll or in the Testaments of the Twelve Patriarchs), not by fundamental opposition to any sort of government that deviated from theocratic ideals.[51]

However, one thing seems to militate against such conclusions. According to historiographical tradition, Pompey was confronted in Damascus not only with the delegations of Hyrcanus and Aristobulus, but also with a third delegation that demanded the abolition of kingship in Judea and its replacement by priestly, non-Hasmonean rule (Diodorus Siculus, *Bibl.* 40.2; Josephus, *A.J.* 14.41–45). According to Diodorus, this delegation consisted of 200 Jewish notables; in the much later version by Josephus, the call for hierocracy is attributed to the Jewish *ethnos* as such. In historical narratives, this incident is usually combined with the Psalms of Solomon; together, they form a pair that gives solid proof for the theocratic, anti-Hasmonean positions that were current in Jewish society of the late Hasmonean period. The two texts reinforce each other; it is therefore not surprising that the majority of scholars believes that the delegation was undertaken by Pharisees, although nothing in Josephus supports that conclusion.[52] However, we have seen that the Psalms of Solomon have often been used in a rather tendentious way, and there is, in my view, much reason to discard the story about the antimonarchic delegation as well.

---

50. As has been argued by Samuel Rocca, "Josephus and the *Psalms of Solomon* on Herod's Messianic Aspirations: An Interpretation," in *Making History: Josephus and Historical Method*, ed. Zuleika Rodgers, JSJSup 110 (Leiden: Brill, 2007), 313–33.

51. See Benedikt Eckhardt, *Ethnos und Herrschaft: Politische Figurationen judäischer Identität von Antiochos III. bis Herodes I.*, SJ 72 (Berlin: de Gruyter, 2013), 197–228.

52. This is the standard view at least since Wellhausen, *Die Pharisäer und die Sadducäer*, 100: "Abgesandte des Volkes, d.h. Pharisäer." For him, it is also clear what the Pharisees wanted: "sie wünschen die Fremdherrschaft, damit der kirchliche Charakter der Theokratie unverfälscht bleibe." For full documentation, see my article cited in the next note.

The historicity of the events is usually held to be beyond any doubt, because Diodorus and Josephus independently agree on the basic facts. But this is not a valid argument.[53] Neither author was an eyewitness, so all we can say is that they may have independently drawn on the same source. The variations in Josephus's version do not prove even that, however, because he may well have adapted a version he had found and which he thought needed correction. Thus, in Diodorus's version the argument of the Judean elite is that Jews never have a king and that Hyrcanus and Aristobulus want to introduce kingship. Josephus of course knew that this was not correct and added the information that Jannaeus had already reigned as king. Diodorus is probably closer to the original source. That source, in my view, was interested in the Jewish constitution for the sole purpose of throwing a positive light on Pompey, who had abolished kingship in Judea and thus effectively replaced the local πάτριοι νόμοι. Under normal circumstances, this would not have been of great concern for Roman observers. But when Pompey returned to Rome in 62 BCE, Lucullus brought the senate to decide that every single measure taken by Pompey in the east was to be considered on its own, instead of accepting the new order as a whole (Plutarch, *Pomp.* 46.3; *Luc.* 42.6; Cassius Dio, *Hist. Rom.* 37.49.4–5).[54] In that situation, it was good to have a report at hand that refuted the possible objection that local

---

53. The following argument (that the delegation is a propagandistic fiction invented by Theophanes of Mytilene) has its roots in short notes by Joshua Efron, *Studies on the Hasmonian Period*, 230–32 and Bezalel Bar-Kochva, "Manpower, Economics, and Internal Strife in the Hasmonean State," in *Armées et fiscalité dans le monde antique: Actes du colloque national, Paris, 14–16 octobre 1976*, ed. A. Chastagnol, C. Nicolet, and H. van Effenterre, Colloques nationaux du centre national de la recherche scientifique 936 (Paris: Éditions du CNRS, 1977), 179–81; it has been rejected by, e.g., David Goodblatt, *The Monarchic Principle: Studies in Jewish Self-Government in Antiquity*, TSAJ 38 (Tübingen: Mohr Siebeck, 1994), 36–40, and revived by me in "Die jüdischen Gesandtschaften an Pompeius (63 v. Chr.) bei Diodor und Josephus," *Klio* 92 (2010): 388–410. The (negative) evaluation of the arguments of Efron and Bar-Kochva by Regev, *The Hasmoneans*, 162–63 does not add much to the discussion. See now Nadav Sharon "The End of the Hasmonean State and the Beginning of Roman Rule in the Land of Israel (67–37 BCE): History, Historiography, and Impact on Jewish Society and Religion" (PhD diss., Hebrew University, 2013), 56–74, who has reached conclusions similar to mine.

54. What matters here is the procedure; it may be conceded that Lucullus's move did not create as much opposition as is suggested by some sources; see Thilo Rising, "Senatorial Opposition to Pompey's Eastern Settlement: A Storm in a Teacup?" *Historia* 62 (2013): 196–221.

πάτριοι νόμοι were changed without reason; rather, Pompey could present himself as the champion of Jewish traditional law, because under normal circumstances, the Jews do not have kings. That is the claim of the Jewish elite as well as of Hecataeus of Abdera in the well-known excursus that follows (Diodorus Siculus *Bibl.* 40.3).[55] The most natural source one could think of is Theophanes of Mytilene, Pompey's propagandist who accompanied him on his eastern campaign. If this conclusion is correct, then the reports about the delegation to Pompey cannot bolster the traditional interpretation of the Psalms of Solomon. Rather, they show that already in antiquity, certain authors were interested in the *construct* of a constant antimonarchic, theocratic tradition in Judea. Theophanes of Mytilene could use it to defend his patron Pompey, and Josephus makes it one of the main themes of his *Antiquities*.[56]

Summing up this testing of hypotheses: The value of the Psalms of Solomon as a historical source has never depended on the information the psalms themselves provide. They were so highly valued because they supposedly proved general assumptions about Judea. If these are deconstructed, as can be done through a reevaluation of the sources, the Psalms hardly tell historians anything about the period of Pompey's conquest. Since all condemnation of Jews is written in retrospect in order to show God's justice, nothing can be learned about attitudes prevalent before the loss of independence. Since the Hasmoneans are not criticized apart from the late passage in Ps. Sol. 17, nothing can be learned about pre-Herodian attitudes towards secular rule in Judea. That passage is important because it shows an early Jewish view on Herod and gives some indication as to when the opposition against the combination of secular and religious authority actually arose. But all in all, the psalms can in no way carry the weight that scholars in the tradition of Wellhausen and Meyer have put upon them.

---

55. The excursus shows close verbal parallels with the argument of the Jewish delegation in Diodorus's report; I therefore think that it has at least been adapted, if not created for this purpose.

56. On the relationship of Theophanes and Pompey, see Barbara K. Gold, "Pompey and Theophanes of Mytilene," *AJP* 106 (1985): 312–27. With regard to Josephus, the third delegation is not mentioned in the *Bellum Judaicum*. The *Antiquitates Judaicae* show many adaptations of earlier material to make it fit that antimonarchical, theocratic discourse; e.g., the new introduction to the king's law of Deuteronomy in *A.J.* 4.223–224, or the antimonarchic delegation sent to Augustus in 4 BCE (*A.J.* 17.304–314), where we have the original version, not concerned with antimonarchic arguments, in a fragment from Nicolaus of Damascus (*FGrHis* 90 F 136).

They do not represent the theocratic zeal of the Jewish populace, but a small group of Jews alienated from the great majority, a group that has found theological explanations for a calamity that has already happened, but even now does not reject politics as such.

4. Nineteeth-Century Legacies

As noted in the introduction, a number of points raised above have already been discussed in some way or another by Joshua Efron. His claims, however, were much more radical. In his attempt to expose the detrimental influence of German theological scholarship on the rest of the scholarly world and to dismantle a method of writing Jewish history that was anti-Semitic, he became extremely skeptical of pseudepigraphical sources. According to his interpretation, there are no references to Pompey or any other recognizable historical event in the Psalms of Solomon, because it is a Christian composition with an anti-Jewish tone; ἄνομος, ἄνθρωπος ἀλλότριος, ἁμαρτωλός etc. are not sobriquets for Pompey, Antipater, or Herod, but all refer to one single character, the antichrist.

Aspects of his analysis are still worth considering, especially because the psalms have only been preserved in Christian traditions. The meaning given to them by their Christian readers may have come close to Efron's reconstruction. Still, his case for Christian authorship and a total lack of references to historical events is unconvincing. This does not, however, mean that Efron's whole argument can be discarded as a curiosity of scholarly history, as has become usual. Given the prevalence even today of an interpretation of the Psalms of Solomon (and of Jewish "theocracy" in general) that has no real basis in the sources, one has to ask for developments in scholarship that have led to the widespread acceptance of such theories.

Efron is correct in pointing to Jewish "pietists" as the main focus of traditional theories about ancient Jewish history. It may well be derived from German theological scholarship, which would place it within the debate on "piety through works" (not highly valued and attributed to Jewish pietists such as the Pharisees) versus "piety through belief" (highly valued and the main attribute of Christians).[57] But the category has long since become

---

57. See Wellhausen, *Die Pharisäer und die Sadducäer*, 19: "ethischer und religiöser Materialismus." But see 118–19, where he is surprised to find that the Psalms of Solomon do value belief and morals, not only rituals; Wellhausen argues that this extraordinary step was called for by the turbulent political developments.

independent from theological scholarship. In historical works, at least in those written in German, "die Frommen" ("the pious ones") is still a general label for all possible groups of opposition towards the Hasmoneans, Herod, or any other political ruler. To give just one example, in a recent Herod biography by Baltrusch, the only one that can hope to replace Schalit's monumental work at least in the German speaking world, "die Frommen" figure solely as a monolithic obstruction to rational rule. The term sometimes expands towards "die Juden" as such. The Hasmoneans, Herod, the Romans—they all fail to rule Judea in the end because "die Frommen" cannot be convinced to accept political rulership.[58]

It is important to recognize some nuances, especially because Efron did not. "Die Frommen" as used by the scholars mentioned can be a pejorative designation, but it can also result from the struggle to come to terms with sources and events that often defy the patterns established in the study of the Graeco-Roman world. The term "theocracy" might also represent this challenge. The problem is that a term like "pious" hardly qualifies as an objective category for historical research, not least because all inhabitants who accept Hasmonean, Herodian, or Roman rule are implicitly denied piety. If it were marked as a self-description used, for example, in the Psalms of Solomon, or as the self-designation of a group such as the Hasidim (who do figure prominently in these models, although we do not know anything about them), things would be different. But using the term as an outside designation for a majority of the Jewish people can lead to nothing else than a reinforcement of traditional scholarly hypotheses about Jewish theocracy and its adherents. To complicate matters, such treatments could easily be described as fulfilling a number of recent criteria for innovative historical scholarship: Interdisciplinarity, sensibility to divergent cultural expectations, and an integration of a bottom-up perspective. It is not without irony that the most "progressive" historical treatments of Hasmonean and Herodian Judea are also most prone to reviving nineteenth-century theological discourses.

In addition to the use and abuse of pietism, another scholarly tradition should be noted that probably determined the assessment of the Psalms of Solomon as a historical source by Wellhausen, Meyer, and later scholars. One should not underestimate the legacy of nineteenth-century

---

58. Ernst Baltrusch, *Herodes: König im Heiligen Land: Eine Biographie* (Munich: Beck, 2012), e.g., 31, 34–36, 81–82, 128. Note that on 34, the "fromme jüdische Kreise" are documented by recourse to Ps. Sol. 17.

state-theoretical discourse. In handbooks on the history of the state, "theocracy" was regarded as characterizing the "oriental state"—the Old Testament being the main source for historically-oriented scholars.[59] It was thus part of the discourse on "oriental despotism" that can of course be traced back to Aristotle and even Aeschylus, but gained new importance as a heuristic device in the nineteenth century, as the "Greek polis" was invented as a positive precursor of the modern, German state, while all oriental phenomena were subsumed under the label "despotism."[60] Apart from the absolute, divine power of the ruler, characteristics of oriental despotism were supposed to be the importance of religion as an irrational, but traditional basis of authority, the apolitical nature of the inhabitants caused both by the Asian climate and the submissiveness towards rulers and gods, and, as a result, stagnancy, which allowed for general remarks on "the oriental" ancient and modern.[61]

This general way of constructing the Orient as the opposite of Greece also left its mark on historical investigations of Jewish history,[62] although the special role of Judaism as the precursor of Christianity (generally associated with the Greek side) was sometimes acknowledged. An additional driving force in historical scholarship, then, besides anti-Semitism, was antiorientalism. Anti-Semitic arguments could certainly be constructed

---

59. A good starting point is Georg Jellinek, *Allgemeine Staatslehre*, ed. W. Jellinek, 3rd ed. (Berlin: Häring, 1914), 288–92, whose call for a more differentiated perspective engages with the by then traditional views.

60. On oriental despotism, see Michael Curtis, *Orientalism and Islam: European Thinkers on Oriental Despotism in the Middle East and India* (Cambridge: Cambridge University Press, 2009); on the invention of the *polis* in the German "Altertumswissenschaften," see Wilfried Gawantka, *Die sogenannte Polis: Entstehung, Geschichte und Kritik der modernen althistorischen Grundbegriffe der griechische Staat die griechische Staatsidee die Polis* (Stuttgart: Steiner, 1985), esp. 119–37 on the connection with German nationalism. On the contrast between the Greek "Staatsidee" and oriental despotism, see Eckhard Meyer-Zwiffelhoffer, "Orientalismus? Die Rolle des Alten Orients in der deutschen Altertumswissenschaft und Altertumsgeschichte des 19. Jahrhunderts (ca. 1785–1910)," in *Getrennte Wege? Kommunikation, Raum und Wahrnehmung in der Alten Welt*, ed. Robert Rollinger, Andreas Luther, and Josef Wiesehöfer (Frankfurt am Main: Verlag Antike, 2007), 514–15.

61. A good example is Edwyn R. Bevan, *The House of Seleucus*, 2 vols. (London: Arnold, 1902), 1:3–8.

62. For a particular aspect and fuller discussion of the scholarly history see Benedikt Eckhardt, "Vom Volk zur Stadt? Ethnos und Polis im hellenistischen Orient," *JSJ* 45 (2014): 199–228.

on the basis of the supposed historical knowledge about the unwillingness of Orientals to adhere to a national state.[63] But this was not always the reason for adhering to the theory of oriental theocracy. Historians believed that they had found, or rather rediscovered in the footsteps of Aristotle, the main dividing line between Eastern and Western peoples, and thereby one of the main mechanisms of world history.

As a model of what to expect from an ancient Jewish text that was not commissioned by hellenized elites, this historical scheme must have also determined the Psalms of Solomon's assessment by multifaceted intellectuals like Wellhausen and Meyer. Their authority then gave credence to the traditional interpretation even after the great Hegelian theories of history were banned from historical scholarship.

5. Conclusion

It is easy to see that the usual understanding of the Psalms of Solomon fits traditional views both on Jewish piety and on oriental despotism very well. What does this mean? No serious scholar working today would regard the degradation of Jewish piety by Christian scholars as a model that should be followed. Nor would he or she deliberately base conclusions on interpretations that were determined by the orientalist discourses of the nineteenth century. The point of returning to the origins of the Psalms of Solomon's career as a historical source is another observation: they simply do not prove what they are said to prove in historical narratives, and the way they are used today—if we leave aside the rhetoric employed—does not fundamentally differ from Wellhausen or Meyer. One cannot help but see it as an unconscious continuation of discourses that every scholar would

---

63. For example, Theodor Nöldeke in his "Zur Characteristik der Semiten," published in 1872 (one year after the foundation of the German Reich) in the journal *Im Neuen Reich*, draws on historical insights into the character of Oriental peoples to reach the conclusion that Semites form a state only under the pressure of either religion or despots, and have no true adherence to that state. I have used the reprint in Theodor Nöldeke, *Orientalische Skizzen* (Berlin: Paetel, 1892), 12. Lurking in the background is the question of the adherence of German Jews to the newly formed German state. Another example, tied to the very same debate, would of course be Mommsen's infamous statement on Judaism as the "Ferment der nationalen Dekomposition" and its (unintended) career as an anti-Semitic slogan, on which see Hoffmann, *Juden und Judentum*, 96–103.

openly and justly reject if confronted with their more explicit articulations (some examples have been adduced above).

Although an awareness of the problematic scholarly history of Judaism can generally be presupposed, the influence of nineteenth-century scholarship should not be underestimated. It was in this period that many important methodological and interpretative advances were made. But it was also a period when a paradigm for the interpretation of oriental—and more specifically Jewish—history evolved that determined not only its general presentation, but also the interpretation of particular sources to such a degree that it is at times difficult to dissociate oneself from it. That the term "theocracy" ultimately goes back to Josephus further complicates the issue: the distinctions between modern and ancient perspectives are often blurred, and it can be difficult to disentangle them.

New approaches cannot hope to convince if they are based simply on eliminating the main sources of the old paradigm by declaring them Christian, as Efron did. But a critical evaluation of the actual contents as well as the generalizability of apocryphal texts is in order, without too many general presuppositions (and without hindsight based on events such as the Jewish War). This may make a sectarian prayer book a less exciting source at least for the reconstruction of political history. But anyone would agree that a critical attitude is a basic condition when working with historical sources—be they candles or cryptic texts such as the Psalms of Solomon.

Reflections on the Original Language of the Psalms of Solomon

Jan Joosten

Although they have come down to us in Greek and Syriac only, there is near unanimity among specialists that the Psalms of Solomon were originally written in Hebrew.[1] This consensus rests on several considerations. The Psalms almost certainly originated in Jerusalem over a rather short period following the conquest by Pompey in 63 BCE. In this time and locale, religious literature may be expected to be written in Hebrew. "Ort und Zweck entscheiden für hebräisches Original," writes Julius Wellhausen in his well-known authoritative style.[2] This general likelihood is taken to be confirmed by a variety of philological data: Hebraisms in the Greek text, indications of mistranslation, and the independent status of the Syriac version. On inspection, however, the specific philological arguments turn out to be weak. The Hebraisms of the Psalms may with more justification

---

1. See, e.g., Matthias Delcor, "Psaumes de Salomon," *DBSup* 9:214–245, in particular 221–22 and 224–25; Joseph L. Trafton, "Solomon, Psalms of," *ABD* 6:115-7; Robert B. Wright, *The Psalms of Solomon: A Critical Edition of the Greek Text*, JCTC 1 (New York: T&T Clark, 2007), 11-13. The only exceptions are Adolf Hilgenfeld in the nineteenth century and, more recently, Joshua Efron; see his "The *Psalms of Solomon*, the Hasmonean Decline and Christianity," in *Studies on the Hasmonean Period*, SJLA 39 (Leiden: Brill, 1987), 230–32. Efron's postulate that the Psalms were written in Greek is a consequence of his thesis that they are Christian texts. It is not argued on philological grounds. In recent times, Kim has also put forward the idea that the Psalms of Solomon were originally written in Greek, but the supposition does not seem to be based on serious research; see Heerak Christian Kim, *Psalms of Solomon: A New Translation and Introduction* (Highland Park, NJ: Hermit Kingdom Press, 2008), viii.

2. Julius Wellhausen, *Die Pharisäer und die Sadducäer: Eine Untersuchung zur inneren jüdischen Geschichte* (Greifswald: Bamberg, 1874), 131.

be called "Septuagintisms."³ Almost all of them find precise parallels in the Septuagint of the translated books. Thus, Ἐβόησα πρὸς κύριον ἐν τῷ θλίβεσθαί με (Ps. Sol. 1:1) could be a literal translation of אקרא ליהוה בצר לי or something similar.⁴ But it could equally well be a Greek creation loosely based on passages such as ἐν τῷ θλίβεσθαί με ἐπεκαλεσάμην τὸν κύριον, Ps 18[17]:7. The suggestion of mistranslation is always precarious when the source text is no longer available. In the case of the Psalms of Solomon it is particularly fragile. The Psalms of Solomon are a text unique in its genre. Moreover, they are known only from late manuscripts. There is no time presently to go through all suggested mistranslations. Suffice it to say that no single case is entirely convincing in regard to both the solution of the problem in Greek, and the reconstructed text in Hebrew.⁵

In recent times, the argument from the Syriac version has enjoyed some popularity. Trafton, hesitatingly, and Ward, more confidently, have tried to show that the Syriac version was not made on the basis of the Greek but independently goes back to a Hebrew text. This would of course clinch the matter. Trafton's arguments were rather tentative, however, as he himself admitted.⁶ As to Ward, his dissertation presents grave methodological deficiencies, making it hard to accept his claims.⁷ On balance, the evidence favoring the view that the Syriac is based on a Greek text close to that of the Greek manuscripts is much more convincing. In Ps. Sol. 13:3, the equivalent of Greek μύλαι "molars" is Syriac ܪܚܘܬܐ "millstones":

Ps. Sol. 13:3 θηρία ἐπεδράμοσαν αὐτοῖς πονηρά ἐν τοῖς ὀδοῦσιν αὐτῶν ἐτίλλοσαν σάρκας αὐτῶν καὶ ἐν ταῖς μύλαις ἔθλων ὀστᾶ αὐτῶν·

---

3. Herbert R. Ryle, and R. James Montague, ΨΑΛΜΟΙ ΣΟΛΟΜΩΝΤΟΣ: *Psalms of the Pharisees, Commonly Called the Psalms of Solomon* (Cambridge: Cambridge University Press, 1891), lxxxv.

4. Wilhelm Frankenberg, *Die Datierung der Psalmen Salomos: Ein Beitrag zur jüdischen Geschichte*, BZAW 1 (Giessen: Ricker, 1896), 66.

5. The Greek text of the Psalms is at times difficult to understand. Translation from Hebrew is not the only way to explain this, however. Note that the manuscripts are very recent and do not always agree with one another.

6. Joseph L. Trafton, *The Syriac Version of the Psalms of Solomon: A Critical Evaluation*, SCS 11 (Atlanta: Scholars Press, 1985).

7. Grant Ward, "The *Psalms of Solomon*: A Philological Analysis of the Greek and the Syriac Texts" (PhD diss., Temple University, 1996).

Evil wild animals rushed upon them, with their teeth they tore their flesh, and with their *molars* they crushed their bones.[8]

The Syriac reading is easily explained as a mistranslation reflecting the primary meaning of the Greek word.[9] The hypothesis that the Syriac reflects Hebrew לחיים "jaws," misread as רחיים "handmill," is gratuitous and explains the facts less well.[10] Many other Syriac renderings indicate dependence on the Greek.[11]

1. Arguments for a Greek Origin of the Psalms of Solomon

In the present paper the question of the original language of the Psalms of Solomon will be reconsidered. Several data would seem to indicate, against the consensus position, that they were composed directly in Greek. A selection of the evidence will be set out with a view to reopening the discussion.

1.1. Literary Allusions Based on the Septuagint

A first argument for a Greek origin can be taken from the literary allusions contained in the Psalms of Solomon. The Psalms of Solomon are full of references to books that today form part of the biblical canon: Psalms, Job, Proverbs, Isaiah, the Minor Prophets, Daniel, the Pentateuch, the historical books, and others. In this respect, the Psalms of Solomon conform to expectation. Other works from the same general period, such as the Qumran Hodayot, are similarly anthological. What is striking in regard to the Psalms of Solomon is that such allusions are generally clothed in the wording of the Septuagint. Let us consider one example:

---

8. Unless otherwise noted, all translations are taken from NETS.

9. Joachim Begrich, "Der Text der Psalmen Salomos," *ZNW* 38 (1939): 131–64, in particular 134–35.

10. Ward, "*Psalms of Solomon*," 150–51. While the parallelism between ὀδούς and μύλη (reflecting שן and מתלעה) is frequent in biblical poetry, the parallelism between teeth and jaw is attested only in Ps 3:8, in a context that is rather unlike that of Ps. Sol. 13:3 (in Ps 3:8, the teeth are broken, in Ps. Sol. 13:3, they bite).

11. Many of these were already pointed out by Harris in his edition of the Syriac text; see Rendel Harris and Alphonse Mingana, *The Odes and Psalms of Solomon*, 2 vols. (Manchester: Manchester University Press, 1916–1920).

Isa 19:14: κύριος γὰρ ἐκέρασεν αὐτοῖς πνεῦμα πλανήσεως
For the Lord mixed for them a spirit of confusion
MT: יְהוָה מָסַךְ בְּקִרְבָּהּ רוּחַ עִוְעִים

Ps. Sol. 8:14: ἐκέρασεν αὐτοῖς ὁ θεὸς πνεῦμα πλανήσεως
God mixed for them a spirit of confusion

As can be seen, the allusion in the psalm reproduces the wording of the Septuagint precisely. Cases like this can be explained on the supposition that the text of the Psalms was translated from Hebrew. One only has to suppose that the original Hebrew text of the Psalms of Solomon contained a reminiscence of the Isaiah passage,[12] which was recognized by the Greek translator, and rendered in accordance with the Septuagint version. The scenario may seem complicated, but it is in fact attested widely, including in Septuagint books that were certainly translated from Hebrew.[13]

In a few passages, however, it appears that the allusion is directly based on the Septuagint version and shows no knowledge of the Hebrew text. In such cases the explanation involving a Hebrew source text is unlikely. This phenomenon suggests that the author of the Psalms was composing his text in Greek. A good example is the following:

Ps 53[52]:6: ὁ θεὸς διεσκόρπισεν <u>ὀστᾶ</u> ἀνθρωπαρέσκων· κατῃσχύνθησαν, ὅτι ὁ θεὸς ἐξουδένωσεν αὐτούς
God scattered bones of men-pleasers; they were put to shame because God despised them
MT: אֱלֹהִים פִּזַּר עַצְמוֹת חֹנָךְ הֱבִשֹׁתָה כִּי־אֱלֹהִים מְאָסָם

Ps. Sol. 4:19: Σκορπισθείησαν σάρκες ἀνθρωπαρέσκων ὑπὸ θηρίων, καὶ <u>ὀστᾶ</u> παρανόμων κατέναντι τοῦ ἡλίου ἐν ἀτιμίᾳ
May the flesh of men-pleasers be scattered by wild beasts, and may the bones of the transgressors of the law lie before the sun in dishonor

---

12. Note that the verse in Isaiah is alluded to in the Hodayot, 1QH^a XIV, 26 and XV, 8.

13. For a study of this feature in the Septuagint of Psalms, see Jan Joosten, "The Impact of the Septuagint Pentateuch on the Greek Psalms," in *XIII Congress of the International Organization for Septuagint and Cognate Studies: Ljubljana 2007*, ed. Melvin K. H. Peters, SCS 55 (Atlanta: Society of Biblical Literature, 2008), 197–205.

Ps. Sol. 4:19 almost certainly alludes to Ps 53[52]:6, as is shown not only by the vocabulary but also by the striking image of the shameful scattering of bones or flesh. The scenario imagined above runs into difficulties here. In fact, it is not clear why a Hebrew author writing something like Ps. Sol. 4 would allude to Ps 53[52]:6 at all. Ps. Sol. 4 is all about hypocrisy and pretense of observing the law. But in the Hebrew tradition, Ps 53[52] has nothing to do with this theme.[14] The notion of hypocrisy comes in only in the Greek translation, notably through the use of the noun ἀνθρωπάρεσκος.

The intertextual dynamics of Ps. Sol. 4:19 suggest a different scenario: the author of the Psalms of Solomon, who was writing in Greek, exploited a literary allusion to the Greek text of Ps 53[52], which he found congenial to his general topic. Since the noun ἀνθρωπάρεσκος is used also in Ps. Sol. 4:7, 8 (as well as in the title), we might say that the reference to the Greek text of Ps 53[52] was a foundation stone for the author of Ps. Sol. 4.

Of course, we do not know what may have happened. Perhaps in some Hebrew tradition, unbeknownst to us, Ps 53[52] *was* connected to the notion of hypocrisy. Or perhaps the Greek translator of the Psalms of Solomon was inordinately creative, and inserted a literary allusion into the translation that was not there in the Hebrew.

Imaginative explanations like this become less likely, however, if they are to be invoked repeatedly. Several other examples confirm the impression that the "Greek scenario" explains the intertextual references of the Psalms of Solomon better than the "Hebrew scenario":

Num 25:4: παραδειγμάτισον αὐτοὺς κυρίῳ ἀπέναντι τοῦ ἡλίου
Make an example [MT הוֹקַע] of them to the Lord before the sun

Ps. Sol. 2:12: ἀπέναντι τοῦ ἡλίου παρεδειγμάτισαν ἀδικίας αὐτῶν
Before the sun they paraded their injustices

The combination of the rare verb παραδειγματίζω and the expression ἀπέναντι τοῦ ἡλίου suggests that there is a literary connection between

---

14. This statement is made not only in view of the MT, but also of the history of its interpretation. Neither the Targum to Psalms nor the Midrash Tehillim reflects any trace of an application of the psalm to hypocrites. The rendering "men-pleasers" is found in the Peshitta of Ps 53[52]:6, but because the Syriac is practically a calque of the Greek, the expression may there with confidence be attributed to influence from the Septuagint.

these two passages. One notes, however, that the implications of this combination are not the same: while Numbers speaks of corporal punishment, the Psalms of Solomon refer to the bringing to light of sins committed in secret. This reinterpretation works in Greek: παραδειγματίζω "to make an example of someone or something" accommodates both usages.[15] But it does not work in Hebrew. The verb הוקע does not mean "to expose, to parade," but rather "to impale" or "to precipitate from a rock" or something similar. A Hebrew writer would hardly have used it in reference to injustices. This means that if there is indeed a literary link, it must have been established in Greek. One could, again, imagine that a creative translator used language he knew from the Greek Pentateuch, even although his Hebrew source text contained no reminiscence of the passage in Numbers. One would be hard pressed to find an analogy for such a procedure. Rather than picture the translator as a creative writer, one is led to accept that the literary allusion was created by an author working in Greek.

An even more interesting example illustrates at once the "Hebrew scenario" and the "Greek" one:

Deut 28:25: καὶ ἔσῃ ἐν διασπορᾷ <u>ἐν πάσαις</u> ταῖς βασιλείαις τῆς γῆς
And you shall be in dispersion in all the kingdoms of the earth
MT: וְהָיִיתָ לְזַעֲוָה לְכֹל מַמְלְכוֹת הָאָרֶץ

Jer 34[41]:17 καὶ δώσω ὑμᾶς εἰς διασπορὰν πάσαις ταῖς βασιλείαις τῆς γῆς
I will give you as a dispersion to all the kingdoms of the earth
MT: וְנָתַתִּי אֶתְכֶם לְזַעֲוָה לְכֹל מַמְלְכוֹת הָאָרֶץ[16]

Ps. Sol. 9:2: <u>ἐν παντὶ</u> ἔθνει ἡ διασπορὰ τοῦ Ισραηλ κατὰ τὸ ῥῆμα τοῦ θεοῦ
Among every nation is Israel's dispersion, *according to the word of God*

In Deut 28:25, the rendering διασπορά, "dispersion," clearly diverges from the meaning of the Hebrew equivalent זועה/זעוה "trembling, terror."[17] The

---

15. The verb is used most often in the meaning "to make a show of someone," as in Ezek 28:17, but it also occurs in the meaning "to parade something," as in Jer 13:22.

16. The Hebrew is given according to the *ketiv*; the *qere* is זְעָוָה. Note that Jer 34[41]:20 also quotes from Deut 28 (v. 26). This may have made the identification of Jer 34[41]:17 as a quote easier.

17. The Hebrew word זועה/זעוה, "trembling, terror" is attested eight times in the Hebrew Bible. It is more or less correctly translated in Jer 15:4; Ezek 23:46; 2 Chr 29:8. In Deut 28:25, the divergence between the Hebrew and the Greek may be explained in

change triggered a rewriting of the entire verse: instead of Israel "becoming an object of terror to all the kingdoms" as in the MT, it will "be in dispersion *among* all the kingdoms" in the Septuagint. Thus, the idea of dispersion is introduced into a verse that originally spoke only of adversity and shame for Israel. The use of the same Greek word in the Septuagint of Jer 34[41]:17, where it again diverges from the Hebrew equivalent, is almost certainly due to influence from the Septuagint of Deuteronomy.[18] This shows the force of the "Hebrew scenario": the translator of Jeremiah identified the reference to Deut 28:25 in the Hebrew text of Jeremiah, and borrowed part of the Greek rendering of that verse, including the word διασπορά, even although it did not correspond to its equivalent in the Hebrew text. As in Deuteronomy, so in Jeremiah, the notion of dispersion has no contextual warrant.

In Ps. Sol. 9:2, the wording of Deut 28:25 is followed less faithfully, yet the use of the word διασπορά makes it likely that there is a literary connection. In addition, the expression "according to the word of God" indicates that the psalm is here referring to a biblical passage, probably none other than Deut 28:25. One might be tempted to explain the use of the word διασπορά in Ps. Sol. 9:2 in the same way as in Jer 34[41]:17. Two facts speak against this, however. The first one is the thought developed in Ps. Sol. 9:1–2. Clearly, the main theme here is Israel's forcible exile far from its own land:

---

different ways. The Hebrew may have been misread, or the translator may have wanted to refer to his own situation and that of his audience; perhaps this is a case where one could argue the Hebrew was "intentionally misread." The rendering has been much discussed in the literature, but the main question has not been why the translator diverged from the Hebrew but whether διασπορά in the Greek text has negative connotations; see, e.g., Willem Cornelis van Unnik, *Das Selbstverständnis der jüdischen Diaspora in der hellenistisch-römischen Zeit*, ed. and rev. Pieter W. van der Horst, AGJU 17 (Leiden: Brill, 1993), 91–92, with literature. More secondary literature is quoted in Martin Karrer and Wolfgang Kraus. eds., *Septuaginta Deutsch: Erläuterungen und Kommentare* (Stuttgart: Deutsche Bibelgesellschaft, 2011), 1:585–6.

18. In Jer 24:9, which also alludes to Deut 28:25, the word זועה/זעוה is rendered with the word διασκορπισμόν "scattering," a near synonym of διασπορά. This is a slender basis, however, for the claim that זועה/זעוה was interpreted to mean "dispersion." What led the translator to use διασκορπισμόν is most probably not the Hebrew word as such, but the perception that the verse alluded to the Deuteronomic curse.

When Israel was led away [ἐν τῷ ἀπαχθῆναι] in exile [ἀποικεσία] to a foreign land,
when they fell away from the Lord who redeemed them,
they were expelled from the inheritance,
which the Lord had given them. (Ps. Sol. 9:1)

If the psalm were written in Hebrew, the author would hardly be led at this point to refer to Deut 28:25, a passage that has nothing to say of exile. Only the Septuagint version, read without reference to the Hebrew, could serve as a justification for Israel's dispersion. Second, it is to be noted that the psalm alludes to the Deuteronomy passage very loosely. Although the thought is the same, practically the only word that is common to the two passages is precisely the word διασπορά. This means that if Ps. Sol. 9 was written in Hebrew, it would have been very hard for the translator to identify the scriptural passage referred to. These considerations lead to the conclusion that the reference to Deut 28:25 was worked into the text in a stage of Greek composition. The simplest explanation of such a phenomenon is to submit that the psalm was created from the start in Greek.

Other examples exist where the Greek text of the Psalms of Solomon shows a connection to original interpretations in the Septuagint.[19] There is no need to discuss them all. The above examples sufficiently demonstrate how it may be argued that the scriptural references of the Psalms of Solomon point to a Greek origin.

1.2. The Greek of the Psalms of Solomon

A second argument in favor of Greek origin can be drawn from the language of the Greek version. In spite of the Hebraistic diction, which may with equal justice be called "Septuagintal" diction, the Psalms of Solomon contain several features that are rare in books translated from Hebrew, and more typical of original Greek composition. Such features tend to indicate that the text was created in Greek. As in the preceding section, only a

---

19. In Ps. Sol. 8:29, καὶ σὺ παιδευτὴς ἡμῶν εἶ "You are our educator" is probably a reminiscence of the Greek version of Hos 5:2, ἐγὼ δὲ παιδευτὴς ὑμῶν "I am your educator"; and Ps. Sol. 8:23, "The pious (servants) of God are like innocent lambs in the midst of the nations of the earth" almost certainly alludes to the Septuagint of Mic 5:6 "The remnant of Jacob among the nations, in the midst of many peoples, shall be like dew falling from the Lord and like lambs in the grass." In both passages the Septuagint version is quite original.

selection of the evidence can be presented. Even a selection will show the force of this line of argument.

1.2.1. Successive Nouns Governing a Single Genitive

Because the construct state is to be followed immediately by a noun phrase, it is difficult in Hebrew to assign two entities to a single "possessor." Instead of saying "the chariots and horsemen of Israel" one says: רֶכֶב יִשְׂרָאֵל וּפָרָשָׁיו "the chariots of Israel and its horsemen." This peculiarity of Hebrew syntax has been carried over into the Greek of the Septuagint. In the translated books, there is hardly an example of two coordinated nouns governed by a single genitive.[20] In the Greek text of the Psalms of Solomon, however, this construction is encountered several times:

> Ps. Sol. 9:4: Τὰ ἔργα ἡμῶν ἐν ἐκλογῇ καὶ ἐξουσίᾳ τῆς ψυχῆς ἡμῶν
> Our works are in the choosing and power of our soul[21]
>
> Ps. Sol. 14:5: ἡ μερὶς καὶ κληρονομία τοῦ θεοῦ ἐστιν Ισραηλ
> For the portion and the inheritance of God is Israel
>
> Ps. Sol. 15:1: ἐλπὶς καὶ καταφυγὴ τῶν πτωχῶν σύ
> You are the hope and the refuge of the poor

None of these Greek phrases can easily be translated into Hebrew. Frankenberg's renderings are simply ungrammatical in these passages.[22] More to the point, the syntax is entirely uncommon in the Septuagint version of the translated books. It is, however, unproblematic in compositional Greek.

---

20. See, however, Tob 4:13 μὴ ὑπερηφανεύου τῇ καρδίᾳ σου ἀπὸ τῶν ἀδελφῶν σου καὶ <u>τῶν υἱῶν καὶ θυγατέρων τοῦ λαοῦ</u>.

21. It has been mooted that the "choosing" referred to is not that of the soul, but of God. The anthropological interpretation is much more likely, however; see Eberhard Bons's contribution in the present volume (where earlier literature is discussed).

22. Frankenberg, *Die Datierung der Psalmen Salomos*, 63–85; e.g., Frankenberg's translation (p. 79) of Ps. Sol. 14:5 is חלק ונחלת־אלהים ישראל, which leaves the word חלק without grammatical connection. The other examples are translated similarly.

1.2.2. Discontinuous Nominal Phrases

In a recent paper Eberhard Bons has drawn attention to an interesting stylistic feature in the Greek text of Ps 33[34]:13b:

τίς ἐστιν ἄνθρωπος ὁ θέλων ζωὴν ἀγαπῶν ἡμέρας ἰδεῖν ἀγαθάς;
What man is there that desires life, loving to see good days[23]?

The discontinuous word order, breaking up the noun phrase ἡμέρας ἀγαθάς "good days," is unremarkable in Greek. In the Septuagint Psalter, however, and in the entire corpus of translated books, it stands out as a highly unusual phenomenon.[24] In the Psalms of Solomon, this type of syntax is found repeatedly:

Ps. Sol. 13:3: θηρία ἐπεδράμοσαν αὐτοῖς πονηρά
Evil wild animals rushed upon them

Ps. Sol. 17:19: πηγαὶ συνεσχέθησαν αἰώνιοι
Eternal spring were held back

Ps. Sol. 17:43: διακρινεῖ λαοῦ φυλὰς ἡγιασμένου
He will judge the tribes of a sanctified people

Note also the following examples where an adnominal genitive is similarly separated from the noun governing it:

Ps. Sol. 4:20: ὀφθαλμοὺς ἐκκόψαισαν κόρακες ὑποκρινομένων
May ravens peck out the eyes of hypocrites

Ps. Sol. 15:1: εἰς βοήθειαν ἤλπισα τοῦ θεοῦ Ιακωβ
I hoped for the help of the God of Jacob

---

23. Literally "days to see good."
24. Eberhard Bons, "Rhetorical devices in the Septuagint Psalter," in *Et sapienter et eloquenter: Studies on Rhetorical and Stylistic Features of the Septuagint*, ed. Eberhard Bons and Thomas J. Kraus, FRLANT 241 (Göttingen: Vandenhoeck & Ruprecht, 2011), 69–79, in particular 70. Bons also refers to Ps 37[36]:16, but the example is less striking because the discontinuity occurs within a single noun phrase. There may be a few other cases of this type of word order in the translated books of the Septuagint, but they are certainly rare and unrepresentative.

The relative frequency of this feature indicates that it is not accidental but really reflects the style of the Psalms of Solomon.

Both of these linguistic features are difficult to account for if the Greek text we have is a translation from Hebrew. Several other syntactic features point in the same direction, but time doesn't permit to present them here.[25] In a pinch, a very free translation might exhibit one or two examples of such typically Greek syntax. This possibility creates another puzzle, however. If Psalms of Solomon were a translation, one would not expect it to be a free one. On the contrary, it would have to be a very literal one to account for all the Hebraisms. Thus, the postulate of a Hebrew source text runs into logical problems. The balance of probability comes down on the side of a Greek origin.

1.3. Provisional Conclusions

The evidence evaluated so far suggests that the Psalms of Solomon, contrary to the current consensus, were originally written in Greek. Allusions to scripture are to the Greek version, whose style and diction are imitated. And the author occasionally lapses into idiomatic Greek, adopting turns of phrase that are hardly attested in the translated books.[26] These considerations tentatively assign the Psalms of Solomon to a literary category in which one also finds the Testament of Abraham, parts of the Gospel of Luke, and according to recent investigations the Book of Judith.[27] These

---

25. The following phenomena deserve to be looked into: the insertion of a prepositional phrase between the article and its noun (Ps. Sol. 1:8 τὰ πρὸ αὐτῶν ἔθνη); the positioning of a genitive before its regens (Ps. Sol. 5:11 πτωχοῦ καὶ πένητος ἡ ἐλπίς); use of the sequence substantive-adjective-genitive (Ps. Sol. 15:3 ἐν ὀργάνῳ ἡρμοσμένῳ γλώσσης); the positioning of πᾶς after its headword (Ps. Sol. 2:10 τὰ κρίματά σου πάντα τὰ δίκαια).

26. An additional argument can be derived from the vocabulary of the Psalms of Solomon, as demonstrated by Eberhard Bons in the present volume.

27. See Jan Joosten, "The Original Language and Historical Milieu of the Book of Judith," *Meghillot 5–6: A Festschrift for Devorah Dimant* (ed. M. Bar-Asher and E. Tov; Jerusalem: The Bialik Institute, 2007), *159–*76; repr. in *Collected Studies on the Septuagint: From Language to Interpretation and Beyond*, FAT 83 (Tübingen: Mohr Siebeck, 2012), with a review of earlier literature. Moulton pointed out long ago that this phenomenon is not unexpected in Greek literature; see James H. Moulton, "New Testament Greek in the light of Modern Discovery," in *The Language of the New Testament: Classic Essays*, ed. Stanley E. Porter, JSNTSup 60 (Sheffield: Sheffield Academic

texts were originally written in Greek, in a style that imitates the translated books of the Septuagint. They reflect the fact that when the Septuagint became Scripture among Greek-speaking Jews and Christians, not only its contents, but also its form became normative. Later authors wishing to link up with the Septuagint adopted much of its diction.

The peculiar stylistic cast of the Psalms of Solomon may account for some of the hard passages that are sometimes invoked to argue for a Hebrew origin. Obscurity in the Greek text may be due to a scriptural allusion that is no longer understood. Alternatively, an allusion may not have been understood in antiquity and may consequently have become corrupted textually.

2. Historical Considerations

At this point in our argument, the question of the historical background must briefly be revisited. Is Greek composition reconcilable with what we know about the author—or possibly, group of authors—and his, or their, epoch? The Jerusalemite origin of the Psalms of Solomon should not be doubted, nor the dating to the period following the year 63 BCE. Also relatively certain, in my view, is the religious identity of the author, whose ideas and social location are close to that of the "Pharisees" (i.e., to proto-Rabbinic Judaism). Would a Jerusalemite Pharisee—if this is the correct term—in the early Roman era write religious poetry in Greek? Most knowledgeable scholars would probably hold that this is unlikely. Apart from Eupolemus—who, as a historian, is really a special case—it is hard to point to a certain example of religious texts written in Greek by Jews in Palestine during the Hellenistic and early Roman periods—Alexandria being of course a different affair.[28] The dominant medium for religious

---

Press, 1991), 60–97. On p. 75: "The reading of the classics soon shows us how the several literary forms attached themselves to dialects associated with their earliest exemplars. Epic poetry, even down to Nonnus, must endeavour to follow the nondescript dialect into which Ionic rhapsodists had transformed the Achaian of Homer. Choral odes in tragedy and comedy must preserve the broad long *alpha* which witnesses to the origin of drama in some region outside the area of the Ionic-Attic *eta*. We can therefore understand the instinct that would lead the educated Greek Evangelist to suit his style under certain conditions to the book which held the same relation to his Gospel as the *Iliad* held to subsequent experiments in epic verse."

28. See John J. Collins, *Jewish Cult and Hellenistic Culture: Essays on the Jewish Eencounter with Hellenism and Roman Rule*, JSJSup 100 (Leiden: Brill, 2005), 30.

texts was Hebrew. The extensive collection of religious writings from this period recovered from the Qumran caves is predominantly written in Hebrew, with a minority written in Aramaic. Greek is attested in Qumran only marginally, and only in translated texts.

Over against all this, two clues may perhaps render the idea of a Greek origin more plausible. The first clue comes from within the text of the Psalms of Solomon itself. The second is connected to a well-known process taking place among Palestinian Jews during the first century BCE.

2.1. The Connection to the Diaspora

In regard to the Psalms of Solomon, the preoccupation of the author with Jerusalem should not obscure the importance of the subtheme of Jewish life in the diaspora. Jerusalem, to the author, is the center of the world, but it is not his entire world. In 9:2–3, the origin of the dispersion is traced back to the Jews's apostasy and God's righteous judgment.[29] In 8:28, God is called upon to gather the diaspora in Jerusalem, and the whole of Ps. Sol. 11 prophesies the return of the exiles. A more recent movement away from Jerusalem seems to be referred to in 17:16–18:

> Those who loved the congregations of the devout fled from them, as sparrows were scattered from their nest. They wandered in wildernesses that their souls be saved from evil, and their saved soul was precious in the eyes of those who sojourned abroad. They were scattered over the whole earth by lawless men.

The presentation of the diaspora is not univocally negative. Ps. Sol. 8:23 states that "the pious servants of God are like innocent lambs in the midst of the nations of the earth." And Ps. Sol. 1:4 evokes the wealth and glory of the sons of Jerusalem that are spread out over the whole earth. Many of these references are more or less traditional and all of them are expressed in conventional language. Yet the fact that the theme recurs so often and with so much variation suggests that it is somehow close to the heart of the author. Without engaging in excessive speculation, we may posit that the author had firsthand knowledge of the Jewish diaspora in his own time. The passage in Ps. Sol. 17:16–18 may even suggest that the author himself spent time away from Jerusalem, in the "wilderness" together with other

---

29. Van Unnik, *Das Selbstverständnis der jüdischen Diaspora*, 71–72.

"lovers of the congregations of the devout." While religious life in Jerusalem was dominantly expressed in Hebrew, in the diaspora Greek was much more important. Thus, the prominence of the diaspora theme in the Psalms of Solomon raises at least the possibility of a connection to a Greek-speaking milieu.

3. Palestinian Revisions of the Greek Bible

The second clue is the demonstrable interest of proto-Rabbinic groups in Palestine during the first century BCE in the Septuagint. The prime exhibit is the Minor Prophets Scroll discovered in Nahal Hever and edited for the first time by Dominique Barthélemy.[30] The text is generally dated to the first century BCE. It clearly attests a revision of the Septuagint towards a Hebrew text closely aligned with the MT. On the basis of its translation technique, Barthélemy hypothesized that the revision followed a hermeneutical approach that would later come to characterize Rabbinic Judaism. Some of the details of his demonstration have been called into question, but the main outline of his thesis has widely been recognized as helpful. The Minor Prophets Scroll testifies to an enterprise that must have spanned centuries and involved many generations of scribes. Later evidence of this enterprise is found in the versions of Theodotion and Aquila. Many translation units within the Septuagint also bear witness to it: the so-called *kaige* sections in the books of Kingdoms, Esdras B, Lamentations, Canticles, and Ecclesiastes, the so-called Theodotionic version of Daniel, additions to the text of Job, and no doubt others. Most of these texts are of uncertain date, but they may roughly be related to the period going from 100 BCE to 100 CE. [31] The scope of the undertaking was to conform the Greek Bible to the Hebrew text and canon that were rising in authority. Although explicit testimonies are

---

30. Dominique Barthélemy, *Les devanciers d'Aquila: Première publication intégrale du texte des fragments du Dodécaprophéton trouvés dans le désert de Juda, précédée d'une étude sur les traductions et recensions grecques de la Bible réalisées au premier siècle de notre ère sous l'influence du rabbinat palestinien*, VTSup 10 (Leiden: Brill, 1963); Emanuel Tov and Robert. A. Kraft, eds., *The Greek Minor Prophets Scroll from Nahal Hever (8HevXIIgr) (The Seiyal Collection I)*, 2nd ed., DJD VIII (Oxford: Clarendon, 1995).

31. For the state of research on this question, see Natalio Fernández Marcos, *The Septuagint in Context: Introduction to the Greek Version of the Bible*, trans. Wilfred G. E. Watson (Leiden: Brill, 2000), 109–22.

lacking, the workshop executing this program must have been situated in Palestine, most probably in Jerusalem. Its time frame overlaps that of the Psalms of Solomon.

Thus, while there is little evidence of original production of Greek religious literature in Jewish Palestine, there is abundant evidence of sustained interest in the Greek biblical text. A potential link between the milieu that produced the revisions of the Septuagint and the author of the Psalms of Solomon may perhaps be found in a few items of vocabulary. Most of the religious vocabulary of the Psalms of Solomon comes straight from the Septuagint. But the Psalms of Solomon also contain a number of words absent from the Septuagint, or attested only in its most recent strata. Some of these words are also prominent in the revisions. A good example is the verb ὑποκρίνω, "to pretend, to deceive," and derived nouns, used in Ps. Sol. 4:6, 20, 22. In the Septuagint, this word group is largely absent, the only exceptions being three occurrences of the verb in Sirach. In Aquila and Theodotion, they are used systematically to render derivatives of the root חנף. Hebrew חנף means "to profane, to be impious" in most of its biblical occurrences. In later Hebrew, however, starting (probably) with Dan 11:32, it is attested with the meaning "to flatter, to deceive." The development of this vocabulary at once in Hebrew and in Greek is an epiphenomenon of the growing emphasis on observance of the law.[32] The fact that both the *kaige*-Theodotion-Aquila school and the Psalms of Solomon attest it suggests a degree of proximity between the two circles.

Another striking piece of evidence is the use of the word καταφορά with the rare meaning "deep sleep, lethargy." This word, unattested in the Septuagint, is found in Ps. Sol. 16:1, "I slipped for a short time, in the *lethargy* of those that sleep far from God." It is also the word used by Aquila to render Hebrew תרדמה "deep sleep, coma" in Gen 2:21 and in other passages.[33]

---

32. See, e.g., Moshe Weinfeld, "The Charge of Hypocrisy in Matthew 23 and in Jewish Sources," *Immanuel* 24/25 (1990): 52–58.

33. This and other similarities in the language use of the Psalms of Solomon and Aquila or Theodotion have been duly noted in the literature, e.g., Ryle and James (*Psalms of the Pharisees*, xci) have noted the presence of καταφορά, Aquila's rendering for תַּרְדֵּמָה. The same authors (ibid., 74) note that the title of Ps. Sol. 8 εἰς νῖκος is found in Theodotion.

There are several other points of contact between the vocabulary of our Psalms of Solomon and that of the revisions.[34] The matter would probably repay more extensive research than could be carried out in the preparation of this paper. The examples cited suffice to illustrate the interest of this approach, and also its limits. There are no grounds for arguing that one or another proto-Theodotion wrote the Psalms of Solomon. The evidence does indicate, however, that Jerusalem in the first century BCE was home to Jewish groups who had a good mastery of Greek and a profound interest in the Greek Bible. Thus, the Jerusalemite origin of the Psalms of Solomon does not preclude their having been written in Greek. The motivation for writing in Greek remains somewhat obscure. But the openness toward the diaspora evinced in several psalms may perhaps show that in this regard, too, the hypothesis of a Greek original is not outrageous.

4. Concluding Remarks

Two sets of observations make it possible to argue for a Greek origin of the Psalms of Solomon. The intense intertextuality of the corpus lends its Hebraic aspect. But a more penetrating analysis shows that the similarity to the Septuagint reflects imitation rather than a similar origin. Equally paradoxically, the language of the Psalms of Solomon is unlike that of any Greek literary text, but it nonetheless evinces traits that are unexpected in a text translated from Hebrew.

The demonstration attempted in the present paper does not suffice, perhaps, to turn around a consensus that has lasted well over a century. On some points, more research will be needed. And some arguments presented may be open to discussion. At the least, however, the present paper should contribute in putting the question of the original language of the Psalms of Solomon back on the agenda. The consensus position positing a Hebrew source text is itself based on hypothetical reasoning, some of which has escaped criticism for too long.

If the thesis of Greek origin should be judged to hold water, it will affect the exegesis of the Psalms significantly. It will also have implications for the evaluation of the historical background of the corpus. As the last part of the paper has tried to show, a Greek origin is not unthinkable in historical terms. It does, however, imply rethinking the social and

---

34. See, e.g., ἀνωφελής (Ps. Sol. 16:8); ἀποικεσία (Ps. Sol. 9:1); ἐκλογή (Ps. Sol. 9:4).

political location of the author of the corpus and of the group to whom it is addressed. Language use is never neutral. It may have been particularly fraught with significance among Jews in Jerusalem during the early Roman age.

Philosophical Vocabulary in the Psalms of Solomon: The Case of Ps. Sol. 9:4*

Eberhard Bons

1. Introduction

One of the most significant features of the Psalms of Solomon is its Greek style. There is no doubt that nearly each psalm of this collection is replete with so-called Hebraisms. It might suffice to quote some examples: the substantivated infinitive, for example, ἐν τῷ ὑπερηφανεύεσθαι τὸν ἁμαρτωλόν "when the sinner became proud" (Ps. Sol. 2:1); the expression οὐκ ... πᾶς ἄνθρωπος "no person" instead of οὐδείς (Ps. Sol. 2:9)[1]; the use of προστίθημι with infinitive in the sense of "to continue" (Ps. Sol. 5:4); the expression καὶ εἶπα ἐν τῇ καρδίᾳ μου "and I said in my heart" (Ps. Sol. 8:3) in the sense of "I thought." Moreover, the terminology of the Psalms of Solomon is largely borrowed from the Septuagint Psalter, as can be illustrated by some expressions of the vocabulary of lamentation: for example, ἐν τῷ θλίβεσθαί με "when I am afflicted" (Pss. Sol. 1:1; 15:1; Ps 18[17]:7); μὴ παρασιωπήσῃς ἀπ᾽ ἐμοῦ "do not pass be my in silence" (Ps. Sol. 5:2; Ps 28[27]:1; cf. Ps 35[34]:22; 39[38]:13; 109[108]:1); πρὸς σὲ κεκράξομαι "to you I will cry" (Ps. Sol. 5:8; Ps 30[29]:9; 86[85]:3).[2] However, the acquaintance with the Septuagint Psalter goes even farther. In the field of theological vocabulary in the strict

---

*I wish to thank my colleages Anna Passoni Dell'Acqua (Milan) and Jan Joosten (Strasbourg) for several remarks and suggestions.

1. For more examples, see Joseph Viteau, *Les Psaumes de Solomon: Introduction, texte grec et traduction, avec les principales variantes de la version syriaque par François Martin*, Documents pour l'étude de la Bible (Paris: Letouzey et Ané, 1911), 119–20.

2. For further examples, see Armin Lange and Matthias Weigold, *Biblical Quotations and Allusions in Second Temple Jewish Literature*, JAJSup 5 (Göttingen: Vandenhoeck & Ruprecht, 2011), 163–78.

sense, a couple of rare words only occur in the Septuagint Psalter and in the Psalms of Solomon, for example, the divine title ὑπερασπιστής "protector" (Ps. Sol. 7:7; cf. Ps 18[17]:3, 31, etc.), as well as the characterization of God as χρηστὸς καὶ ἐπιεικής "kind and gentle" (Ps. Sol. 5:12; Ps 86[85]:5). Finally, scholars have observed that the Greek language of the Psalms of Solomon displays various features which are typical of translation Greek[3]: on the level of vocabulary expressions like ἰδοὺ δή "see" (Ps. Sol. 8:25) and ἀποστρέφω τὸ πρόσωπον "to turn away the face" (Ps. Sol. 2:8); on the level of syntax the fact that the genitive absolute is very rare (Ps. Sol. 8:11, 30) while subordinate clauses are a little more frequent.[4] Be this as it may, these and other significant stylistic features of the Psalms of Solomon have prompted scholars to draw the following conclusion: the Greek text of the Psalms of Solomon represents a word-for-word translation from a Hebrew *Vorlage* which is no longer available. This result could be corroborated by a striking phenomenon: The Psalms of Solomon uses the terms ἔξοδος and εἴσοδος as synecdoche for a person's everyday activities (Ps. Sol. 4:14). It is noteworthy that this word order—that is, mentioning going out before coming in—corresponds to biblical models (see 2 Kgdms 3:25; Isa 37:28). In this regard, the Psalms of Solomon would be even more literal than the Septuagint Psalter, which quotes the two nouns ἔξοδος and εἴσοδος in reverse order (Ps 121[120]:8).[5]

The idea that the Psalms of Solomon represents a translation from Hebrew is an *opinio communis* shared by the majority of contemporary scholars.[6] Nevertheless, several questions remain open.[7] The Psalms of

---

3. Gerard Mussies, "Greek in Palestine and the Diaspora," in *The Jewish People in the First Century: Historical Geography, Political History, Social, Cultural and Religious Life and Institutions*, ed. Shemuel Safrai and Menahem Stern, CRINT 2 (Assen: Van Gorcum, 1976), 2:1048–49.

4. See the list in Viteau, *Les Psaumes de Salomon*, 109.

5. For detailed information about this LXX reading and its Greek background, above all in Egyptian papyri, see Thomas J. Kraus, " 'Der Herr wird deinen Eingang und deinen Ausgang bewahren': Über Herkunft und Fortleben von LXX Psalm CXX 8A," *VT* 56 (2006): 58–75.

6. See already Julius Wellhausen, *Die Pharisäer und die Sadducäer: Eine Untersuchung zur inneren jüdischen Geschichte* (Greifswald: Bamberg, 1874), 131–38; Viteau, *Les Psaumes de Salomon*, 120. As for contemporary research, see, e.g., Albert-Marie Denis and Jean-Claude Haelewyck *Introduction à la littérature religieuse judéo-hellénistique*, 2 vols (Turnhout: Brepols, 2000), 1:521: "La langue de composition a été probablement l'hébreu."

7. See Jan Joosten's contribution in the present volume.

Solomon include some rare words that are completely missing in the Septuagint, for example, ἀκρασία "lack of self-control" (Ps. Sol. 4:3), αὐτάρκεια "sufficiency, self-sufficiency" (Ps. Sol. 5:16), ἀμαθία "ignorance" (Ps. Sol. 18:4). Needless to say the quoted examples are compound words. Therefore, the question arises which Hebrew equivalents were underlying such renderings. Did the translator create these equivalents ad hoc, that is, without depending on a translation vocabulary of Hebrew-Greek equivalents already available at his time?[8] If so, did he borrow these nouns from his Hellenistic socio-cultural environment? Admittedly, it is difficult to give a clear-cut answer to these questions. In particular, it seems impossible to specify with which works or ideas the translator would have been familiar. However, this should not prevent us from looking for other criteria to better define the language and the background of the Psalms of Solomon.

In this paper I will focus on Ps. Sol. 9:4 without paying particular attention to its immediate context.[9] In the past, this verse has attracted the attention of scholars because it defends the idea of the freedom of the will. This idea served as criterion for attributing the Psalms of Solomon to the different currents of contemporary Palestinian Judaism, either to the Sadducees or to the Pharisees.[10] Leaving aside this question, I would like to address another issue, especially two nouns of this verse, ἐκλογή and ἐξουσία, and their exact meaning. The first noun is attested once more in the Psalms of Solomon (Ps. Sol. 18:5), whereas the second is quite frequent in the LXX (e.g., Sir 9:13; Dan 3:2). However, nowhere else in the LXX and in cognate literature are the two nouns used in parallel. On the other hand, the points of contact between the Psalms of Solomon and Hellenistic thinking are much more obvious.

---

8. See Emanuel Tov, "The Impact of the Septuagint Translation of the Torah on the Translation of Other Books," in *The Greek and Hebrew Bible: Collected Essays on the Septuagint*, VTSup 72 (Leiden: Brill, 1999), 184.

9. For a more detailed analysis of the Psalm, see Joachim Schüpphaus, *Die Psalmen Solomos: Ein Zeugnis Jerusalemer Theologie und Frömmigkeit in der Mitte des Vorchristlichen Jahrhunderts*, ALGHJ 7 (Leiden: Brill, 1977), 50–53; Mikael Winninge, *Sinners and the Righteous: A Comparative Study of the Psalms of Solomon and Paul's Letters*, ConBNT 26 (Stockholm: Almqvist & Wiksell, 1995), 69–77.

10. For the Sadducees, see, e.g., Ferdinand Hitzig in the nineteenth century; see also Viteau, *Les Psaumes de Salomon*, 200; for the Pharisees, see Herbert R. Ryle and Montague R. James, *ΨΑΛΜΟΙ ΣΟΛΟΜΩΝΤΟΣ: Psalms of the Pharisees, Commonly Called the Psalms of Solomon* (Cambridge: Cambridge University Press, 1891), l.

2. Ps. Sol. 9:4 in the Light of Its Philosophical Background

To begin with, a look on the complete verse will be helpful:

τὰ ἔργα ἡμῶν ἐν ἐκλογῇ καὶ ἐξουσίᾳ τῆς ψυχῆς ἡμῶν[11]
τοῦ ποιῆσαι δικαιοσύνην καὶ ἀδικίαν ἐν ἔργοις χειρῶν ἡμῶν
καὶ ἐν τῇ δικαιοσύνῃ σου ἐπισκέπτῃ υἱοὺς ἀνθρώπων.

Our works are in the election and power of our soul,
to do righteousness or injustice in the works of our hands,
and in your righteousness you visit the sons of men. (NETS, slightly modified)

It goes without saying that the verse addresses the question of free will, particularly by claiming that man is fully responsible for his acting, be it just or unjust.[12] No mention is made of other "factors," whose influence on human actions was debated in antiquity, for example, εἱμαρμένη or μοῖρα.[13] The third line underscores the idea of human responsibility: it is before God that humans have to give account of what they do because he will "visit," that is "call," them to account for their deeds.[14]

The two words to be dealt with in this paper are ἐκλογή and ἐξουσία. It is my contention that both are borrowed from contemporary philosophy, especially from Stoicism. To the best of my knowledge, this hypothesis has not yet been put forward. However, one methodological problem has to be tackled: The Psalms of Solomon probably dates from the second half of the first century BCE, or at the latest from the first decades of the first

---

11. Robert R. Hann, *The Manuscript History of the Psalms of Solomon*, SCS 13 (Chico, CA: Scholars Press, 1982), 29.83, mentions two slight variants: (1) the omission of the preposition ἐν in the manuscript group 253 as well as in ms 336, (2) μῶν instead of ἡμῶν in ms 471 (this second variant is present in neither Oscar von Gebhardt, ed., ΨΑΛΜΟΙ ΣΟΛΟΜΩΝΤΟΣ: *Die Psalmen Salomo's zum ersten Male mit Benutzung der Athoshandschriften und des Codex Casanatensis*, TUGAL 13/2 (Leipzig: Hinrichs, 1895], nor Robert B. Wright, *The Psalms of Solomon: A Critical Edition of the Greek Text*, JCTC 1 (New York: T&T Clark, 2007).

12. For a more nuanced position, see Schüpphaus, *Die Psalmen Salomos*, 51; Winninge, *Sinners and the Righteous*, 73–75; Kenneth Atkinson, *I Cried to the Lord: A Study of the Psalms of Solomon's Historical Background and Social Setting*, JSJSup 84 (Leiden: Brill, 2004), 189–90.

13. E.g., Dorothea Frede, "Schicksal," *DNP* 11:156–58.

14. For this use of the verb ἐπισκέπτομαι see, e.g., Sir 2:14; Ps. Sol. 15:12.

century CE.¹⁵ By contrast, many texts and ideas of Stoic philosophers are only accessible in documents of more recent times, for example, in summaries or quotations given by authors like Diogenes Laërtius, Stobaeus, or the fathers of the church. For this reason, it is impossible to prove a direct dependence between a passage of the Psalms of Solomon and a specific Stoic philosopher or a specific Stoic text. On the other hand, it cannot be excluded that Jewish authors living in Jerusalem had a certain knowledge of contemporary hellenistic philosophy.¹⁶

2.1. The Use of ΕΚΛΟΓΗ in Ethical Contexts

As for ἐκλογή and its underlying verb ἐκλέγω, "to single out, to choose," it is without any doubt a key term in Stoic ethics.¹⁷ Its main ideas are explained by Diogenes Laërtius in a brief outline he gives in the seventh book of his *Vitae philosophorum*. In this context, the idea of "choice" is crucial, man choosing continuously between values whose importance for his own life he has to find out, for example, on the field of the so-called indifferent things (τὰ ἀδιάφορα). Accordingly, he has to choose a value (ἐκλέγω) or choose to avoid it (ἀπεκλέγω), as Diogenes Laërtius explains (*Vit. philos.* 7.105).¹⁸ For Chrysippus, the decisive criterion to be put forward in these issues is εὐδαιμονία: Does a value contribute to it or does it not? The corresponding consequence is either ἐκλογή "choice" or ἀπεκλογή "rejection" (fr. 118 *apud* Stobaeus, *Ecl.* 2.7.7). In short, because humans are enabled

---

15. Robert B. Wright, "*Psalms of Solomon*," OTP 2:645; Denis and Haelewyck, *Introduction à la littérature religieuse judéo-hellénistique*, 1520–21.

16. E.g., Martin Hengel, *Judentum und Hellenismus: Studien zu ihrer Begegnung unter besonderer Berücksichtigung Palästinas bis zur Mitte des 2. Jh.s v. Chr.*, 3rd ed., WUNT 1/10 (Tübingen: Mohr Siebeck, 1988), 160.

17. Pace Felix Perles, *Zur Erklärung der Psalmen Salomos*, SOLZ 5 (Berlin: Peiser, 1902), 30, who claims: "Das Wort ἐκλογή findet sich in diesem Sinne auch noch einmal im NT (Rom 9,11 …) sonst aber nirgends in der gesamten Gräzität; see, e.g., Max Pohlenz, *Die Stoa: Geschichte einer geistigen Bewegung*, 7th ed. (Göttingen: Vandenhoeck & Ruprecht, 1992), 187: "Diogenes [von Babylon] verstand darunter die subjektive Stellungnahme, durch die wir positiv die naturgemäßen Dinge wählen, negativ die naturwidrigen verwerfen (ἐκλογή und ἀπεκλογή)." See the commentary by Robert Dobbin, ed., *Epictetus: Discourses Book 1*, Clarendon Later Ancient Philosophers (Oxford: Clarendon, 1998), 77.

18. A translation is available in Arthur A. Long and David N. Sedley, *The Hellenistic Philosophers*, 2 vols. (Cambridge: Cambridge University Press, 1987), 58B.

to use the freedom of will (Arrian, *Epict. diss.* 1.1.5), they have to practice ἐκλογή.

Among the Jewish authors of the Hellenistic and Roman period, only Josephus seems to be familiar with the ethical use of ἐκλογή. The noun appears in his brief description of the philosophical and religious convictions of the Sadducees in *B.J.* 2.164–165:

> Σαδδουκαῖοι δέ, τὸ δεύτερον τάγμα, τὴν μὲν εἱμαρμένην παντάπασιν ἀναιροῦσιν καὶ τὸν θεὸν ἔξω τοῦ δρᾶν τι κακὸν ἢ ἐφορᾶν τίθενται· φασὶν δ' ἐπ' ἀνθρώπων ἐκλογῇ τό τε καλὸν καὶ τὸ κακὸν προκεῖσθαι καὶ κατὰ γνώμην ἑκάστου τούτων ἑκατέρῳ προσιέναι.
>
> But the Sadducees are those that compose the second order, and take away fate entirely, and suppose that God is not concerned in our doing or not doing what is evil; and they say, that to do what is good, or what is evil, is at men's own choice, and that the one or the other belongs so to everyone, that they may act as they please.[19]

It is obvious that this passage reflects the following idea: good and evil are –according to the vocabulary of the text—lying before the choice of humans—so that it is up to them to make the right decision. At any rate, they cannot shift the responsibility of their actions to God.

2.2. The Use of ΕΞΟΥΣΙΑ in Ethical Contexts

The word ἐξουσία has a wide range of meanings going from "power, authority" to "office, magistracy." In ethical contexts, ἐξουσία means "power" in the sense that humans are able to have something at their disposal and command.[20] Probably some decades after the redaction of the Psalms of Solomon, the Stoic philosopher Epictetus (ca. 50–125 CE)[21] makes a sharp

---

19. Translation by William Whiston in Paul L. Maier, ed., *The New Complete Works of Josephus* (Grand Rapids: Kregel, 1999).

20. Klaus Scholtissek, *Vollmacht im Alten Testament und im Judentum: Begriffs- und motivgeschichtliche Studien zu einem bibeltheologischen Thema*, Paderborner theologische Studien 24 (Paderborn: Schöningh, 1993), 80. According to Joseph L. Trafton, *The Syriac Version of the Psalms of Solomon: A Critical Evaluation*, SCS 11 (Atlanta: Scholars Press, 1985), 101, the Peshitta strengthens the idea of free will by reading ܚܐܪܘܬܐ "liberty" (Ps. Sol. 9:4[7]).

21. See the overview of Epictetus's ethics by Adolf Bonhöffer, *Epictet und die Stoa: Untersuchungen zur stoischen Philosophie* (Stuttgart: Enke, 1890), 232–81; Pedro Pablo Fuentes González, "Épictète," *DPA* 3:130–32.

distinction between things which are in our power and things which are not and which therefore must not trouble us (Arrian, *Epict. diss.*, 1.25.2-3):

περὶ ἃ ἐσπουδάκαμεν, τούτων ἐξουσίαν οὐδεὶς ἔχει ὧν ἐξουσίαν οἱ ἄλλοι ἔχουσιν, τούτων οὐκ ἐπιστρεφόμεθα. ποῖον ἔτι πρᾶγμα ἔχομεν;
The things about which we have been busied are in no man's power: and the things which are in the power of others, we care not for. What kind of trouble have we still?[22]

Needless to say these things do not require any kind of ἐκλογή. Such an idea emerges elsewhere in Epictetus's *Dissertationes*: if things belong to one person who has been entrusted the ἐξουσία of them, nobody else can have them at his disposal so as to claim their ἐκλογή (Arrian, *Epict. diss.* 4.10.30):

τίς εἰμι ὁ θέλων αὐτὰ οὕτως ἔχειν ἢ οὕτως; μὴ γάρ μοι δέδοται ἐκλογὴ αὐτῶν; μὴ γὰρ ἐμέ τις αὐτῶν διοικητὴν πεποίηκεν; ἀρκεῖ μοι ὧν ἔχω ἐξουσίαν. ταῦτά με δεῖ κάλλιστα παρασκευάσαι.
Who am I who wish to have them in this way or in that? is a power of selecting them given to me? has any person made me the dispenser of them? Those things are enough for me over which I have power: I ought to manage them as well as I can.[23]

In conclusion, it is only ἐξουσία over something that qualifies us to make a decision so as to choose or to avoid something.[24] Without ἐξουσία no one is capable of practicing ἐκλογή.

3. Does Ps. Sol. 9:4 Have a Biblical Background?

In the light of the preceding observations, it is possible to draw the following conclusion: Ps. Sol. 9:4 employs a philosophical vocabulary typical of Stoic thinkers. Whether a person acts justly or injustly is not the result of destiny or determination. The author of Ps. Sol. 9:4 makes a similar claim:

---

22. For a short commentary of this passage, see Dobbin, *Epictetus*, 205.
23. Translation in George Long, *The Discourses of Epictetus* (London: Bell, 1890), 365.
24. See Arrian, *Epict. diss.* 2.2.26: τίς δ' ἐστὶ κύριος; ὁ τῶν ὑπὸ σοῦ τινος σπουδαζομένων ἢ ἐκκλινομένων ἔχων ἐξουσίαν "And who is the master? He who has the power over the things which you seek to gain or try to avoid."

human acting is fundamentally rooted in the power and in the choice an individual makes use of in a given situation. If this interpretation is correct, it is not necessary to take into consideration one that would attribute ἐξουσία to humans while this choice is determined by a divine ἐκλογή.[25]

It should be highlighted that the expression ἐν ἐκλογῇ καὶ ἐξουσίᾳ belongs to abstract philosophical terminology. This is all the more true if we compare Ps. Sol. 9:4 with one of the very few Jewish texts of the Hellenistic epoch dealing with human responsibility, Sir 15:11–17.[26] Unlike this passage, Ps. Sol. 9:4 is quite concise. However, the differences between both texts are not solely on the quantative level. On the one hand, Sir 15:11–17 has almost nothing in common with the vocabulary of Ps. Sol. 9:4, on the other hand, Sir 15:11–17 introduces biblical subjects which are not mentioned by Ps. Sol. 9:4: the idea of leading astray (v. 11), fear of the Lord (v. 13), creation (v. 14), the commandments (v. 15). In particular, the idea that God as creator has enabled humans to act freely and to keep the commandments has its biblical background in the creation narrative, especially Gen 2–3.[27] Furthermore, the idea of choice is explained in a different manner. Choice is considered a matter of εὐδοκία, "favourable estimation" (v. 15, cf. v. 17: ὃ ἐὰν εὐδοκήσῃ δοθήσεται αὐτῷ; "whatever one desires will be given to him"). Lastly, the human has the choice between fire and water. It depends on human will (verb θέλω, v. 16) as to which of the two is preferred. Obviously, this idea is influenced by biblical texts like Deut 30:15, 19.[28]

---

25. For this possibility, see Ryle and James, *Psalms of the Pharisees*, 95.

26. For the idea of human responsibility in Sir 15:11–17, see, e.g., Gian Luigi Prato, *Il problema della teodicea in Ben Sira: Composizione dei contrari e richiamo alle origini*, AnBib 65 (Rome: Biblical Institute Press, 1975), 234–36: see also 240: "'al principio' l'uomo è essenzialmente libero, anche se di fatto poi sceglie il male." See Ursel Wicke-Reuter, *Göttliche Providenz und menschliche Verantwortung bei Ben Sira und in der frühen Stoa*, BZAW 298 (Berlin: de Gruyter, 2000), 111–22, p. 115: "Nachdem Ben Sira im theologischen Teil seiner Argumentation gezeigt hat, daß Gott nicht der Urheber der Sünde ist, muß er umgekehrt begründen, daß der Mensch selbst die Verantwortung für sein Tun trägt;" Pancratius C. Beentjes, "Theodicy in the Wisdom of Ben Sira," in *"Happy the One Who Meditates on Wisdom" (Sir. 14,20): Collected Essays on the Book of Ben Sira*, ed. Pancratius C. Beentjes, CBET 43 (Leuven: Peeters, 2006), 266–270.

27. Prato, *Il problema della teodicea*, 246.

28. Wicke-Reuter, *Göttliche Providenz*, 121; Prato, *Il problema della teodicea*, 245–46.

In conclusion, the comparison between Sir 15:11–17 and Ps. Sol. 9:4 sheds some more light on the literary features of the latter quotation. To be sure, the latter of the two texts mentions the hands and the soul, which could be a reminiscence of Hebrew thought. Nevertheless, there is no doubt that a typical biblical background is missing in the first two lines of Ps. Sol. 9:4.

4. Can We Reconstruct the Hebrew *Vorlage* of Ps. Sol. 9:4?

As we have seen, Ps. Sol. 9:4 reveals a direct or at least indirect knowledge of Greek philosophical terminology, especially of the currents of Stoic philosophy. This leads to another question: Can we reconstruct an underlying Hebrew text?

In the past, scholars have suggested to read words such as בְּחִירָה "choice,"[29] חֵפֶץ "delight, pleasure" or רָצוֹן "favor, will"[30] as possible Hebrew equivalents of ἐκλογή. As for ἐξουσία, the Hebrew equivalents are mostly מֶמְשָׁלָה "rule, realm, dominion"[31] (e.g., Ps 114[113]:2) and nouns of the root שׁלט (e.g., Eccl 8:8). Of course, we cannot exclude from the outset that these or other words could have been included in a Hebrew *Vorlage* of the verse. However, in the absence of any trace of a Hebrew text of the Psalms of Solomon, it is useless to engage in such speculations. Moreover, the question arises whether the two mentioned Greek terms introduced slight philosophical overtones which were extraneous to a possible Hebrew *Vorlage*.

Perhaps, the terminological evidence of Ps. Sol. 9:4 suggests a consideration of a hypothesis that diverges largely from the *opinio communis*: Nobody can deny that the Psalms of Solomon is written in a Hebraizing style. Analyzing the texts carefully, we find the whole range of characteristics of Biblical Greek, even rare phenomena that are typical of the LXX Psalter. Nevertheless, here and there the texts exhibit literary features, in particular on the level of vocabulary, which appear to be fully incompatible with Biblical Hebrew.[32] In certain cases, it turns out to be impossible to

---

29. Eduard Ephraem Geiger, *Der Psalter Salomo's herausgegeben und erklärt* (Augsburg: Wolff, 1871), 184; Perles, *Zur Erklärung der Psalmen Salomos*, 29.
30. See Gottlob Schrenk, "ἐκλογή," *TDNT* 4:176.
31. Perles, *Zur Erklärung der Psalmen Salomos*, 30.
32. For other arguments that could confirm these observations, see Jan Joosten's contribution in the present volume.

find a corresponding Hebrew word that was already known in the Hellenistic and Roman epoch. The case of Ps. Sol. 9:4 is a good example, which shows that at least its first line is not directly influenced by biblical models. This twofold evidence—Hebraizing style on the one hand and on the other a vocabulary that is not attested in biblical Greek—requires an explanation. Therefore a new hypothesis deserves careful consideration: despite the Hebraizing style of the Psalms of Solomon, some words or expressions betray a Greek background. Thus it seems conceivable that the Psalms of Solomon is not (or not completely) a word-by-word-translation but that it has been rewritten or composed—at least partially—in Greek and not in Hebrew, though imitating Hebrew style and diction.

Some Thoughts on and Implications from Genre Categorization in the Psalms of Solomon

Brad Embry

1. Introduction

The aim of this paper is to reevaluate the genre classification of the Psalms of Solomon. Need for such a reevaluation is evidenced by recent treatments of the document in which it is variously classified as psalmic, apocalyptic, and Deuteronomic. All of these classifications lack, more or less, a degree of accuracy that might aid in both the interpretation of the document by specialists and, perhaps more critically, the placement of the Psalms of Solomon as an interpretive partner for scholars of Second Temple period Jewish socio-religious movements and literary productions, including work on the New Testament. In 1991, Marinus de Jonge sounded a word of caution that, while specifically addressing views of the future in the Psalms of Solomon, holds implications for the critical study of Second Temple period texts more generally, "We cannot trace the essential characteristics of the Jewish expectation of the future by analysing it in its literary form in a dogmatic-classifying way."[1] The attempt in what follows is to get at some of the "essential characteristics" of the Psalms of Solomon by looking beyond the immediate literary form and to itemize some of the features of the document by way of thematic categories.

This essay will argue that the document espouses a worldview and theo-philosophical orientation that resonates with that of biblical prophecy. By addressing the particular historical situation that he and his community faced—the invasion and dominance of Rome—through the

---

[1]. Marinus de Jonge "The Expectation of the Future in the *Psalms of Solomon*," in *Jewish Eschatology, Early Christian Christology and the Testaments of the Twelve Patriarchs: Collected Essays of Marinus de Jonge*, NovTSup 63 (Leiden: Brill, 1991), 5.

"religious utilization of history," the author was able to produce a document that addressed this crisis with a certain, theo-historical sangfroid.[2] A prophetic worldview, in addition to providing an ideological or theological narrative source thread for the "anointed of the Lord" in Ps. Sol. 17 as heir to the Davidic line, also provides a *Weltanschauung* that can accommodate the catastrophe of Roman invasion and dominance. The messianic impulse, which reads "against the grain" of the historical reality of Roman might, is a fluid continuation of this prophetic worldview: restoration, through miraculous and interventive means, follows from God's punishment, which is a response to the sins and covenantal infidelity on the part of the community of God.

There are a number of reasons to allow for an association between biblical prophecy and the Psalms of Solomon despite the document's literary similarities with the biblical Psalter. The first is that psalmic and poetic discourses are familiar literary forms for the prophetic corpus and are therefore not exclusive property of the biblical Psalter.[3] Habakkuk comes to mind as a prophetic text that contains psalmic forms, and every prophetic text is replete with poetic discourse. So, the literary form of psalms or poetry finds expression in the medium of prophecy as well as in psalms.

More important, the Psalms of Solomon shares core, thematic features with biblical prophecy. In his treatment of prophetic literature from the Hebrew Bible, Gerhard von Rad was careful to stress that, while there exists no singular "message" of biblical prophecy that unifies all prophetic expressions, certain salient features were common to most prophetic utterances. These, he identifies, as three: "[T]he new eschatological word with which Yahweh addresses Israel, the old election tradition, and the personal situation, be it one which incurred penalty or one which needed comfort, of the people addressed by the prophet."[4] All three rubrics could

---

2. I will be using the singular "author" throughout for clarity and ease, even though it is likely that the Psalms of Solomon was shaped by numerous hands.

3. In particular, see Susan E. Gillingham, *The Poems and Psalms of the Hebrew Bible*, Oxford Bible Series (Oxford: Oxford University Press, 1994), who notes the overlap between psalmic expression and prophetic content.

4. Gerhard von Rad, *The Message of the Prophets*, trans. D. M. G. Stalker (London: Oliver & Boyd, 1965; repr. San Francisco: HarperSanFrancisco, 1972), 101. For a critique of von Rad's tradition-historical approach, see Christopher Seitz, *Prophecy and Hermeneutics: Towards a New Introduction to the Prophets* (Grand Rapids: Baker Academic, 2007), 163–71. In his critique of von Rad's efforts to provide a comprehensive analysis without flattening out the individual prophetic voices, Seitz comments:

be used to categorize points of interest for the Psalms of Solomon. But, before looking in greater detail at the appearance of these features in the Psalms of Solomon, a few words should be said to address contemporary genre classifications for the Psalms of Solomon.

2. Common, Contemporary Treatments of the Psalms of Solomon

Categorization of Second Temple documents essentially takes on the idiosyncratic qualities of that era of Jewish literature. So, Jewish testamentary or apocalyptic literature from this period have their own literary forms. But, all categories of literature in this period can be traced to biblical models. For instance, apocalyptic literature of this period, while evincing its own, distinctive qualities, owes much to biblical base models such as Ezekiel or Daniel. For the Psalms of Solomon, a common approach is to suggest that the biblical Psalter functions as that biblical base.[5] There is much to commend this association, even apart from the title of the document. The psalms in the Psalms of Solomon are written in psalmic form; they are poetic and contain evidence that suggests that they were accompanied by music in a liturgical setting.[6] The presence of chapter titles is also a psalmic gesture.

"While one can defend von Rad as not seeking to write a commentary or give a full examination of the literature of the prophets, it at the same time remains the case that he has invented a genre of interpretation that stands aloof in a great many ways from the prophetic literature in the form in which we actually receive it. This new genre is something like 'the historical-theological development of Israel's traditions, as they move toward the New Testament.' But in what way is this selection from the canonical prophetic corpus an accurate reflection of what Israel came to regard as the Nebiim...?" (164). This question may benefit from an evaluation of how the author of the Psalms of Solomon may have viewed his own writing.

5. See, e.g., Robert B. Wright, "*Psalms of Solomon*," in *OTP* 2:636–70 and Kenneth Atkinson, *An Intertextual Study of the Psalms of Solomon: Pseudepigrapha*, SBEC 49 (Lewiston, NY: Mellen, 2001).

6. The manner in which these psalms may have been used is complicated by two factors. First, the Psalms of Solomon is not part of any canonical tradition—whether that is an existing tradition or, as research in the area of Second Temple period Judaism often implies, an implicit "scriptural" tradition in which numerous texts that are noncanonical today circulated with a "canonical authority" in first century Judaism. George Brooke, "Between Authority and Canon: The Significance of Reworking the Bible for Understanding the Canonical Process," in *Reworking the Bible: Apocryphal*

Beyond this literary classification, the biblical Psalter also holds the character of David in high regard, giving expression to a Davidic theology that stresses David's special place in the pantheon of Israelite kings in addition to numerous authorial ascriptions. Psalms 2 and 110 are two examples illustrating David's importance, which then functioned as source threads for messianic texts later (e.g., 4Q174 [4QFlor]; 4Q285 fr. 5 lines 2–3), of which Ps. Sol. 17 would be a premier example.

However, these similarities are not uniquely shared by the Psalms of Solomon and the biblical Psalter. Interest in Davidic theology is not limited to the biblical Psalter. For both of the major histories of the Hebrew Bible, that of the Deuteronomist and the Chronicler, as well as all of the major prophetic texts (Isaiah, Jeremiah, and Ezekiel), several of the Minor Prophets (Hos 3:5; Amos 6:5, 9:11; and especially Zechariah's vision of the future restoration in Zech 12–13) and postexilic literature (Ruth, Ezra/Nehemiah), the character of David is an important theological figure in Israelite history. He is the best of Israel's kings and, in the historical memory of Israel, is emblematic both of Israel's glorious past and her idealized future. The exilic and postexilic communities in particular looked to the return of David as evidence of Israel's full restoration in the land. Importantly for prophets such as Ezekiel, this included a restored temple and a unified nation (see Ezek 37–48), both of which are features for the

---

and Related Texts at Qumran: Proceedings of a Joint Symposium by the Orion Center for the Study of the Dead Sea Scrolls and Associated Literature and the Hebrew University Institute for Advanced Studies Research Group on Qumran, 15–17 January, 2002, ed. Esther G. Chazon, Devorah Dimant, and Ruth A. Clements, STDJ 58 (Leiden: Brill, 2005), 85 referred to this process as moving from "authority to canon." This makes it impossible to associate the Psalms of Solomon with a broader liturgical tradition, the use of which in a community can aid in interpreting the contents of the document or the communal awareness of its message. Second, manuscript evidence suggests that the Psalms of Solomon was connected, at one point and in some fashion, with the Odes of Solomon and that the document was preserved, as was the case with many of the ancient writings, by the Christian community. But the Odes of Solomon, while originally Jewish, contain obvious Christian editorial additions. The deliberate connection between Odes of Solomon and the Psalms of Solomon, which did not save the Psalms of Solomon from being excised from the major MS traditions (e.g., Alexandrinus), seems to suggest that this connection was due to Christian interpretive methods. But, the Psalms of Solomon shows no invasion of Christian religious perspectives. It may be the case that the Psalms of Solomon simply did not fit, ideologically, with either the Odes of Solomon or the Christian view of prophetic discourse. That is, the Psalms of Solomon was simply not Christian enough.

Psalms of Solomon. All this suggests that the form of Davidic theology expressed in the Psalms of Solomon is better explained through intertextual connections with the prophetic tradition than through connections with the biblical Psalter.[7]

In fact, when it comes to assessing issues of genre and the influence of biblical narrative or worldview for the Psalms of Solomon, commentators rarely deploy the biblical Psalter in a systematic way to explain the content or ideological outlook of the Psalms of Solomon; comparisons between the two tend to have much more to do with literary form than they do with thematic content and narrative development or structural form. This may be due to the fact that the biblical Psalter is notoriously difficult to summarize by way of an overarching theological or ideological trajectory, no matter how general that rubric might be.[8] This in turns makes the biblical Psalter difficult to "use" as an intertextual guide for assessing content or theme-driven issues for later texts. To be sure, the biblical Psalter was an important resource for later Jewish and Christian communities. But, these references tend to occur in florilegial constructions.

---

7. One interesting aspect for the Psalms of Solomon, which has yet to be explored fully, is the theological ramifications for choosing the name Solomon as the pseudepigraphic author best suited to introduce the messiah in the line of David in Ps. Sol. 17. This may speak to Solomon's characterization in the Second Temple period as a prophetic figure from the Hebrew Bible; see Bradley J. Embry, "Solomon's Name as a Prophetic Hallmark in Jewish and Christian Texts," *Henoch* 28 (2006): 47–62.

8. See, e.g., Hermann Gunkel, *The Psalms: A Form-Critical Introduction*, trans. Thomas M. Horner, FBBS 19 (Philadelphia: Fortress, 1967); Sigmund Mowinckel *The Psalms in Israel's Worship*, trans. D. R. Ap-Thomas (New York: Abingdon, 1962; repr. Grand Rapids: Eerdmans, 2004); Claus Westermann, *The Psalms: Structure, Content and Message* (Minneapolis: Augsburg, 1980); Walter Brueggemann, *The Message of the Psalms: A Theological Commentary*, OTS (Minneapolis: Augsburg, 1984); and Norman Whybray, *Reading the Psalms as a Book*, JSOTSup 222 (Sheffield: Sheffield Academic Press, 1996). For Mowinckel, the effort was to pinpoint the historical and situational setting for the Psalms, which would, in Mowinckel's view, allow for greater access to the compositions. But, he also notes in his introduction (1): "Incidentally, in my view, this difference in time has not been of any great importance for their real place and function in the religious life of the congregation." Despite Mowinckel's effort to distance the prophetic corpora from the psalmic on this note—that in the Psalms the "human heart has found its counterpart at all times"—the same approach may be made of the prophetic texts. This is much more a question of hermeneutical theory than it is of biblical, textual criticism.

Recent work on the Psalms of Solomon proposes a high degree of unity and cohesion for the document.⁹ This suggests that the author(s) was(were) not interested simply in creating a document that responded to the historical calamity of the era by way of a series of loosely arranged references to the Hebrew Bible. Rather, it seems as though the author was driven by a theo-philosophical vision that set his community's experiences within the biblical tradition in a more organic way. That is, the concern was not simply to offer comfort, but to stress that he and his community stood on the cusp of a revision of the historical order, something that the Hebrew Bible addresses in the prophetic traditions. This community was, so to speak, living in that moment of God's restorative plans. Given the frenetic nature of the biblical Psalter, it seems unlikely that the relatively unified composition of the Psalms of Solomon used the biblical Psalter as its primary source for articulating this response.

In his recent exploration of the placement of the Psalms of Solomon in wisdom and apocalyptic traditions, Rodney A. Werline comments in his critique of the association of the Psalms of Solomon with apocalyptic material that the "proper literary category for the Psalms of Solomon is a collection of psalms."¹⁰ But, when Werline addresses the ideological and theological content of the Psalms of Solomon as to its perspective on historical factors, messianism, and notions of sovereignty and rule, he only refers to the biblical Psalter once, and there in a footnote.¹¹ Instead, Werline always refers (and

---

9. Kenneth Atkinson, "Theodicy in the *Psalms of Solomon*," in *Theodicy in the World of the Bible*, ed. Antti Laato and Johannes C. de Moor (Leiden: Brill, 2003) 546–75. George W. E. Nickelsburg (*Jewish Literature between the Bible and the Mishnah: A Historical and Literary Introduction*, 2nd ed. [Minneapolis: Fortress, 2005], 238) has suggested that the Psalms of Solomon displays a "didactic character" that distinguishes the Psalms of Solomon from the biblical Psalter.

10. Rodney A. Werline, "The *Psalms of Solomon* and the Ideology of Rule" in *Conflicted Boundaries in Wisdom and Apocalypticism*, ed. Lawrence M. Wills and Benjamin G. Wright III, SBLSymS 35 (Atlanta: Society of Biblical Literature, 2005), 83.

11. In fact, even this reference should be discarded. Werline cites Ps 106[105]:21 as evidence of a widespread biblical understanding of God as "savior" (σωτήρ). But Ps 106[105]:21 is crediting God as "saving" (σῴζων) Israel ("They forgot the God who saved them"), thus as an activity of God and not necessarily as a title for God. Each of his other references in the footnote are from Isaiah (43:3, 11, and 60:16, σῴζων; Isa 45:15, 21, σωτήρ; and 49:26, ὁ ῥυσάμενος), all of which use these terms as a title for God and which is Werline's point in regards to its usage in the Psalms of Solomon.

I believe rightly) to the prophetic corpus or to Deuteronomy when dealing with the ideology of the Psalms of Solomon. Werline's instinct to cite from the prophetic material and not the biblical Psalter should indicate that genre issues cannot be solved simply by reference to literary form.

Another view of the Psalms of Solomon, popularized by Robert B. Wright, is that the Psalms of Solomon uses apocalyptic themes and is, therefore, closely associated with that genre.[12] This thesis has not won wide support.[13] While I agree with this rejection of Wright's thesis, it may be that he has identified important thematic motifs for the Psalms of Solomon that had previously gone without proper attention.[14]

Academic treatments of apocalyptic literature have long noted the close connection between prophetic and apocalyptic discourse. Paul Hanson's influential work suggests that the origins of apocalyptic traditions were to be found in the biblical prophetic tradition from the late sixth century BCE.[15] As heir to the worldview of biblical prophecy, one would expect apocalyptic thought to share ideas and outlook with its older brother. John J. Collins has clarified this view by stressing the uniqueness of apocalyptic thought and demonstrating that the differences suggest a new reality in apocalyptic thought that cannot be explained simply by recourse to the prophetic model.[16] However, Collins too notes that the differences between apocalyptic and prophetic thought do not mitigate their shared characteristics. Thus, Hanson may have simply overstated the case, missing the matter quantitatively rather than qualitatively. Wright may have done the same with regard to his assessment of the Psalms of

---

12. Wright, "*Psalms of Solomon*," 2:642–43. Wright (643) also refers to the Psalms of Solomon as "crisis literature."

13. Atkinson, "Theodicy," 551; Werline, "The *Psalms of Solomon* and the Ideology of Rule" 83; John J. Collins, "Introduction: Towards the Morphology of a Genre," *Semeia* 14 (1979): 9, and idem, *The Apocalyptic Imagination: An Introduction to the Jewish Matrix of Christianity* (Grand Rapids: Eerdmans, 1998), 143; Bradley J. Embry "The *Psalms of Solomon* and the New Testament: Intertextuality and the Need for a Re-Evaluation" *JSP* 13 (2002): 122–26.

14. For instance, I believe that Wright is correct when he notes that the depictions of the foreign conqueror in the Psalms of Solomon are "concrete to a degree paralleled only in Daniel" (Robert B. Wright, *The Psalms of Solomon: A Critical Edition of the Greek Text*, JCTC 1 [London: T&T Clark, 2007], 4).

15. Paul D. Hanson, *The Dawn of Apocalyptic: The Historical and Sociological Roots of Jewish Apocalyptic Eschatology*, rev. ed. (Philadelphia: Fortress, 1979).

16. John J. Collins, *The Apocalyptic Imagination*.

Solomon and Jewish apocalyptic literature from this era. He has identified themes and structures in the Psalms of Solomon that resonate with the apocalyptic genre, but has, perhaps, simply overstated this connection. Since both apocalyptic and prophetic literature share similarities, such as a prioritization of covenantal fidelity, identification of the sinful acts of the community, the subsequent punishment of the community by God, and the ultimate fulfillment or restoration of history as part of God's actions on behalf of the community, it could be that Wright has identified not a shared apocalyptic worldview between the Psalms of Solomon and the biblical text, but rather a shared prophetic vision of history. This would free commentators from having to accommodate for the distinctive features of Jewish apocalyptic literature during this period while retaining the conceptual characteristics noted by Wright.

On linguistic grounds, the Psalms of Solomon seems to part company from the biblical Psalter in other, important ways. One example of this is the author's use of Deuteronomic language.[17] There is one final view of the Psalms of Solomon that has recently surfaced in scholarship and which is, I believe, working in the right direction towards a better understanding of the ideological framework for the document. Werline has suggested that the Psalms of Solomon expresses a "Deuteronomic" resonance in its ideology.[18] This view is supported by William Horbury whose recent work on the remembrance of God in the Psalms of Solomon draws on numerous references to this concept from the biblical Psalter as well as the Pentateuch (in particular Deut. 8:18) and Isaiah.[19] These two

---

17. Werline, "The *Psalms of Solomon* and the Ideology of Rule," 69–87; and William Horbury "The Remembrance of God in the *Psalms of Solomon*" in *Memory in the Bible and Antiquity: The Fifth Durham-Tübingen Research Symposium (Durham, September 2004)*, ed. Steven C. Barton, Loren T. Stuckenbruck, and Benjamin G. Wold, WUNT 1/212 (Tübingen: Mohr Siebeck, 2007), 111–28; e.g., the term παιδεία occurs in the Psalms of Solomon approximately the same number of times that it occurs in the biblical Psalter (noted by P. Pouchelle "Critique textuelle et traduction du treizième *Psaume de Salomon*" *JSJ* 42 [2011]: 510 n. 9, so as to emphasize the great frequency of παιδεία in the Psalms of Solomon in comparison with the Psalms). Obviously, this could not indicate that the author of the Psalms of Solomon was consciously attempting to replicate the biblical Psalter, as the term appears approximately the same number of times in the biblical prophetic texts. Hence, issues of influence must rest on other criteria.

18. Werline, "The *Psalms of Solomon* and the Ideology of Rule," 72–74.

19. Horbury, "'The Remembrance of God," 111–28.

works identify an important theological and narratological superstructure that may have influenced the author of the Psalms of Solomon in constructing his reaction to the historical crisis of Roman invasion and domination, one that is more cohesive and definable than allowed for by reference to the biblical Psalter. The author may have been articulating a view of history that was determined by this biblical template, which gave a prominent place to Deuteronomic theology and ideology, rather than simply pulling scriptural references piecemeal from the Hebrew Bible. Given the references to David in the major prophetic texts and the association of David as a model for messianic foundations in the historical books, both preexilic (D-History) and postexilic (Chronicler), the author of the Psalms of Solomon may have been giving voice to this tradition as a method of encouraging his community in the face of this crisis. That is, the historical memory of both Israel's traditions (its history) and the projection of those traditions in a recycled form onto a current context (prophecy) functioned as a means of addressing a present conundrum. The activity of Pompey and the Romans was merely the first step in unlocking the historical process that would culminate, as Isaiah, Jeremiah, or Ezekiel might have it, in the arrival of "David," the anointed figure responsible for instituting Yahweh's kingdom on earth and restoring Israel. This fits comfortably with a covenantal perspective articulated by the D-Historian, who would have sympathized with the Psalms of Solomon's program of punishment for disobedience. The ideological complex of punishment-restoration is a prophetic *Tendenz*, one that forms a core thematic element in the Psalms of Solomon. This theme cannot be captured or articulated solely by literary form and, even if present in the biblical Psalter in degrees, does not identify a programmatic superstructure that may be extruded from it.

3. Why Prophecy Might be a More Accurate Genre Description for the Psalms of Solomon and Why This Matters

If there are limitations to associating the Psalms of Solomon with biblical prophecy as a method for understanding the historical vision of the author, how might biblical prophecy help? More immediately, do structural elements exist within the Psalms of Solomon that resonate with biblical prophecy in a programmatic way? If we take von Rad's outline from above and its three categories for biblical prophecy, perhaps we can detect in the Psalms of Solomon a superstructure for the document.

3.1. The Personal Situation and the Historicization of Prophetic Hope

While some debate may yet remain over the precise details of the historical milieu of the Psalms of Solomon, a general consensus remains that the Psalms of Solomon address a period of history from approximately 63 BCE to 37 BCE. [20] Ps. Sol. 2, along with Pss. Sol. 1, 8, and 17, captures elements from this historical period of Roman invasion and assertion of hegemony in the region. I would agree with Nickelsburg in adding Pss. Sol. 7 and 18 to this category, which fall into his designation "Psalms of the Nation,"[21] which for him means the historical reality of the nation. Three of these psalms (1, 2, and 8) have been referred to as expressions of dismay and lamentation. Ps. Sol. 17 has avoided this description owing to the presence of the "anointed of the Lord" and the eschatological vision of reordering and restoration that occasions his advent. Ps. Sol. 7 focuses on the disciplinary and corrective value of the conquest while appealing to God to protect his people from the gentiles. Ps. Sol. 18 seems to address the future for Israel and to suppress discussions of the historical crisis of 63 BCE.

However, the fact that these psalms express different reactions to the same historical occasion and are understood as the historical foundations for the document should suggest that a common theme, and not simply a common occasion, transects the document. Owing to the presence of Ps. Sol. 17 in the category of historical psalms, lamentation cannot be the unifying feature of these psalms. A single, historical occasion generates two different results. The first is punishment and the second restoration.

---

20. See Wright *"Psalms of Solomon"* 2:640–642; and Robert B. Wright, "The Psalms of Solomon: The Pharisees and the Essenes," in *1972 Proceedings for the International Organization for Septuagint and Cognate Studies and the Society of Biblical Literature Pseudepigrapha Seminar*, ed. Robert A. Kraft, SCS 2 (Missoula, MT: Society of Biblical Literature, 1972), 150 n. 8; Atkinson, *An intertextual Study*, 397–98. Nickelsburg, *Jewish Literature*, 238–47, suggestively places his discussion of the Psalms of Solomon in the chapter concerning the rise of the house of Herod.

21. Nickelsburg, *Jewish Literature*, 241, also adds Ps. Sol. 11 to this category, which speaks to the return of those in the Diaspora. Since his category is "Psalms of the Nation," this makes sense. But, this notion of restoration is a key, prophetic theme that does not necessarily have a specific, historical moment. If the Psalms of Solomon fits the prophetic model, then Ps. Sol. 11 would be an example of this hope in future restoration, which is such an important motif for the biblical prophets (see, e.g., Isa 11 or Ezek 40–48), and a fitting prelude to Ps. Sol. 17.

Set within this two-part response, the author also routinely returns to the motif of God's sovereignty and gives expression to an assurance that, despite appearances to the contrary, the author's God, the God of Israel and his community, is orchestrating these events. This motif of punishment-restoration, along with the hope that it can generate when grounded in a view of God's universal sovereignty, is part of the prophetic worldview. In this way, a primary motif is that of God's sovereignty, and one can well imagine how crucial this theme would be for the author's community. For the sake of space, Ps. Sol. 2 will function as the test case for this punishment-restoration motif and its ability to articulate assurances in God's sovereignty and hope. In this psalm, the author uses an effective point-counterpoint system to establish his perspective on the historical crisis.

Ps. Sol. 2:1–9: A Psalm of Solomon Concerning Jerusalem[22]

1 Arrogantly the sinner broke down the strong walls with a battering ram and you did not interfere.
2 Gentile foreigners went up to your place of sacrifice; they arrogantly trampled (it) with their sandals.
3 For the sons of Jerusalem defiled the sanctuary of the Lord; they were profaning the offerings of God with lawless acts;
4 Because of these things he said, "Remove them far from me; they are not sweet-smelling."
5 The beauty of his glory was despised before God; it was completely disgraced.
6 The sons and the daughters (were) in harsh captivity, their neck in a seal, a spectacle among the gentiles.
7 He did (this) to them according to their sins, so that he abandoned them to the hands of those who prevailed.
8 For he turned away his face from their mercy; (from) young and old and their children once again, for they sinned once again by not listening.
9 And the heavens were weighed down, and the earth despised them, for no one on (the earth) had done what they did.

The historical situation was the conquest of Jerusalem by Pompey in 63 BCE, which clearly evoked deep and profound emotions from the author. The first nine lines read as a lament. However, they also provide a rationale for the conquest, one that is carefully inserted by way of a cause and effect clause in

---

22. The translation is taken from Wright, *OTP* 2:651–54, unless otherwise noted.

v. 4 as well as an explanatory comment in v. 8 for why God had turned his face from mercy. The conquest is punishment for the sinful activities of the people of Jerusalem. Thus, the punishment is rooted in a cause-effect relationship, which draws on covenantal language and perspective (e.g., Deut 28–30 and Lev 26) and which is very important to the biblical prophetic texts. Ps. Sol. 2:10 evokes this covenantal framework:

> 10 And the earth shall know all your righteous judgments, O God.

The point-counterpoint here is in the form of judgment and vindication of this judgment. This is also an assertion of God's sovereignty; God was responsible for this catastrophe and it is a form of judgment. The point (punishment/dismay) played against the counterpoint (universal recognition of God's sovereignty/God's righteous actions) creates a view of the historical crisis, terrible though it may be, as an organic extension of God's relationship with this community; sin and the rejection of God leads to punishment. Ps. Sol. 2 continues by reverting to the theme of punishment/dismay in verses 11–14:

> 11 They set up the sons of Jerusalem for derision because of her prostitutes. Everyone passing by entered in in broad daylight.
> 12 They derided their lawless actions even in comparison to what they themselves were doing; before the sun they held up their unrighteousness to contempt.
> 13 And the daughters of Jerusalem were profane,[23] according to your judgments, because they defiled themselves with improper intercourse.
> 14 My heart and my belly are troubled over these things.

We are back to the "point." The author continually provides an explanation as to why these events have befallen Jerusalem. The sons of Jerusalem consult prostitutes (v. 11); the people are "unrighteous" (v. 12); the daughters of Jerusalem practice illicit sexual unions (v. 13). The author is clearly disturbed by these things—both the sins and the resulting punishment—for in v. 22 the author would plead for God's judgment to come to an end, evocative of Amos 7:1–6. However, note the counterpoint in verse 15:

---

23. My translation; Wright has "available to all."

15 I shall prove you right, O God, in uprightness of heart; for your judgments are right, O God.

The connection between the punishment and God's sovereignty can be seen in the judgment of God, which are both the cause of Jerusalem's misfortunes and the substance of the author's praise. In this way, Ps. Sol. 2 is not simply a lament or "literature of crisis," but rather extols God's righteous actions in bringing punishment upon Jerusalem. By implication, it is also an assertion of God's universal sovereignty, a point made clear later in the chapter by the subjection of the gentile ruler (Pompey) to God's punishment owing to Pompey's hubris (Ps. Sol. 2:26–27). Perhaps more importantly, this view also forms a foundation upon which the author can begin to build a vision of the future. The conquest of Jerusalem—an act of punishment in concert with covenantal parameters of Israel's past—unlocks a process that leads to the future restoration in which those who are faithful to God's will and covenant will realize the coming of God's kingdom. Importantly, the arrival of God's kingdom develops out of this assertion of universal sovereignty and, as a result, necessarily implicates the known historical order.

The rejection of God produces a reflexive response from God to punish the community. This is wedded in the Psalms of Solomon to the arrival of a foreign conqueror and the attendant assertion of God's sovereignty in the form of puppeteer to world history and foreign nations.[24] This is a prophetic *Tendenz*. Moreover, the language use in Ps. Sol. 2:11–14 seems to indicate a strong reliance on the prophetic literature. For instance, in v. 11, the noun used for "prostitute" (πόρνη) appears nowhere in the biblical Psalter. However, this term is used fourteen times in biblical prophecy.[25] In v. 13, the term βέβηλοι (translated here as "profane") appears in

---

24. E.g., Ps. Sol. 8 (compare 1–6 [point] with 7 [counterpoint] and 11–22 [point] with 23–32 [counterpoint]) and Ps. Sol. 17 (compare 5–9 [point] and 10 [counterpoint]); 9:1–3; and 15:10–13. In biblical prophecy, foreign nations are viewed as evidence of God's activity in history (e.g., Assyria: Isaiah 10; Babylon: Isaiah 39 [see Jer 20:4]; Persia: Isaiah 13 [see Jer. 51:11]).

25. There is no nominal use of "prostitute" in the biblical Psalter. The verb πορνεύω does appear in the biblical Psalter in two places, Ps 73[72]:27 and Ps 106[105]:39. Psalm 106[105] uses some of the same techniques as found in Hebrew Bible prophecy and the Psalms of Solomon for accommodating for Israel's punishment. In biblical prophecy, the concept of Israel's infidelity as a form of prostitution appears approximatively sixty-eight times (this includes nominal and verbal forms).

the Hebrew Bible as a noun only fifteen times and never in the Psalter.[26] The term appears in the prophetic corpus only in Ezekiel (Ezek 21:30, 22:26, and 44:23) and four times in the Psalms of Solomon.[27] Finally, the unusual term φυρμός ("disorder") in v. 13 appears twice (once as a noun and once in a verbal form) in the Psalms of Solomon (2:13 and 8:9).[28] It is not used in the biblical Psalter and appears only once in the biblical text (Ezek 7:23). Notably, that section of Ezek 7 discusses the sins of Israel and the coming punishment: Yahweh sees the idolatry and uncleanness of the people (Ezek 7:20) and sends a foreign nation as conqueror (Ezek 7:24). A specific constellation of terms appear in Ps. Sol. 2 that suggest that the author was influenced by this specific portion of Ezekiel: ὑπερηφανία (Ps. Sol. 2:2, 25 and Ezek 7:20); ἀλλότριος (Ps. Sol. 2:2 and Ezek 7:21); βεβηλόω (Ps. Sol. 2:3 and Ezek 7:21 [βέβηλος appears in Ps. Sol. 2:13]); ἀποστρέφω used the same phrasing (Ps. Sol. 2:8 [ἀπέστρεψεν γὰρ τὸ πρόσωπον αὐτοῦ] and Ezek 7:22 [ἀποστρέψω τὸ πρόσωπόν μου]); μιαίνω (Ps. Sol. 2:3 and Ezek 7:22, 24).

It is here that Wright's emphasis on the precision with which the Psalms of Solomon and Daniel identify the historical situation sets the document apart from the biblical Psalter and positions it more as an heir to the prophetic tradition. By the time the author reaches the end of his work, the means by which the restoration of Israel and the installation of Yahweh's kingdom on earth as a universal kingdom is resolved is through the advent of the anointed of the Lord. This is the final counterpoint in the document, suggesting that this thematic complex of punishment for

---

26. As a verb, the term occurs six times in the biblical Psalter and thirty-seven times in the prophetic corpus.

27. The term appears to be almost exclusively priestly in application. Of the fifteen occurrences (Lev 10:10; 1 Kgdms 21:5–6; 2 Macc 5:16; 3 Macc 2:2, 14; 4:16; 7:15; Pss. Sol. 2:13; 4:1; 8:12; 17:45 and the references in Ezekiel), only 3 Macc 4:16 and 7:15 appear to use the term apart from a cultic context. Its appearance in the Psalms of Solomon represents a greater concentration than any other biblical text except for 3 Maccabees.

28. This concept of mixing as a process of defilement is also important to the prophets. For instance, in Hos 4:14, the term συμφύρω appears alongside the term for prostitute (both πορνεύω and πόρνη). Συμφύρω occurs elsewhere only in Sir 12:14 and Ps. Sol. 8:9. Illicit sexual unions are highlighted in the Psalms of Solomon as one of the key problems in Israel, and the combination of "mixing/prostitution" also appears as an important motif for several other prophets (Jer 3:2 and Ezek 16:22). This concept does not appear in the biblical Psalter.

sin-restoration may function as a superstructural element for the entire document.

3.2. The Old Election Tradition

As is commonly noted, the Psalms of Solomon is replete with references to the Hebrew Bible and to traditions that define the Israelite community as the chosen people of God. Zion theology is important for the author with this motif appearing in Ps. Sol. 1:1–3; 2:1–5 (esp. 4–5 and the "glory" of Jerusalem), 19–23; 7:1–2; 8:4; 11; and 17:22–31. The election tradition may also be expressed in the author's use of terms or phrases such as "Israel" (5:18; 7:8; 8:26 and 28; 9:1–2, 8 and 11; 10:5–8; 11:1, 6–9; 12:6; 14:5 [here particularly in connection with the law in 14:2–4]; 16:3 [author's soul "was drawn away from the Lord God of Israel"]; 17:4, 21, 42, 44–45; 18:1, 5), "house of Jacob" or "Jacob's God" (7:10; 15:1 ["Jacob's God"]), "descendants of Abraham" (9:9; 18:3 [importantly, Abraham is referred to here as an Israelite]), "covenant" (9:10; 10:4—with reference to "a covenant with our ancestors" in 9:10 [inheritance of the Lord's promises in 12:6]).[29]

The phrases "descendants of Abraham" and "covenant" or "covenant with our ancestors" in particular lay bare the author's rearticulation of the election tradition.[30] It may be of some note that this reference occurs in Ps. Sol. 9, which forms the medial point in the document, and then again at the end. Importantly, the Psalms of Solomon also contains a reference to the exile and loss of the inheritance (9:1–2), which directly contradicts the patriarchal promises. By invoking the election tradition, the author

---

29. It may also be the case that "beloved son" (Ps. Sol. 13:9), and "firstborn (son)" (Pss. Sol. 13:9 and 18:4 [in connection with "only child" in Ps. Sol. 18:4]) give voice to a tradition in which Israel is viewed as God's beloved son (e.g., Exod 4:22). See Jon D. Levenson's treatment of this tradition and its evolution in the Hebrew Bible in *The Death and Resurrection of the Beloved Son: The Transformation of Child Sacrifice in Judaism and Christianity* (New Haven: Yale University Press, 1993).

30. The appearance of "Jacob" as a surrogate for "Israel" is also important. In the Balaam oracles from Num 23–24, the term Jacob is used to collectively refer to Israelite identity and, importantly is wed to notions of Israel's function in relationship to God. See Num 23:7, 10, 21, 23 (where Jacob and Israel are paired); 24:5, 17, 19. Num 24:17 is particularly important given its messianic interpretation by later Jewish communities alongside Ps 2:9 and Isa 11:4. The name is used to designate Israel approximatively thirty-four times in the biblical Psalter and seventy-five times in biblical prophecy.

reengages these past promises as a method of accommodating their loss and does so with the point-counterpoint motif found elsewhere.

Of course, it goes almost without saying that biblical prophecy was grounded fundamentally in covenantal relationship. All prophetic utterances that had Israel as their primary subject matter (e.g., not including Nahum) held to a view of covenantal infidelity as the primary issue in Israelite society. To be sure, this was articulated idiosyncratically; Ezekiel's vision of this infidelity differs from that of Amos. However, covenantal infidelity and the reaction of punishment as a corrective remains a salient feature for biblical prophecy.

3.3. The New Eschatological Word with Which Yahweh Addresses Israel

The presence of the old tradition in the thought world of the author of the Psalms of Solomon stresses the point that this author understood a line of continuity between the Israel of the biblical tradition and that of his present community. Importantly, this allowed the author to draw on that sacred tradition as a means of offering comfort and direction during a period of great historical upheaval. In this way, the author was a traditionalist, holding on to core concepts from this biblical tradition, such as Zion and David theology; it also explains the author's resilient commitment to the temple.

But traditional views are elements with which the author gets at the contemporary religious (and socio-political) issues that are particularly at stake for him and his community. It is the recasting of these traditions in the light of the historical reality that galvanizes them into a "new word" modality for the author. This is every bit a matter of interpreting the biblical text; so the author of the Psalms of Solomon is offering a form of midrash on biblical traditions in a contemporary setting. However, this form of interpretation is also generative of a new manner of speaking or addressing the current historical situation and, as such, goes beyond the category of commentary.[31]

The most obvious instance of this is the reference to the anointed of the Lord in Ps. Sol. 17. There, the Davidic theology evident in pre- and postexilic literature ranging across historical, psalmic, and prophetic

---

31. Shani Berrin, "Pesher Nahum, *Psalms of Solomon* and Pompey," in Chazon, Dimant, and Clements, *Reworking the Bible*, 65–84.

lines, is reengaged as a means by which the current historical crisis will be addressed. However, this is neither *sui generis* nor simple parroting; the author sees his particular historical moment as a time in which this new reality—that of the advent of the Davidic messiah who will rescue Israel, reinstitute the proper religious activities in Jerusalem, and function as a leader to the entire world community—will unfold.

One of the features often noted by von Rad in his treatment of Isaiah's prophecy is that not one of the prophet's utterances about Zion came true.[32] Von Rad then uses this piece of information not as a criticism of the veracity of the prophet's message, but as a method of further characterizing Isaiah as a person, his understanding of the word of Yahweh, and his ultimate role as a prophet. One implication of this is that that prophetic discourse is partly aimed at meeting a contemporary crisis with the armament at one's disposal and is nuanced in historically and personally idiosyncratic ways. In the case of Isaiah, Zion and Davidic theology (the two primary categories of von Rad's treatment of Isaiah) exert an irrepressible influence on the prophet and his work. However, given the reality of the historical failures of both his community and elements of his prophetic utterance, Isaiah is led to a revelation of a "new word" in which the "stump of Jesse" (Isa 11) or the so-called "Suffering Servant" (Isa 53) arrives and restores Israel and institutes Yahweh's kingdom.

For the Psalms of Solomon, the nuance is aimed at viewing the arrival of the Davidic messiah as a cumulative act in the on-going interaction between God, the community of God, and the wider world. In either case, that of Isaiah or that of the Psalms of Solomon, the worldview is similar. The prophetic model of managing the historical situation in which the community of God (Israel) seems irretrievably consigned to servitude to a dominant power (Assyria, Babylon, Rome) by way of the inbreaking power of God to rearrange the historical situation through the rescue of Israel and the subjugation and exertion of sovereignty over the entire world (through the "stump of Jesse," the "Suffering Servant," or the "anointed of the Lord") helps explain the coordination of historical and eschatological features in the Psalms of Solomon, all the while honoring the document's overall continuity. This prophetic framework can easily accommodate the author's rejection of certain segments of his immediate community (the sinners), the punishment of gentile oppressors, and the continual refer-

---

32. Von Rad, *The Message of the Prophets*, 137.

ence to the educative, disciplinary effect of God's activity in relationship to the author's community. Given the right ideological orientation on the part of the author, which I am here suggesting is a prophetic orientation, the collision between the traditional views of Israelite identity and society, the author's own communal self-awareness, and the immediate historical reality leads to the generation of a "new word."

4. Conclusions and the Effect of Biblical Prophecy for Understanding the Psalms of Solomon

The importance of accurately assessing genre categories for contemporary scholarship on the Psalms of Solomon is twofold. First, the activity of interpreting ancient communal notions of religious identity, worldview, social, and political issues is based almost entirely on literary artifacts from that period, and genre expectations and classification is an area of great importance in promoting an accurate assessment of the content of any document. If the Psalms of Solomon was considered a prophetic expression, then our understanding of the author's worldview, not to mention his views on key social aspects of Israelite (Jewish) identity during his day, might become more refined.

Second, a more far-reaching (and admittedly ambitious) effect of this view of the Psalms of Solomon is that it may hold implications for our understanding of how the author of the Psalms of Solomon understood the work that he produced. If this author was cognizant of a prophetic framework of history and was keen to deploy this model in addressing his own historical crisis, which includes such an overt reference to the Davidic messiah, it may be possible that the author viewed his work as participating, directly and organically, in this biblical tradition. If so, this may suggest that the author viewed his work as a "biblical" text, extending the tradition of the prophets by locating the (potential) fulfillment of the prophetic model of history in his own day and age. This point is all the more significant given the text from Zech 13:1–4 in which the prophet announces the cessation of the prophetic office once a set of criteria was met. The elements that lead to the cessation of the prophetic office were the opening of a "fountain for the house of David and the inhabitants of Jerusalem" (13:1), the cleansing of Jerusalem from "sin and impurity" (13:1), and the eradication of idolatry (13:2). Significantly, these events occur for Zechariah after the activity of the "pierced one" (Zech 12:10), a text that would become an important messianic reference in the New Testament, particularly for John (see John 19:34 and Rev 1:7). For Zechariah, the terminal point for the prophetic office was located in the restoration of Jerusalem and the house of David, both features central to the ideological portrait for the Psalms of Solomon. Is it possible that the author of the Psalms of Solomon had in mind that he was composing at the very least an extension of the prophetic corpora if not its terminus, one that contained all the necessary ingredients to see the arrival of God's kingdom on earth?

This would suggest that the biblical prophetic view of history in which God was set to break into human history in a revelatory manner was a vibrant theological idea in at least one expression of Judaism of the first century BCE. This resonates with portions of the New Testament's view of history and the work of Jesus, who was understood as the fulfillment of the prophetic view of history. To be sure, the differences of opinion over the nature of the messiah are stark between the Psalms of Solomon and the New Testament. But, a shared outlook suggests a common theme; namely, that the writing of additional books, such as the Psalms of Solomon or the gospels, was a continuation of the biblical tradition of expectation, and in particular a prophetic one, in which human history would be altered by the activity of God on earth through the "anointed one of the Lord."[33]

In conclusion, three points may be made to underscore this connection between biblical prophecy and the Psalms of Solomon. First, the name of Solomon became associated with prophecy in the Second Temple period and beyond, allowing for the possibility that writings associated with his name were to be understood as prophetic.[34] Second, the recent work by Rodney Werline and William Horbury suggests that the Psalms of Solomon relied heavily on Deuteronomic thought and language parameters as a means of giving expression to its view of history, suggesting that genre categorization must be attentive to factors other than literary expressions or forms. Deuteronomic thought and its close association with prophetic thought does provide a superstructural view of history that can move from point (covenantal infidelity and punishment as Yahweh's response to this) to counterpoint (vindication of Yahweh's judgments and the restoration of Israel). This would better explain trajectory issues in the Psalms of Solomon than correlation to the biblical Psalter and firmly ground the Davidic messiah in Ps. Sol. 17 within the larger framework of the book.

---

33. See Joel Willitts "Matthew and *Psalms of Solomon*'s Messianism: A Comparative Study in First-Century Messianology" *BBR* 22 (2012): 27–50.

34. Embry "Solomon's Name," 47–62.

Finally, I want to draw attention to an insightful article by Shani Berrin, in which the author suggests that the Psalms of Solomon and Pesher Nahum share a common tradition.[35] Berrin comes to this conclusion based on allusions in the pesher that suggest a historical provenance shared with the author of the Psalms of Solomon. This shared experience then governed the author's diachronic interpretation of Nahum. This means that, at least in this one case, Jewish authors of that period were reacting to the Roman invasion and conquest under Pompey by recourse to the prophetic traditions. Of course, Pesher Nahum has a specific genre category of pesher, one that is fairly well defined, and clearly interpretive of a biblical source text within the prophetic tradition. But, the shared features between Pesher Nahum and the Psalms of Solomon suggested by Berrin indicate that the Psalms of Solomon may also have been produced with connections to the biblical prophetic traditions in mind. The difference, however, may be that the Psalms of Solomon was written as prophecy, whereas Pesher Nahum is interpretive of a prophetic book. This may help to explain why the Psalms of Solomon was excised from the Christian codices. Understood as a book of prophecy, one that takes a more direct line on the militaristic vision of the messiah and makes implicit claims to stand in the prophetic tradition through a shared worldview and linguistic field, the Psalms of Solomon intones a vision of the Davidic messiah inconsistent with the New Testament articulation of Jesus; the messiah from the Psalms of Solomon simply did not look enough like the Messiah from the gospel records to fit within the Christian tradition.[36]

---

35. Berrin, "Pesher Nahum," 65.

36. Joel Willitts "Matthew and *Psalms of Solomon*'s Messianism," suggests that Matthew and the Psalms of Solomon are part of a common tradition. Of course, the connection over a "common messianic conception" suggested by Willitts has limitations insofar as the Messiah of Matthew is killed by the Romans whereas the messiah of Ps. Sol. 17 is not.

Perceptions of the Temple Priests in the Psalms of Solomon

Kenneth Atkinson

The eighteen poems known as the Psalms of Solomon are a unique Second Temple period composition. They recount a Jewish community's theological struggles to explain suffering and their response to a siege of Jerusalem by a foreign army. Written before the temple's 70 CE destruction, they provide a rare glimpse of contemporary religious disagreements over halakah as well as internal Jewish political disputes.[1] What perhaps makes this collection of eighteen poems most interesting is its genre. Rather than a narrative account of the tumultuous events of the first century BCE, the writers of the Psalms of Solomon use the medium of poetry to express their criticisms of the temple cult and to explain their present suffering at the hands of Jewish sinners and foreign oppressors. This collection of poems is a valuable document for understanding Second Temple Jewish history and theology. This study focuses on one of the most prominent and unique themes in the Psalms of Solomon: the perceptions of its authors toward the temple priests.

1. The Problem

The sanctity of the temple was central to the authors of the Psalms of Solomon and the ancient Jewish faith. The temple was the symbol of God's very presence. It was a physical affirmation of the covenant promise that God would never reject the nation of Israel. The problem that the community of the Psalms of Solomon shared with groups such as the Qumran sectarians was that the individual Jew could not fulfill the Torah alone.

---

1. For the dates, historical background, and contents of these poems, see Kenneth Atkinson, *I Cried to the Lord: A Study of the Psalms of Solomon's Historical Background and Social Setting*, JSJSup 84 (Leiden: Brill, 2004).

Although Jews could pray and worship in their local synagogues, the temple was the focus of Second Temple Judaism. God mandated that all sacrifices and certain holidays had to be observed there. Most important of these was the Day of Atonement, during which the high priest sought expiation for the sins of the nation (Lev 23:27–32; Num 29:7–11).[2] The priests were the divinely chosen mediators of the covenant. Their job was to serve as intercessors between God and Israel. They performed the temple sacrifices, they oversaw the temple rituals, and they determined who was pure enough to enter the temple's innermost courts. But the Psalms of Solomon's authors were convinced there was a problem with this biblical institution.

Because the priests controlled access to God, any halakic infractions by them effectively severed the divine connection between God and the covenant community. If the priests were impure, then the temple compound was defiled as well. If the temple complex was polluted, then ordinary Jews were contaminated and could not fulfill the biblical laws.[3] Ritual purity was, therefore, important in Second Temple Judaism since both priests and ordinary Jews were required to be in a state of ritual cleanliness in order to participate in the temple cult. Disagreements over the proper observance of halakah was a major factor in the formation of Jewish sectarianism because it dominated virtually every facet of Jewish life.[4] Different Jewish groups used the laws of ritual purity to regulate every aspect of life for their followers, such as clothing, meals, and worship. These rules served to distinguish between Jews that were members of a particular sect from those that were not.[5] Sectarian communities like

---

2. See Roland de Vaux, *Ancient Israel: Its Life and Institutions*, 2 vols. (New York: McGraw-Hill, 1961; repr., Grand Rapids: Eerdmans, 1997; trans. from *Les institutions de l'Ancien Testament* Paris: Cerf, 1958–1960), 2:507–10.

3. This study accepts Philip Davies's definition of halakah as a body of law governing Jewish behavior that not only derives from Scripture but that also acquires its authoritative status from it (Philip R. Davies, "Halakhah at Qumran," in *A Tribute to Geza Vermes: Essays on Jewish and Christian Literature and History*, ed. Philip R. Davies and Richard T. White [Sheffield: JSOT Press, 1990], 37–50).

4. See Hannah K. Harrington, "Purity," in *Encyclopedia of the Dead Sea Scrolls*, ed. Lawrence H. Schiffman and James C. VanderKam (Oxford: Oxford University Press, 2000), 724–28; Jodi Magness, *Stone and Dung, Oil and Spit: Jewish Daily Life in the Time of Jesus* (Grand Rapids: Eerdmans, 2011), 1–15.

5. Albert I. Baumgarten, *The Flourishing of Jewish Sects in the Maccabean Era: An Interpretation*, JSJSup 55 (Leiden: Brill, 1997), 5–23, 81–113.

those at Qumran often derived their halakic interpretations from their theological reflections on contemporary events. For this reason, the traditional law-centered approach to the study of halakah must be expanded to include an analysis of the influence of historical developments on Jewish ritual observances during the Second Temple period. Specifically, halakic research needs to explore how historical events caused some Jewish groups to separate themselves from other Jews. It also needs to investigate how some Jewish communities sought alternative ways to atone for sin apart from the temple cult.[6] The eighteen Psalms of Solomon are a unique document for understanding the development of Second Temple halakah since the authors of these poems responded to historical events and sectarian disputes through the creation of some distinctive Jewish practices. Like their contemporaries at Qumran, they believed the temple priests had defiled Judaism's most sacred shrine. Consequently, to worship with them in this holy place was a sacrilege. But how did the temple priests pollute the sanctuary? To understand the portrayals of the temple priests in the Psalms of Solomon, this study will focus on three topics: the covenant, the crimes of the temple priests, and the theological solution offered by the authors of these poems.

2. The Covenant

The covenant is a central theme throughout the Psalms of Solomon. The authors appeal to the covenant to explain their present suffering. They believe the covenant guarantees that God will always look after Israel (Pss. Sol. 7:8; 9:8–11; 11:7; 14:5; 17:4). The writer of Ps. Sol. 9 expresses this traditional confidence in God's covenant when he writes:

> And you chose the offspring of Abraham above all the nations,
> and you placed your name upon us, O Lord,
> and you will not reject us forever.
> You made a covenant with our ancestors concerning us,
> and we shall hope in you when we return our souls toward you.
> The mercy of the Lord is upon the house of Israel forever and ever. (Ps. Sol. 9:9–11)[7]

---

6. Jonathan Klawans, *Josephus and the Theologies of Ancient Judaism* (Oxford: Oxford University Press, 2012), 14–43, 137–79.

7. Translations from Atkinson, "*Psalms of Solomon*," in NETS, 763–76.

In this passage the psalmist emphasizes that God has promised never to reject Israel.[8] Yet, the collection is written against the backdrop of human suffering. The destruction of Jerusalem by a foreign army is the cause of many of the afflictions described in these poems. This could be viewed as a sign that God has failed to fulfill his covenant promises. Because Jerusalem is the city God has chosen to house his temple and to represent his presence among Israel, its current desolation and occupation by gentiles demands an explanation.

The authors of the Psalms of Solomon clearly do not believe that the gentiles who have attacked Jerusalem belong to the covenant. Rather, they denounce these gentiles as "lawless nations" (ἔθνη παράνομα, Ps. Sol. 17:24); God has rejected them (Ps. Sol. 7:2). However, the writer of Ps. Sol. 9:6-7 implies that gentiles can be righteous since righteousness is dependent upon acknowledging God's justice.[9] This attitude should not be surprising, for God's covenant has always been extended to gentiles who believe in God, accept the Torah, and live according to its precepts. Nevertheless, the collection displays a fairly hostile attitude toward gentiles, largely because they have destroyed the holy city. The Psalms of Solomon's authors view Jews and gentiles as two peoples in perpetual conflict. They look forward to the arrival of the Davidic messiah, whose purity will enable him to be victorious over the gentiles and successfully restore the Davidic throne (Ps. Sol. 17:21-25). The Davidic messiah will also destroy the Psalms of Solomon's enemies with an iron rod and the word of his mouth (Ps. Sol. 17:23-24). At that time the gentiles will serve under his yoke and bring him gifts in Jerusalem (Ps. Sol. 17:30-31).[10] But there is a theological problem with this expectation. The difficulty is the identity of those the Davidic messiah will favor. It is clearly not gentiles. That is to be expected. However, what is surprising is that the authors of the Psalms of Solomon were convinced that God will not favor all Jews.

---

8. See *Septuaginta Deutsch: Erläuterungen und Kommentare*, ed. Martin Karrer and Wolfgang Kraus (Stuttgart: Deutsche Bibelgesellschaft, 2011), 2:926-7.

9. Although this poem has been the focus of much attention because of its apparent description of free will (Ps. Sol. 9:4), the poet emphasizes human choice and responsibility to stress that sinners who repent will receive God's mercy; see Joachim Schüpphaus, *Die Psalmen Solomos: Ein Zeugnis Jerusalemer Theologie und Frömmigkeit in der Mitte des Vorchristlichen Jahrunderts*, ALGHJ 7 (Leiden: Brill, 1977), 50-53, 99-105.

10. For the portrayal of the Davidic messiah in the Psalms of Solomon, see Atkinson, *I Cried to the Lord*, 129-79.

Although the writers of the Psalms of Solomon denounce the gentiles who have attacked Jerusalem and now occupy their country, the collection primarily focuses on the actions of sinful Jews that have affected their community. The poets use the Greek words "sinner" (ἁμαρτωλός) and "righteous" (δίκαιος) to describe Jews more frequently than the Septuagint and the Greek Pseudepigrapha.[11] Much of the rhetoric in the Psalms of Solomon is directed towards sinful Jews. According to the poets of the Psalms of Solomon, these sinners will perish on the day of judgment (Pss. Sol. 12:4–6; 15:12–13) when the righteous receive God's salvation (Pss. Sol. 2:22–36; 4:23–25; 13:10–12; 14:9–10; 15:12–13). Although the authors of these poems recognize that the righteous sin, they maintain there is a difference. They insist that the transgressions of the pious are unintentional (Pss. Sol. 3:7–8; 13:7, 10; 18:4). This is because the devout continually search their homes to remove injustice arising from their transgressions (Pss. Sol. 3:7–8; 13:7, 10; 18:4). It is their vigilance, and their constant effort to atone for their sins, that sets the community of the Psalms of Solomon apart from other Jews. For this reason, God forgives the devout for their unintentional sins. Sinners who fail to atone properly for their transgressions do not merit God's justice.[12] The authors of the Psalms of Solomon maintain that Jews who have violated the covenant are worse than gentiles (Pss. Sol. 1:8; 8:13; 17:15). The writer of Ps. Sol. 17 even accuses the "sons of the covenant" (οἱ υἱοὶ τῆς διαθήκης; Ps. Sol. 17:15) of lawless behavior that has resulted in the forfeiture of their covenantal status.[13] Like the gentiles who have besieged Jerusalem (Ps. Sol. 2:28–31), these Jewish sinners have abandoned the Lord (Pss. Sol. 4:1, 21; 14:7).

The authors of the Psalms of Solomon recognize that their community has suffered greatly while wicked Jews have prospered. The suffering of the pious has not diminished with the passing of time, but has only increased as a result of the siege of Jerusalem. However, the writers of these poems believe that their present distress and their poverty are actually a sign of

---

11. The words ἁμαρτωλός and δίκαιος both appear approximately thirty-five times each in the Psalms of Solomon. In contrast they respectively occur seventy and fifty times in the biblical Psalter. See Mikael Winninge, *Sinners and the Righteous: A Comparative Study of the Psalms of Solomon and Paul's Letters*, ConBNT 26 (Stockholm: Almqvist & Wiksell, 1995), 3.

12. Herbert Braun, "Vom Erbarmen Gottes über den Gerechten: Zur Theologie der Psalmen Salomos," *ZNW* 43 (1950/51), 32–42.

13. Winninge, *Sinners and the Righteous*, 126–27.

God's favor (Pss. Sol. 1:6; 5:2, 11; 10:6; 15:1; 18:2). Merely belonging to the covenant community does not guarantee salvation or prosperity. Rather, God disciplines the devout through adversity, as a form of divine chastisement, to test their faithfulness (Pss. Sol. 3:4; 7:3, 9; 8:26, 29; 10:1-4; 13:7, 10; 16:4, 11-15).[14] For this reason, these poems encourage the pious to accept righteous suffering (Ps. Sol. 13:10) as a sign of God's blessing. It atones for sins—both deliberate and unintentional—and prevents the righteous from committing future transgressions.[15] However, the difficulty with this theological concept is that the sacrificial system is intended to remove both intentional and unintentional sins.

The eighteen Psalms of Solomon were largely written to deal with what its community perceived to be a crisis with the temple. Its priests, through their defilement of the sanctuary, have rendered the sacrificial system ineffective. In lieu of the temple cult, the authors of the Psalms of Solomon promote other ways to worship God, atone for sin, and remain in the covenant community without the mediation of the temple priests. However, in order to accomplish this, they must first convince their audience to reject the efficacy of the temple priests to atone for sin. Consequently, the writers of these poems vehemently denounce the temple priests for their religious and political transgressions. But what crimes have these priests committed?

3. The Crimes of the Temple Priests

The authors of the Psalms of Solomon denounce the temple priests for a variety of sins and halakic transgressions. Their polemic is often harsh and vicious. Such bitter language suggests a close relationship between the writers of these poems and the priests, since the accusations leveled against them often seem personal. There are several passages that suggest that at least some of the authors of the Psalms of Solomon were once connected with the temple, and likely priests and members of the upper class. One example is the seventeenth psalm (Ps. Sol. 17:4-6) where the poet writes:

---

14. Kenneth Atkinson, "Enduring the Lord's Discipline: Soteriology in the *Psalms of Solomon*," in *This World and the World to Come: Soteriology in Early Judaism*, ed. Daniel M. Gurtner, LSTS 74 (London: T&T Clark, 2011), 145-66.

15. Winninge, *Sinners and the Righteous*, 137-40.

You, O Lord, you chose David king over Israel,
and you swore to him concerning his offspring forever,
that his palace would never fail before you.
And, because of our sins, sinners rose up against us,
they attacked us and thrust us out, to whom you did not promise,
they took possession by force and they did not glorify your honorable name.
They set up in glory a palace corresponding to their loftiness,
they laid waste the throne of David in arrogance leading to change.

This passage appears to presuppose that some members of the community behind this poem once occupied positions of high status, from which they had been expelled by the Hasmoneans. The usurpers who removed them from their former privileged ranks are described throughout these poems as insolent and wealthy (Ps. Sol. 1:6). They have committed numerous sexual improprieties (Pss. Sol. 2:13; 4:4; 8:9–10). But the most important accusation against them is that they have corrupted the temple cult (Pss. Sol. 1:8; 2:3; 8:12–13). The interest in cultic matters throughout the Psalms of Solomon reflects priestly concerns. The poets often connect the crimes of the temple priests with halakic transgressions that are frequently rooted in sexual misconduct. The interest in priestly behavior and the knowledge about the temple priests reflected in these poems suggest that the community of the Psalms of Solomon, like their contemporaries at Qumran, originated from members of the priesthood.[16]

The authors of the Psalms of Solomon do not emphasize their former high status, but consistently refer to their community as the "poor" (Pss. Sol. 5:2, 11; 10:6; 15:1; 18:2). This term appears interchangeable with "the devout." One example of this is found in the tenth poem whose author proclaims:

καὶ ὅσιοι ἐξομολογήσονται ἐν ἐκκλησίᾳ λαοῦ, καὶ πτωχοὺς ἐλεήσει ὁ θεὸς ἐν εὐφροσύνῃ Ισραηλ. (Ps. Sol. 10:6)
And the devout shall confess in the assembly of the people, and God will show pity upon the poor to the joy of Israel.

The collection frequently contrasts the poverty of the devout community of these poems with the moral state of their wealthy opponents (Pss. Sol.

---

16. Robert R. Hann, "The Community of the Pious: The Social Setting of the *Psalms of Solomon*," SR 17 (1988): 176.

1:6; 5:2, 11; 10:6; 15:1; 18:2). The emphasis on privation throughout the collection does not necessarily mean that the writers of the Psalms of Solomon emanated from the lower class. Rather, the knowledge of the crimes of the temple priests and Jerusalem's political institutions suggests that the authors of these poems were once affluent, but have adopted a lifestyle of poverty. In this respect the community of the Psalms of Solomon is similar to the group reflected in the Qumran texts. Both communities emphasize their material poverty. At Qumran the utilitarian pottery, the archaeological evidence of simple living accommodations, the absence of imports, and the plain graves in the adjacent cemeteries provide physical evidence of the actual poverty of this site's inhabitants. They deliberately adopted a simple lifestyle with minimum possessions.[17] The community of the Psalms of Solomon appears to have adopted a similar lifestyle of simplicity.

Like the Psalms of Solomon, the authors of the Dead Sea Scrolls display some hostility towards the temple priests. Most notable is the Habakkuk Pesher, which recounts the occasion when the Wicked Priest traveled to Qumran to persecute the Teacher of Righteousness (1QpHab VIII, 8; XI, 4).[18] However, this event is unique and was apparently never repeated. The Qumran community otherwise appears to have had little actual contact with the temple priests. They sought a degree of physical separation from them and chose to move to the wilderness. Nevertheless, they were obsessed with the behavior of the temple priests. The document MMT is similar to Ps. Sol. 8. Both works condemn the temple priests for their defilement of the sanctuary.[19] However, the tension between the com-

---

17. Catherine M. Murphy, *Wealth in the Dead Sea Scrolls and the Qumran Community*, STDJ 40 (Leiden: Brill, 2002), 293–326. The anthropological analysis of some of the Qumran skeletons reveals that the site's inhabitants were in excellent health. None display any sign of having engaged in heavy physical labor. This evidence, and the simple graves in which these skeletons were found, suggests that the individuals buried at Qumran were from the upper class but adopted a lifestyle of poverty; see Orlav Röhrer-Ertl, Ferdinand Rohrhirsch, and Dietbert Hahn, "Über die Gräberfelder von Khirbet Qumran, inbesondere die Funde der Campagne 1956 I: Anthropologische Datenvorlage und Erstauswertung aufgrund der Collectio Kurth," *RevQ* 19 (1999): 3–46.

18. The Qumran *yaḥad* and the community of the Psalms of Solomon associate the temple with the Hasmoneans in a negative sense; see Eyal Regev, *The Hasmoneans: Ideology, Archaeology, Identity*, JAJSup 10 (Göttingen: Vandenhocek & Ruprecht, 2013), 93–98.

19. Atkinson, *I Cried to the Lord*, 64–84.

munity of the Psalms of Solomon and the temple priests is more intense than what we find in MMT or other Dead Sea Scrolls. The authors of the Dead Sea Scrolls, as evident in MMT and the pesharim, sought to justify their decision to leave Jerusalem and abandon the temple cult. They produced halakic writings and other texts that espoused their distinctive interpretations of biblical law. They also maintained their own calendars that kept track of the priestly courses that also determined the correct times for the celebration of the temple festivals.[20] Many of the Dead Sea Scrolls were intended to prepare the devout for the day when God would allow the Qumran community to take over the temple and restore rightful worship there.

Although the Psalms of Solomon is reminiscent of many Dead Sea Scrolls, the composition espouses a slightly different attitude toward the temple priests. The temple priests were a daily problem for the community of the Psalms of Solomon because they chose to remain in Jerusalem (Pss. Sol. 2:3, 6, 13; 8:20, 21). They were constantly reminded of the sins of the temple priests because the Temple Mount literally towers over the city. Unlike the Qumran covenanters, the community of these poems lived alongside Jews who accepted the legitimacy of the temple priests. The community of the Psalms of Solomon also experienced the siege of Jerusalem in 63 BCE and the Roman occupation of their country. They also encountered much persecution at the hands of the powerful. For this reason, the poets direct their rhetoric towards the wealthy, from whose ranks the temple priests appear to have been drawn.

The writers of the eighteen Psalms of Solomon often denounce the Hasmonean rulers for their unlawful establishment of a non-Davidic monarchy (Ps. Sol. 17:4–6).[21] Yet, they emphasize that the people bear the blame for this illegitimate rule. Jerusalem's citizens failed to heed the Deuteronomic exhortation to "listen and obey" God's commandments.[22]

---

20. Jonathan Ben-Dov and Stéphane Saulnier, "Qumran Calendars: A Survey of Scholarship 1980–2007," *CurBR* 7 (2008): 124–68.

21. Johannes Tromp, "The Sinners and the Lawless in *Psalm of Solomon 17*," *NovT* 35 (1993): 344–61, proposes that the sinners in Ps. Sol. 17:5–6 and 11–14 are not the Hasmoneans, but the Romans. The claim in this poem that these sinners set up a non-Davidic monarchy makes it more probable that the writer focuses on Jewish sinners throughout this composition. The author distinguishes the Romans, although sinners, from those who established the non-Davidic monarchy in verses 4–14; see Atkinson, *I Cried to the Lord*, 133–39.

22. Rodney A. Werline, "The *Psalms of Solomon* and the Ideology of Rule" in

According to the writers of the Psalms of Solomon, the Hasmonean monarchs committed numerous sins such as incest, adultery, theft from the temple, and the pollution of the sacrifices (Ps. Sol. 8:9–13). The authors of these poems condemn the Hasmonean monarchy not only for these transgressions and their illegitimate rule, they also denounce them because they were temple priests and therefore ultimately responsible for the nation's spiritual welfare.

Because the Hasmoneans descended from the priestly order of Jehoiarib (Joarib, 1 Macc 2:1) and served as high priests, the Psalms of Solomon's authors often do not distinguish their crimes from those of other temple priests. But what are some of the offenses of the temple priests?

The author of Ps. Sol. 8 condemns them for three specific transgressions: adultery, theft from the sanctuary, and the defilement of the temple (Ps. Sol. 8:10–12). The Damascus Document (CD IV, 15–18) also lists these same three sins in the same order, namely, fornication, wealth, and defilement of the temple.[23] The similarities between these two compositions show that the criticisms of the temple priests were quite widespread in the Second Temple period. This common list of crimes in Ps. Sol. 8 and the Damascus Document also reveal that many of the charges made against the temple priests in these texts are not mere polemic, but are rooted in historical reality.

The Psalms of Solomon's authors emphasize three motifs: the profanation of the temple, secret sins, and transgressions that are worse than those committed by gentiles. These themes are not separate, but are connected with one another throughout the composition. The writer of the first poem sets the tone for the entire collection when he links these three sins to denounce the temple priests and declares:

> Their sins were in secret,
> and I had no knowledge of them.
> Their lawlessness surpassed those of the nations before them;

Conflicted Boundaries in Wisdom and Apocalypticism, ed. Lawrence M. Wills and Benjamin G. Wright III, SBLSymS 35 (Atlanta: Society of Biblical Literature, 2005), 72.

23. This list, "The nets of Belial," is also alluded to in 4Q171 II, 1–10. Similar lists of vices are also found in the following texts: Sib. Or. 1.172; 2.65–75, 255–260; 4:30–35; T. Mos. 5.4–6. See Robert B. Wright, "The *Psalms of Solomon*: The Pharisees and the Essenes," in *1972 Proceedings for the International Organization for Septuagint and Cognate Studies and the Society of Biblical Literature Pseudepigrapha Seminar*, ed. Robert A. Kraft, SCS 2 (Missoula, MT: Society of Biblical Literature, 1972), 136–54.

they profaned with profanity the sanctuary of the Lord. (Ps. Sol. 1:7-8)

The writers of the Psalms of Solomon claim to know these secret halakic transgressions. In the second psalm (Ps. Sol. 2:3), the author asserts: "the sons of Jerusalem had defiled the sanctuary of the Lord, had profaned the gifts of God with lawlessness." It was through their lawlessness and their secret sins that the priests polluted the temple when they approached the sacred altar.

The writers of the Psalms of Solomon emphasize that God has now revealed the sins that had been committed in secret (Pss. Sol. 2:17; 4:7; 8:8; 9:3; 14:8). In several instances the poets connect these clandestine transgressions with sexuality.[24] In the eighth psalm (Ps. Sol. 8:11-13), the writer lists some of the crimes the priests have committed at the altar and states:

> They would plunder the sanctuary of God,
> as though there was no heir who redeems.
> They would trample the altar of the Lord because of all kinds of uncleanness,
> and with menstrual blood they defiled the sacrifices as if they were profane meat.
> They left no sin, which they did not do more than the nations. (Ps. Sol. 8:11-13)

The writers of the Psalms of Solomon and the Dead Sea Scrolls were convinced that sexual contact with impure women and incest defiles the sanctuary morally. Unlike ritual purity, which is to a great extent unavoidable, moral impurity is the result of deliberate sin and pollutes the land and its occupants.[25] For this reason, the writers of the Psalms of Solomon denounce the temple priests for their sexual transgressions.

---

24. William Loader, *The Pseudepigrapha on Sexuality: Attitudes Towards Sexuality in Apocalypses, Testaments, Legends, Wisdom, and Related Literature* (Grand Rapids: Eerdmans, 2011), 344.

25. Jonathan Klawans, "Idolatry, Incest, and Impurity: Moral Defilement in Ancient Judaism," *JSJ* 29 (1998): 391-415. Klawans also comments that moral impurity not only defiles the sanctuary, but it even affects the temple from afar. The author of *Jubilees*, like the poet of Ps. Sol. 8, believes that sexual wrongdoing, especially incest, defiles the temple; see William Loader, *The Dead Sea Scrolls on Sexuality: Attitudes Towards Sexuality in Sectarian and Related Literature at Qumran* (Grand Rapids: Eerdmans, 2009), 107-25.

The poets accuse them of illicit marriages and improper adherence to the laws of cleanliness that pertain to sexuality. The writers of these poems also condemn visits to prostitutes by priests and politicians, especially within the Sanhedrin (Pss. Sol. 2:11–13; 4:5). In the fourth psalm (Ps. Sol. 4:9–13), the author describes predatory adulterous behavior that transgresses the Torah, and which destroys the homes of the innocent. The poets of the Psalms of Solomon believe that sexual transgressions by the temple priests were a major reason why God had allowed Pompey's invasion of Jerusalem in 63 BCE to occur. God permitted the Romans to terminate the Hasmonean monarchy because the temple priests had defiled the sanctuary.[26]

The authors of the Psalms of Solomon know much about these secret sins and the personal lifestyles of the temple priests that compelled God to punish all Jewish inhabitants of Jerusalem. This suggests that the Psalms of Solomon's authors were priests who had witnessed these transgressions. Because the priests had become ritually defiled, the authors accuse them of having polluted the sacrifices when they entered the temple compound to perform their sacred duties (Pss. Sol. 1:7–8; 2:3–4; 8:9–13; 16:18–19). For this reason, God has scorned them and their offerings (Pss. Sol. 2:3–4; 8:12). It was now impossible to atone for sin in the temple since the priests no longer had the authority to mediate between God and the nation.

The community of the Psalms of Solomon was convinced that God had rejected the validity of temple priests to preside over the offerings.[27] However, the authors of these poems are obsessed with the temple. They do not reject temple cult or the institution of the temple priesthood. They frequently plead with God to protect the temple from foreign armies (Pss. Sol. 1:8; 2:2; 7:2; 8). The writers denounce the temple priests only because they have failed in their duties; their incorrect purification rituals and profane lifestyle have rendered the temple cult ineffective. The crimes of the priests merit their exclusion from the covenant community. Their transgressions also require that the righteous separate themselves from the temple priests lest they too become polluted and excluded from the covenant community. This conviction led the community of the Psalms

---

26. Atkinson, *I Cried to the Lord*, 55–87.
27. Ibid., 20; Sven Holm-Nielsen, *JSHRZ* 4:63; see also 1 En. 89:56; Jub. 23:21; 30:15–16.

of Solomon to formulate a rather unique solution to the problem of how to atone for sin and approach God without the intercession of the temple priests.

4. The Solution

The writers of the Psalms of Solomon believe that the temple is not necessary to maintain the covenant relationship. They also believe that the laws for the atonement of intentional and unintentional sins, as mandated in Leviticus, are still in effect. However, they cannot fulfill these biblical laws because they are convinced the temple cult is ineffective.[28] The authors of the Psalms of Solomon make the unique claim that the pious can atone for sins without the temple rituals. Daily piety through fasting (Ps. Sol. 3:8) and prayer (Pss. Sol. 3:3; 5:1; 6:1-2; 7:6-7; 15:1) has replaced the sacrificial system. Sins are now cleansed through confession and penance.[29] Discipline and suffering are the means through which the righteous atone for sin and remain within the covenant.

The belief that prayer and fasting can atone for sins appears to have been one of the main theological tenets of the community behind the Psalms of Solomon. The authors of these poems connect fasting with atonement to espouse a lifestyle in which ordinary Jews effectively take on many of the functions reserved for the priests. The author of Ps. Sol. 3 makes this clear when he states:

> The righteous always searches his house,
> to remove his injustice in transgression.
> He made atonement for sins of ignorance by fasting and humiliation of
>   his soul,
> and the Lord cleanses every devout man and his house. (Ps. Sol. 3:7-8)

---

28. Kenneth Atkinson, *An Intertextual Study of the Psalms of Solomon: Pseudepigrapha*, SBEC 49 (Lewiston, NY: Mellen, 2001), 425-26.

29. The Qumran community also believed that prayer had replaced sacrifice in the Jerusalem temple (1QS IX, 3-6; 4Q174 I, 6-7); see Robert A. Kugler, "Rewriting Rubrics: Sacrifice and the Religion of Qumran," in *Religion in the Dead Sea Scrolls*, ed. John J. Collins and Robert A. Kugler (Grand Rapids: Eerdmans, 2000), 90-112; Lawrence H. Schiffman, "The Dead Sea Scrolls and the Early History of Jewish Liturgy," in *The Synagogue in Late Antiquity*, ed. Lee I. Levine (Philadelphia: American Schools of Oriental Research, 1987), 33-48.

Here, the author alludes to the Day of Atonement rituals. This holiday was the only occasion when the high priest entered the holy of holies to sprinkle it with the blood of the sacrificial bull. He also offered a goat for the sin of the people, and scattered its blood over the mercy seat. Through this ritual the high priest expiated the sins of the priests and the people. This ritual also cleansed the sanctuary and the altar, which too received a smattering of blood (Lev 23:11–19, 33).[30]

The author of Ps. Sol. 3:8 reinterprets the Day of Atonement rituals, as described in Lev 16, to espouse a new lifestyle. One of the passages the poet alludes to is Lev 16:29. This verse does not use the traditional Hebrew designation for fasting (צום), but the phrase ענה נפש, "to humble" or "afflict one's soul."[31] In several places, the author of Leviticus urges the people not to be passive during the Day of Atonement ritual, but to "humble their souls" (Lev 16:31; 23:27; Num 29:7). This humbling includes fasting. Through a creative reading of Leviticus, the author concludes that through prayer and fasting ordinary Jews can accomplish the ritual functions formerly granted to the temple priests—the atonement of sin.[32] In this respect, the community of these poems bears some similarities with the Qumran sect, whose members viewed their settlement as a substitute temple and worshiped apart from the temple priests.[33] For the writers of the Psalms of Solomon, their community and their homes have become a physical and spiritual substitute for the temple.

---

30. See de Vaux, *Ancient Israel*, 2:507–8.

31. Dieter Lührmann, "Paul and the Pharisaic Tradition," *JSNT* 36 (1989): 83; Herbert R. Ryle, and Montague R. James, *ΨΑΛΜΟΙ ΣΟΛΟΜΩΝΤΟΣ: Psalms of the Pharisees, Commonly Called the Psalms of Solomon* (Cambridge: Cambridge University Press, 1891), 35; Joseph Viteau, *Les Psaumes de Solomon: Introduction, texte grec et traduction, avec les principales variantes de la version syriaque par François Martin*, Documents pour l'étude de la Bible (Paris: Letouzey et Ané, 1911), 269.

32. Kenneth Atkinson, "Toward a Redating of the *Psalms of Solomon*: Implications for Understanding the *Sitz im Leben* of an Unknown Jewish Sect," *JSP* 17 (1998): 108–9; Paul N. Franklyn, "The Cultic and Pious Climax of Eschatology in the *Psalms of Solomon*," *JSJ* 18 (1987), 8; Hann, "The Community of the Pious," 169–89; Winninge, *Sinners and the Righteous*, 176.

33. The Dead Sea Scrolls and the archaeological finds from Qumran reveal that the sectarians who lived there practiced an excessively strict interpretation of halakah because they conceived of their community as a substitute temple. For texts and examples, see Kenneth Atkinson and Jodi Magness, "Josephus's Essenes and the Qumran Community," *JBL* 129 (2010): 326–41.

The focus on the temple priests, the temple rituals, and the unique solution to worship and sacrifice offered by the writers of the Psalms of Solomon tells us much about the community behind these poems. Rodney A. Werline has noted that the composition reflects a social situation similar to that found in some apocalyptic texts. This leads him to conclude that the poets were likely dissident scribes.[34] The focus on cultic matters and the accusations against the priests throughout the Psalms of Solomon reflect priestly concerns. This implies that at least some of the authors were likely priests and therefore highly literate. The poets describe their expulsion from the temple as a past event. This suggests that these poems contain the recollections of the founding generation, whose members were not from the lower classes, but likely priests.[35] This thesis leads to some significant ramifications for the chosen genre through which these writers decided to communicate their message.

The eighteen Psalms of Solomon are similar to the genre of writings sometimes called "rewritten Bible."[36] Each individual psalm abounds with allusions to Scripture, as well as biblical phrases and vocabulary.[37] This shows that authors of these poems regarded the biblical text as authoritative. They considered it essential to work within the framework of existing Scripture rather than write an entirely new composition. However, at the same time, the writers of the Psalms of Solomon add to the authority of the Bible. This is because all rewriting implies a particular interpretation of the reference text. The Psalms of Solomon, therefore, should not be viewed merely as a rewriting of scripture. Rather, they are a collection of poems that espouse a particular interpretation of the Bible that is meant to adapt the sacred text to a new historical situation.

What makes the Psalms of Solomon unique is that its authors use scripture to propose new religious practices in lieu of the biblical commandment to observe the temple cult. Most notable is their teaching that prayer and fasting can atone for sins without the mediation of the temple priests. This type of exegesis is reminiscent of the Qumran pesharim. In

---

34. Werline, "The *Psalms of Solomon* and the Ideology of Rule," 81–85.

35. Hann, "The Community of the Pious," 176.

36. This type of writing uses Scripture as a source, and often claims an authoritative status for both the scriptural text and its interpretation. For the appropriateness of this term, see Sidnie W. Crawford, *Rewriting Scripture in Second Temple Times* (Grand Rapids: Eerdmans, 2008), 1–18.

37. Viteau, *Les Psaumes de Salomon*, 105–25.

the pesharim, the authors present their scriptural interpretations as departures from the biblical texts that are nevertheless based on their exegesis of the scriptural texts.[38] In the pesharim, both the scriptural passages and the interpretation are considered authoritative.[39] Did the authors of the Psalms of Solomon regard their poems as authoritative? Did the writers of the Psalms of Solomon use scripture to enhance their own authority? Or, did they intend these poems to constitute a new revelation?

A few clues embedded in the collection suggest that the authors of the Psalms of Solomon viewed these poems as authoritative writings. The Psalms of Solomon appear to have been produced for use in worship. Only Pss. Sol. 2, 3, 5, 13, 15, 17, and 18 are designated as a "Psalm" (Ψαλμός). Pss. Sol. 15, 17 contain the heading "with song" (μετὰ ᾠδῆς) while Pss. Sol. 10, 14, and 16 bear the superscription "hymn" (ὕμνος). The Psalms of Solomon contain a few musical notations (διάψαλμα, Pss. Sol. 17:29; 18:9). The headings of many of these poems imply a liturgical use, and suggest that the collection was recited in worship services.[40]

The Syriac translation of the Psalms of Solomon may help us to learn more about the original community behind these poems. In two of the Syriac manuscripts the Psalms of Solomon follow the forty-two Odes of Solomon and the first Psalm of Solomon is numbered as the forty-third Ode.[41] This suggests that the collection was used liturgically by Syriac-speaking Christians. This presupposes a similar use among earlier Jewish communities, likely for both the Hebrew original and its Greek translation. The communal identity throughout the Psalms of Solomon and the reference to the "synagogues of the pious" (συναγωγὰς of ἐκλογῇ ὁσίων; Ps. Sol. 17:16) suggest that the Psalms of Solomon was written for a synagogue community.[42]

---

38. Timothy H. Lim, *Pesharim*, CQS 3 (Sheffield: Sheffield Academic, 2002), 24–53.

39. Florentino García Martínez, "Parabiblical Literature from Qumran and the Canonical Process," *RevQ* 100 (2012): 535–37, 548–49.

40. The ancient catalogues and two of the extant Syriac manuscripts demonstrate that the Psalms of Solomon also circulated as part of the Odes of Solomon, showing that the collection was used by the Syriac speaking Christian Church as part of their liturgy; see Atkinson, *An Intertextual Study*, 411–12.

41. For the Syriac text and manuscript evidence, see Willem Baars, "Psalms of Solomon," part 4.6 of *The Old Testament in Syriac according to the Peshiṭta Version* (Leiden: Brill, 1972), ii–vi.

42. Atkinson, "Toward a Redating," 109–10; Burton L. Mack, "Wisdom Makes a

Texts, especially liturgical texts, are written for manipulative purposes. This is true even if such manipulation is the endorsement or confirmation of a particular perspective that has already been acknowledged by an audience.[43] It is important to consider the function and authority of the Psalms of Solomon. If these poems emanated from dissident priests, then their use in liturgy was likely intended to espouse the authoritative interpretation of scripture held by their authors. These poems incorporate scriptural allusions and language to advocate a lifestyle of piety apart from the temple cult. Their unique teachings about how to atone for sin suggests an authoritative stance by the Psalms of Solomon's writers. They espouse a new interpretation of scripture that they believe fulfills the intent of the covenant.

If the authors of the Psalms of Solomon wrote these poems for use in worship, this suggests that they chose poetry as a mechanism to endorse their authoritative interpretations of scripture. The recitation of these poems in worship would have served both to create a community and to teach a distinctive lifestyle apart from the temple cult. Those who later joined this group would have relived the experiences of the early members of the Psalms of Solomon's community through the recitation of these poems. Frustrated at their suffering and position in Jerusalem, some newer members of this group undoubtedly took some consolation from the knowledge that their leaders once held high positions of religious authority. Through the genre of poetry, the teachings of these founders would have attracted new converts, who had not enjoyed the privileged status of the group's originators, and who were not involved in the crises that precipitated their expulsion and separation from the temple.[44] The lack of any reference to a specific founder of this group may suggest that the Psalms of Solomon in their present form represent the writings of the second, or later, generation of a Jewish community that resided in Jerusalem.

Difference: Alternatives to 'Messianic' Configuration," in *Judaisms and Their Messiahs at the Turn of the Christian Era*, ed. Jacob Neusner, William S. Green, and Erich S. Frerichs (Cambridge: Cambridge University Press, 1987), 15–38; Svend Holm-Nielsen, "Religiöse Poesie des Spätjudentums," *ANRW* 19.1:156–57.

43. George J. Brooke, "Authority and the Authoritativeness of Scripture: Some Clues from the Dead Sea Scrolls," *RevQ* 100 (2012): 523.

44. Hann, "The Community of the Pious," 176–77.

5. Conclusion

The focus on the temple priests in the Psalms of Solomon tells us much about Jewish disputes over the operation of the sanctuary during the Hasmonean period, some of which are also reflected in the Dead Sea Scrolls. It also provides a great deal of information about the community behind the Psalms of Solomon. For the poets who produced this unique collection, atonement was more than the mere elimination of individual sins. It restored Jews to the original and proper relationship with God. God promised to protect the people of Israel providing they follow the Torah and seek repentance for their sins. In exchange for their obedience to the Torah, God once a year promised to wipe out all their transgressions on the Day of Atonement. However, atonement requires a prior good standing in the covenant community. For this reason, the authors of the Psalms of Solomon, like the Hodayot and other Dead Sea Scrolls, emphasize the covenant of a restricted group within Israel. This perspective represents an acute self-consciousness of being chosen not as a nation, but as individuals. The temple priests by their actions have forsaken the covenant and therefore have not only lost their covenantal standing, but their status as priestly intermediaries. For the authors of the Psalms of Solomon, it is the covenant of their group within Israel that is of paramount importance. The community of the Psalms of Solomon believed that they were both chastised and saved because their lifestyle, unlike that of the temple priests, atoned for sins without the temple.[45]

The eighteen Psalms of Solomon are an invaluable witness to the diversity and vitality of Second Temple Judaism. These poems contain the teachings of an unknown group of Jews who were confident that if they remained within the covenant, by acknowledging their sins and accepting divine punishment, then God would carry out justice in the resurrection if it was not administered in this world. The collection as a whole urges perseverance in difficult times. Its authors are firm in their belief that God will save the truly devout.

---

45. Ed P. Sanders, "Covenantal Nomism Revisited," *JSQ* 16 (2009): 23–55.

Die Rede vom Schlaf in den Psalmen Salomos und ihr traditionsgeschichtlicher Hintergrund

Sven Behnke

Abstract: Speech about "sleep" occurs several times and in various ways in the corpus of the Psalms of Solomon. This paper analyzes how it is used and provides a brief outline of its background from a traditio-historical perspective. Through this analysis it will be demonstrated that the semantic field of "sleep" serves (1) as a vehicle for negatively portraying the sinner and positively depicting the faithful; (2) to illustrate the remoteness of God and the experience of death as well as the hope of resurrection and; (3) to reinforce the notion of wakefulness (and praise) as an ideal for a pious way of living. In this respect the imagery of sleep proves to be a very efficient instrument for verbalizing important theological concepts of the writers' community.

(1) Die Rede vom Schlaf in den Psalmen Salomos

Innerhalb der Psalmen Salomos ist die Rede vom Schlaf weder Gegenstand einer vertieften systematisch-theologischen Reflexion noch lässt sie sich sprachlich oder inhaltlich als Einheit fassen. Sie stellt auch kein zentrales Thema der Gebetssammlung dar und dennoch verdient der Topos *Schlaf* besondere Aufmerksamkeit, da er innerhalb des Salomopsalters relativ breit bezeugt ist. So begegnet das Phänomen des Schlafes, zunächst ohne erkennbaren Zusammenhang, in fünf der insgesamt 18 Psalmen Salomos (Pss. Sol. 2,31; 3,1–2; 4,15–16; 6,3–4; 16,1–4).

Wenn im Folgenden vom Schlaf in den Psalmen Salomos gesprochen wird, dann ist damit ein Wortfeld angesprochen, dessen Spektrum sich in dreifacher Hinsicht gliedern lässt. Es umfasst:

(1) Ausdrücke für den Schlaf im engeren Sinne bzw. das Einschlafen/ Einschlummern (vgl. die Substantive ὁ ὕπνος [Pss. Sol. 4,15.16; 6,4;

16,1], ἡ καταφορά [Ps. Sol. 16,1] sowie die Verben ὑπνόω [Ps. Sol. 3,1], κοιμίζω [Ps. Sol. 2,31] und νυστάζω [Ps. Sol. 16,1]),
(2) Begriffe, die die Bewegung des Aufstehens bzw.—eschatologisch formuliert—des Auferstehens ausdrücken (vgl. das Substantiv ἡ ἐξέγερσις [Ps. Sol. 4,15] sowie die Verben ἐξανίστημι [Ps. Sol. 6,4] und ἀνίστημι [Ps. Sol. 2,31; vgl. Pss. Sol. 3,10.12; 11,8; 17,21.42]) und
(3) Wörter, die die Wachsamkeit bzw. das Wachen artikulieren (vgl. das Substantiv ἡ γρηγόρησις [Pss. Sol. 3,2; 16,4] und das Verb γρηγορέω [Ps. Sol. 3,2]).

Kommen wir nun zu den Textpassagen im Einzelnen und werfen wir zunächst einen Blick auf die unreflektierte Rede vom Schlaf in den Psalmen Salomos:

Ps. Sol. 4,15–16[1]
15 ἐν ὀδύναις καὶ πενίᾳ καὶ ἀπορίᾳ ἡ ζωὴ αὐτοῦ, κύριε
ὁ ὕπνος αὐτοῦ ἐν λύπαις καὶ ἡ ἐξέγερσις αὐτοῦ ἐν ἀπορίαις
16 ἀφαιρεθείη ὕπνος ἀπὸ κροτάφων αὐτοῦ ἐν νυκτί,
ἀποπέσοι ἀπὸ παντὸς ἔργου χειρῶν αὐτοῦ ἐν ἀτιμίᾳ.

15 In Schmerzen und Armut und Mangel [sei] sein [des Sünders] Leben, Herr,
sein Schlaf in Sorgen und sein Erwachen in Mängeln.
16 Schlaf möge von seinen Schläfen nachts weggenommen werden,
er möge herabfallen/scheitern durch jedes Werk seiner Hände in Schande.

Betrachtet man die vier vom Sünder (vgl. V. 8) sprechenden Verszeilen in Ps. Sol. 4,15–16 als eine Sinneinheit, so steht die Rede vom Schlaf im Zentrum des Doppelverses (V. 15b.16a) und wird durch die Vv. 15a und 16b gerahmt: Die rahmenden Verszeilen beschreiben dabei mit den Begriffen „Leben" (V. 15a) und „Werk" (V. 16b) die aktiv-gestaltende Sphäre

---

1. Soweit nicht anders angegeben beruht hier und im Folgenden der griechische Text der Psalmen Salomos auf der kritischen Ausgabe von Oscar von Gebhardt, ed., ΨΑΛΜΟΙ ΣΟΛΟΜΩΝΤΟΣ: Die Psalmen Salomo's zum ersten Male mit Benutzung der Athoshandschriften und des Codex Casanatensis, TUGAL 13/2 (Leipzig: Hinrichs, 1895). Die Übersetzung des griechischen Textes ins Deutsche habe ich selbst angefertigt.

menschlichen Wirkens, während mit dem Schlaf (V. 15b.16a) die passiv-ruhende Sphäre menschlicher Existenz ausgedrückt wird.

Das Fluchwort Ps. Sol. 4,15–16 zielt auf eine Verwünschung aller Lebensbereiche des Sünders, der Tag und Nacht gleichermaßen Mangel (ἀπορία) leiden soll. Der Beter des Psalms weiß um die Wichtigkeit eines gesunden Schlafes, wenn er um einen sorgenvollen Schlaf (V. 15b) bzw. Schlaflosigkeit (V. 16) für den Sünder bittet. Im Wunsch des Beters mündet der Schlaf (ὁ ὕπνος) des Gottlosen in die Perspektivlosigkeit: Bereits während des Aufstehens (ἡ ἐξέγερσις) am Morgen soll er sich in einer Aporie-Situation wiederfinden (V. 15b). Der in V. 16b formulierte Wunsch nach dem Scheitern der Taten des Sünders erscheint als logische Konsequenz aus der in der ersten Vershälfte des Parallelismus membrorum vom Beter für den Sünder eingeforderten Schlaflosigkeit und drückt eine Lebenserfahrung aus: Wer selbst nachts keine Erholung von körperlichen Leiden (ὀδύνη) findet und Gedanken an materielle Not (πενία) nicht zurück lassen kann (vgl. V. 15a), dem fehlt die Kraft, um tagsüber das eigene Geschick wenden zu können.

Deutlich unterschieden von der Schilderung von Schlaflosigkeit und sorgenvollem Erwachen des Sünders in Ps. Sol. 4 erscheint die Beschreibung des Schlafs des Frommen, die sich in Ps. Sol. 6,3–4 im Kontext einer Seligpreisung des von Jhwh beschützten Beters findet:

³ Ἀπὸ ὁράσεως πονηρῶν ἐνυπνίων αὐτοῦ οὐ ταραχθήσεται ἡ ψυχὴ αὐτοῦ,
ἐν διαβάσει ποταμῶν καὶ σάλῳ θαλασσῶν οὐ πτοηθήσεται.
⁴ Ἐξανέστη ἐξ ὕπνου αὐτοῦ καὶ ηὐλόγησεν τῷ ὀνόματι κυρίου,
ἐπ'εὐσταθείᾳ καρδίας αὐτοῦ ἐξύμνησεν τῷ ὀνόματι τοῦ θεοῦ αὐτοῦ.

³ Vom Anblick seiner bösen Träume wird seine Seele nicht aufgewühlt werden,
an der Flüsse Furt² und durch Meereswogen wird er nicht erschreckt werden.
⁴ Er steht auf von seinem Schlaf und preist den Namen des Herrn,
mit Festigkeit seines Herzens lobsingt er dem Namen seines Gottes.³

---

2. So mit Eduard Ephraem Geiger und gegen *LXX.D*: „διάβασις ist nicht ‚das Hinübergehen' als Handlung, sondern der Ort, wo man hinübergeht, ‚die Furth' eines Flusses" (Eduard Ephraem Geiger, *Der Psalter Salomo's herausgegeben und erklärt* [Augsburg: Wolff, 1871], 122).

3. Vgl. Steins zu Ps. Sol. 6,4: „Die Aoriste in V. 4–5 explizieren die ‚Beständigkeit'

Keineswegs wird hier der Schlaf des frommen Beters als sorgenfrei beschrieben, ja auch er kann offenbar unter negativen Vorzeichen stehen; denn sogar der Fromme bleibt „vom Anblick böser Träume" (V. 3a) nicht verschont. Entscheidend ist für den Psalmisten aber, dass die nächtlichen Traumerlebnisse nicht zu einer Beunruhigung des Frommen führen: „seine Seele wird nicht aufgewühlt werden" (V. 3a). Die Seele des Frommen erscheint als ruhiger Gegenpol zu den Bildern, die in der zweiten Vershälfte (V. 3b) durch die Begriffe „Flussfurt" und „Meereswogen" aufgerufen werden. Die Gefahr tosender Wasser vermag den Beter ebenso wenig wie böse Träume zu erschrecken.[4]

Wie bereits in Ps. Sol. 4 neben dem Schlaf auch das Erwachen thematisiert wurde, so wird in Ps. Sol. 6,3–4 neben der nächtlichen Verfassung während des Traumes auch das Aufstehen vom Schlaf (ἐξανίστημι ἐξ ὕπνου) reflektiert. Während Ps. Sol. 4,15–16 vom Negativbild der Schlaflosigkeit und des sorgenvollen Aufstehens am Morgen bestimmt ist, nimmt Ps. Sol. 6,4 die Vorstellung von Schlaf und Aufstehen in positiver Weise auf, um den Alltag des Frommen zu charakterisieren.

Der mit dem Erwachen aus dem Schlaf beginnende Tag des Frommen führt nicht—wie in Ps. Sol. 4,15b—ἐν ἀπορίαις („in Ausweglosigkeiten/Mängel"), sondern hebt mit dem Lobpreis des Namens Jhwhs an. Ein besonderes Interesse an einer positiven Qualifizierung des Schlafes des Gerechten zeigt der Text dabei nicht. Dieser Verzicht auf jede Näherqualifizierung des Schlafes der Frommen kann als Indiz für eine eher abwertende Haltung gegenüber dem Schlaf verstanden werden. Zumindest lässt sich feststellen: *Wie* der Fromme schläft, liegt nicht im Interesse des Psalmisten, entscheidend ist vielmehr, dass der nächtlichen Ruhe—oder

---

(V. 4) des Gerechten und sind gnomisch zu übersetzen." (Georg Steins, „Psalmoi Solomontos / Die Psalmen Salomos," in *LXX.D-E* 2:1922).

4. Die Schlüsselbegriffe „Furt" (διάβασις) und „Woge" (σάλος) in V. 3b spielen auf zentrale Ereignisse in der Jakobs- und der Exoduserzählung an. So verweist διάβασις auf die in Gen 32,23 berichtete nächtliche Überquerung der Jabbok-Furt (LXX: ἡ διάβασις τοῦ Ιαβοκ) durch Jakob und seine Familie, während σάλος auf die Meerwundererzählung in Exod 14,15-31 anspielt, in der vom Zurückweichen der Meereswogen „während der ganzen Nacht" (LXX: ὅλην τὴν νύκτα, V. 21) die Rede ist. Die Einspielung der nächtlichen Bilder vom Durchzug Jakobs und seiner Familie durch den Jordan und dem Gang Moses und des Volkes durch das Schilfmeer lassen Jakob und Mose als paradigmatisch fromme Helden erscheinen, in deren Reihe sich der Beter gestellt wissen darf. Der Folgevers (Ps. Sol. 6,5) ruft dem Rezipienten die vorbildhafte Fürbitte Hiobs für seine Söhne (vgl. Job 1,5) in Erinnerung.

angesichts „böser Träume" vielleicht eher der nächtlichen Unruhe — mit dem Aufstehen des Frommen Lobpreis (εὐλογέω) und -gesang (ἐξυμνέω) folgen. Für den Frommen ist das Gotteslob das erste Werk des Tages.

Das Gegenüber von Schlaf als passiver Ruhephase und Lobpreis Jhwhs als aktivem Handeln des Menschen findet sich bereits im Aufgesang von Ps. Sol. 3 ausgeführt:

Ps. Sol. 3,1–2
¹ Ἵνα τί ὑπνοῖς, ψυχή, καὶ οὐκ εὐλογεῖς τὸν κύριον;
ὕμνον καινὸν ψάλατε τῷ θεῷ τῷ αἰνετῷ.
² ψάλλε καὶ γρηγόρησον ἐπὶ τὴν γρηγόρησιν αὐτοῦ,
ὅτι ἀγαθὸς ψαλμὸς τῷ θεῷ ἐξ ἀγαθῆς καρδίας.

¹ Weshalb schläfst du, Seele, und preist nicht den Herrn?
Ein neues Loblied singt Gott, dem Gelobten!
² Singe und erwache zur Wachsamkeit für ihn,
denn ein guter Psalm für Gott [kommt] aus gutem Herzen!

Die in Form der didaktischen Du-Anrede gehaltene rhetorische Frage in V. 1a beschreibt in ihrer zweiteiligen Struktur eine semantische Opposition zwischen „schlafen" (ὑπνόω) einerseits und „preisen" (εὐλογέω) andererseits. Die final aufzufassende Konjunktionalverbindung ἵνα τί, die vermutlich dem hebräischem Wort לָמָה entspricht und nach Sinn und Zweck fragt, unterstreicht die Kritik an der schlafenden Seele. Der Psalmist fordert zum Lobpreis Gottes, „des Hochgelobten" (ὁ αἰνετός), auf, wobei V. 1b mit V. 2a durch das Verb „singen" (ψάλλω), welches den Modus des Gotteslobs angibt, verklammert ist. In V. 2b erscheint ἀγαθὸς ψαλμός als Synonym zu ὕμνος καινός in V. 1b: „guter Psalm" und „neues Loblied" entsprechen sich. Die Haltung, in der dieses Loblied anzustimmen ist, wird in V. 2a mit dem Begriff der Wachsamkeit (ἡ γρηγόρησις) festgehalten: Wach—und das heißt wohl: aufmerksam und konzentriert—soll sich der Mensch lobend und preisend zu Gott wenden.

Offensichtlich denkt Ps. Sol. 3,1–2, anders als die uns zuvor begegnende Rede vom Schlaf in Ps. Sol. 4,15–16 und Ps. Sol. 6,3–4, nicht an den physischen Schlaf, sondern nutzt die metaphorische Redeweise von Schlaf und Wachsamkeit zur Beschreibung einer geistigen Haltung, wobei die schlafende Seele, dem wachsamen, lobsingenden Beter antitypisch gegenüber tritt.

Diese Art der theologisch reflektierten Rede vom Schlaf begegnet auch in Ps. Sol. 16,1–4:

¹ Ἐν τῷ νυστάξαι ψυχήν μου ἀπὸ κυρίου παρὰ μικρὸν ὠλίσθησα,
ἐν καταφορᾷ ὕπνου τῷ⁵ μακρὰν ἀπὸ θεοῦ
² παρ' ὀλίγον ἐξεχύθη ἡ ψυχή μου εἰς θάνατον,
σύνεγγυς πυλῶν ᾅδου μετὰ ἁμαρτωλοῦ
³ ἐν τῷ διενεχθῆναι ψυχήν μου ἀπὸ κυρίου θεοῦ Ἰσραήλ
εἰ μὴ ὁ κύριος ἀντελάβετό μου τῷ ἐλέει αὐτοῦ εἰς τὸν αἰῶνα.
⁴ ἔνυξέν με ὡς κέντρον ἵππου ἐπὶ τὴν γρηγόρησιν αὐτοῦ,
ὁ σωτὴρ καὶ ἀντιλήπτωρ μου ἐν παντὶ καιρῷ ἔσωσέν με.

¹ Während meine Seele einnickte, bin ich beinahe weg vom Herrn gefallen,
in Tiefschlaf, weit weg von Gott.
² Beinahe wurde meine Seele in den Tod ausgegossen,
nahe den Pforten des Hades mit dem Sünder,
³ als meine Seele umhergetrieben wurde, weg vom Herrn, dem Gott Israels,
wenn nicht der Herr mir geholfen hätte durch sein Erbarmen in Ewigkeit.
⁴ Er spornte mich wie mit einem Pferdestachel zur Wachsamkeit für ihn,
mein Retter und Beistand rettet(e) mich zu jeder Zeit.

Wie schon in Ps. Sol. 3 findet sich auch hier die Rede vom Schlaf gleich zu Beginn des Psalms und wieder ist die Seele (ἡ ψυχή) des Beters das Subjekt des Geschehens (V. 1a.2a.3a). Während Ps. Sol. 3,1–2 als Anrede formuliert war, wird hier nun von einem Geschehen berichtet, das den Beter in die Gottesferne, „weit weg von Gott" (τῷ μακρὰν ἀπὸ θεοῦ) führte (V. 1a). Dieser Zustand der Gottesferne wird dann in doppelter Weise entfaltet: zunächst in V. 1b durch das Bild des Tiefschlafs (ἡ καταφορὰ ὕπνου⁶), sodann in V. 2 durch die Vorstellung der Todesnähe. Die umhertreibende Seele (V. 3a) kann schließlich nur durch Gottes „spornendes" (νύσσω) Eingreifen errettet werden (V. 3b.4a), das den Beter „zur Wachsamkeit für ihn" (ἐπὶ τὴν γρηγόρησιν αὐτοῦ, V. 4a) ruft. Die Temporalbestimmung „zu jeder Zeit" (ἐν παντὶ καιρῷ, V. 4b) verdeutlicht, dass Gottes rettendes Han-

---

5. Vgl. Robert B. Wright, *The Psalms of Solomon : A Critical Edition of the Greek Text*, JCTC 1 (New York: T&T Clark, 2007), 168. Ich folge der (übereinstimmenden) Lesart der handschriftlichen Textzeugen und konjiziere den Halbvers nicht mit von Gebhardt zu ἐν καταφορᾷ ὑπνούντων μακρὰν ἀπὸ θεοῦ. Zur Diskussion der Textstelle vgl. von Gebhardt, *Die Psalmen Salomo's*, 82–83.

6. Vgl. Geiger, *Der Psalter Salomo's*, 148, wonach ἡ καταφορά bei Symmachus hebräisch תַּרְדֵּמָה wiedergibt (so in Gen 2,21; Jes 29,10; Prov 19,15).

deln nicht in einer einmaligen Tat besteht, sondern sich immer wieder, alle Morgen neu ereignet.

Die im Zentrum von Ps. Sol. 16,1–4 stehende Schilderung der Todesnähe in den Vv. 2a–3a wird nach vorne durch das Motiv vom Seelenschlaf (V. 1) und nach hinten durch das Motiv der Wachsamkeit (V. 4a) gerahmt. Während das Einschlummern der Seele (V. 1a) den Menschen von Gott weit weg, ja sogar bis an die Pforten des Hades (σύνεγγυς πυλῶν ᾅδου, V. 2b) führen kann, bedeutet Wachsamkeit die Rettung vor dem Todesschicksal des Sünders (V. 4a). Ohne Zweifel bildet die in der Antike breit bezeugte Vorstellung vom Todesschlaf den Traditionshintergrund von Ps. Sol. 16,1–2.

Diese Tradition der Identifikation vom Schlaf mit dem Tod könnte auch hinter Ps. Sol. 2,30–31 stehen:

³⁰ Αὐτὸς βασιλεὺς ἐπὶ τῶν οὐρανῶν
καὶ κρίνων βασιλεῖς καὶ ἀρχάς·
³¹ ὁ ἀνιστῶν ἐμὲ εἰς δόξαν
καὶ κοιμίζων ὑπερηφάνους εἰς ἀπώλειαν αἰῶνος ἐν ἀτιμίᾳ,
ὅτι οὐκ ἔγνωσαν αὐτόν.

³⁰ Er [Gott] ist König über die Himmel,
und richtet Könige und Herrscher,
³¹ der mich auferstehen lässt zur Herrlichkeit
und Hochmütige entschlafen lässt zu ewiger Vernichtung in Schande,
weil sie ihn nicht (er)kannten.

Der hymnische Lobpreis in Ps. Sol. 2,30–31 artikuliert zunächst Gottes Herrschaft über Himmel (V. 30a) und irdische Gewalten (V. 30b), um dann sein richtendes Handeln am Menschen zu schildern (V. 31): Während Gott Hochmütige (οἱ ὑπερήφανοι), die sich durch ihre Ignoranz gegenüber ihm auszeichnen (V. 31c), entschlafen lässt (κοιμίζω, V. 31b) und ewiger Vernichtung (ἡ ἀπώλεια αἰῶνος, V. 31b) preisgibt, lässt er den Psalmisten „zur Herrlichkeit" (εἰς δόξαν, V. 31a) aufstehen oder besser: auferstehen (ἀνίστημι).

Das Zusammentreffen der euphemistischen Rede vom Entschlafen (κοιμίζω, V. 31b) und des Verbs ἀνίστημι (V. 31a), das innerhalb der Psalmen Salomos ausschließlich in eschatologischem Kontext begegnet,[7]

---

7. Durchgängig begegnet das Verb ἀνίστημι innerhalb der Psalmen Salomos in eschatologischem Kontext: Vom gestürzten Sünder heißt es in Ps. Sol. 3,10, dass er

deutet darauf hin, dass hinter V. 31 die Vorstellung des Todesschlafes steht. Dabei bezeichnet ἀνίστημι die Gegenbewegung zu κοιμίζω. Begrifflich unterschieden ist dieses *Auferstehen* (ἀνίστημι) vom Tod in den Psalmen Salomos vom allmorgendlichen *Aufstehen* (ἐξανίστημι, Ps. Sol. 6,4).

Die genannten Beobachtungen am Text lassen folgendes Zwischenfazit zu: (1) Das Wortfeld „Schlaf" findet sich in fünf der 18 Psalmen Salomos und erstreckt sich in seiner Verbreitung über weite Teile des Gebetskorpus' (Pss. Sol. 2; 3; 4; 6; 16). Die Reflexion über das Phänomen des Schlafes darf daher als durchaus bedeutsam für den oder die Verfasser der Psalmen Salomos betrachtet werden und kann möglicherweise Aufschluss über die Frage nach dem Sitz im Leben der Texte geben.[8]

(2) Die in den Psalmen Salomos begegnende Rede vom Schlaf ist weder terminologisch noch inhaltlich einheitlich. Ihr Bedeutungsspektrum reicht von der Darstellung des sorgenvollen Schlafs und der Schlaflosigkeit des Sünders (Ps. Sol. 4), über die Zeichnung des unerschrockenen Schlafs des Frommen (Ps. Sol. 6) und die mahnende Anrede an die schlafende Seele (Ps. Sol. 3), bis hin zum Bild des Schlafes als Ausdruck von mangelndem Gottesbewusstsein, Gottesferne und Todeserfahrung (Pss. Sol. 2 und 16).

(3) Dieser im Einzelnen durchaus unterschiedlichen Rede vom Schlaf in den Psalmen Salomos ist eine konsequent negative Bewertung des Schlafes gemeinsam. Selbst der Schlaf des Frommen kann nicht positiv beschrieben werden, auch dem Gerechten bleibt der „Anblick seiner bösen Träume" nicht erspart. Der Schlaf erscheint als lebensfeindliche Sphäre menschlicher Existenz. Dem mit Gottesferne und Tod assoziierten

---

nicht auferstehen wird. Hingegen heißt es von den Gottesfürchtigen, dass „sie auferstehen werden zum ewigen Leben" (ἀναστήσονται εἰς ζωὴν αἰώνιον, Ps. Sol. 3,12), und für Israel bleibt die Zuversicht, dass Gott einst seine Verheißungen erfüllt und Israel auferstehen lässt (ἀναστῆσαι κύριος τὸν Ισραηλ, Ps. Sol. 11,8). Schließlich wird auch die Hoffnung auf das Auferstehen eines endzeitlichen Königs aus dem Hause Davids mit dem Verb ἀνίστημι ausgedrückt (Ps. Sol. 17,21.42).

8. Letzteres wird besonders deutlich mit Blick auf Ps. Sol. 3,1–2 und Ps. Sol. 6,4, die die beiden Gebete (Ps. Sol. 3; 6) deutlich in der Situation des Morgenlobs verorten. Vgl. zu dieser Beobachtung auch Sverre Aalen, *Die Begriffe „Licht" und „Finsternis" im Alten Testament, im Spätjudentum und im Rabbinismus*, SUNVA 1 (Oslo: Dybwad, 1951), 112: „Nicht ohne Interesse ist die Feststellung, daß die Morgenandacht die einzige liturgische oder kultische Situation ist, von der in diesen Psalmen [i.e., die Psalmen Salomos] gesprochen wird. Dies zeugt von der zentralen und beherrschenden Stellung gerade dieser Situation in der Tradition."

Phänomen Schlaf treten Wachsamkeit, tägliches Aufstehen zum Gotteslob und endzeitliches Auferstehen positiv gegenüber.

(2) Traditionsgeschichtliche Anknüpfungspunkte in biblischer und ausserbiblischer Literatur

In aller Kürze möchte ich erläutern, dass sich die zuvor dargestellte Redeweise vom Schlaf innerhalb der Psalmen Salomos traditionsgeschichtlich in einen breiten Strom biblischer und außerbiblischer Aussagen zum Schlaf fügt.[9] Dabei verfolge ich nicht das Ziel traditionsgeschichtliche Abhängigkeiten aufzuzeigen, sondern will lediglich anhand von zwei Beispielen darlegen, dass die Verfasser der Psalmen Salomos an traditionsgeschichtlich geläufigen Vorstellungen ihrer jüdischen und paganen Umwelt partizipiert haben.

2.1. Das Ideal der Wachsamkeit und die Abwertung des Schlafes

In Pss. Sol. 3,2; 16,4 tritt der Rede von der schlafenden Seele die im Imperativ formulierte Aufforderung zur Wachsamkeit bzw. die Darstellung des Anspornens zur Wachsamkeit als rettendem Handeln Gottes am Menschen gegenüber. Auch Ps. Sol. 6,4 legt nahe, dass der nach dem Aufstehen vom Schlaf lobsingende Beter seinem Gott wach begegnet—und das bedeutet hier ἐπ'εὐσταθείᾳ καρδίας („mit Festigkeit des Herzens"). Man könnte auch sagen: ‚bei vollem Verstand'.

Das Ideal der Wachsamkeit impliziert zugleich eine Abwertung des Schlafes, wie sie sich schon früh in der philosophischen Tradition der Griechen, etwa bei Heraklit oder Homer findet.[10] Nach Plato taugt derjenige, der schläft, nicht mehr als ein Toter und diejenigen, die wirklich leben und denken (νοεῖν) wollen, sollten auf den üblichen Schlaf verzichten.[11] Im Hintergrund dieser Geringschätzung des Schlafes dürfte die im

---

9. Für eine grundlegende Untersuchung zur Thematik des Schlafes in der Literatur der griechischen Antike sei verwiesen auf Georg Wöhrle, *Hypnos, der Allbezwinger: Eine Studie zum literarischen Bild des Schlafes in der griechischen Antike*, PMTKA 53 (Stuttgart: Steiner, 1995). Das Phänomen des Schlafes im Alten Testament findet sich eingehend untersucht bei Thomas H. McAlpine, *Sleep, Divine & Human, in the Old Testament*, JSOTSup 38 (Sheffield: Sheffield Academic Press, 1987).

10. Vgl. Horst Balz, „ὕπνος κτλ," *TDNT* 8:547–48.

11. Vgl. *ibid.*

14. Buch der Ilias beschriebene Anschauung stehen, dass der Schlaf auf die Bereiche des Überlegens und Wahrnehmens, νόος und φρένες (Homer, Il. 14,253 bzw. 14,165), einwirkt.[12]

Die Hochschätzung der Wachsamkeit im Alten Testament ist eng mit der Konzentration auf die Tora verbunden: Jos 1,8 und Ps 1,2 fordern gleichermaßen das Nachdenken über die Tora bei Tag und Nacht (ἡμέρας καὶ νυκτός). Wie der Fromme über der Tora wacht, so wacht die elterliche Weisung nach Prov 6,22 über ihn und auch der Hüter Israels „schläft und schlummert nicht" (Ps 121[120],3). Neben dem Torastudium (vgl. auch Ps 119[118],148) rufen das Nachdenken über Jhwh und das Gebet zu ihm den Frommen in der Nacht zur Wachsamkeit auf: „Mitten in der Nacht stehe ich auf, um dich zu preisen wegen der Ordnungen deiner Gerechtigkeit" (Ps 119[118],62).[13]

Neben der idealisierten Darstellung des wachenden Torastudenten oder Beters, der seinen Augen keinen Schlaf gestattet (Ps 132[131],4; vgl. auch Prov 6,4), begegnet im Alten Testament aber auch ein kritisches Bewusstsein für die Kostbarkeit des Schlafs. So bemerkt Othmar Keel zu Ps 127[126]: „Sich einen ausreichenden Schlaf zu gönnen, in jungen Jahren Kinder zu zeugen, werden als Annahme göttlicher Geschenke, als Ausdruck der Hingabe und des Vertrauens gewertet."[14] Wer sich abends niederlegt, die Nacht zum Schlafen nutzt und am Morgen bei Sonnenaufgang aufsteht, um sich der Arbeit des Tages zu widmen, fügt sich in die vom Wechsel von Tag und Nacht geprägte Schöpfungsordnung ein, wie sie sich exemplarisch in Ps 104[103],19–23 beschrieben findet.[15] Hingegen fällt der Faule, der zu lange schläft und häufig ruht, aus dieser Ordnung, weshalb er Armut und Mangel leiden wird (vgl. Prov 6,9–11).

Doch nicht jedem ist der nächtliche Schlaf vergönnt: So klagt Jakob dem Laban, dass er während seines zwanzigjährigen Dienstes bei ihm in der Kälte der Nächte nicht zum Schlaf fand (Gen 31,40), und noch eindringlicher ist die in 1 Makk 6,10 geschilderte Klage des Seleukidenkönigs Antiochus [IV. Epiphanes] gegenüber seinen Freunden im Ange-

---

12. Vgl. Wöhrle, *Hypnos*, 16.

13. Vgl. auch Ps 42[41],9; 63[62],7; 119[118],55.

14. Othmar Keel, „Psalm 127: Ein Lobpreis auf Den, der Schlaf und Kinder gibt," in *Ein Gott, eine Offenbarung: Beiträge zur biblischen Exegese, Theologie und Spiritualität: Festschrift für Notker Füglister OSB zum 60. Geburtstag*, ed. Friedrich V. Reiterer (Würzburg: Echter, 1991), 162.

15. Vgl. zur Stelle McAlpine, *Sleep*, 152.

sicht seines nahenden Todes: „Der Schlaf fällt von meinen Augen ab und mein Herz zerfällt vor Beunruhigung."[16] So widerfährt dem Antiochus aufgrund der Erinnerung an „die schlimmen Dinge, die ich in Jerusalem tat" (1 Makk 6,12) das Schicksal der Schlaflosigkeit, das der Beter in Ps. Sol. 4,15 dem Sünder wünscht.

Als zentral für das Verständnis des Wachsamkeitsideals in den Psalmen Salomos erscheint das Nomen γρηγόρησις, das neben Pss. Sol. 3,2; 16,4 innerhalb der Septuaginta nur noch in der Daniel-Version nach Theodotion begegnet und dort in einer Reihe mit σύνεσις und σοφία zur Charakterisierung des weisen Daniel gegenüber dem König Baltasar (Belschazzar) verwendet wird (DanTh 5,11.14).

Die enge Verbindung zwischen Wachsamkeitsideal einerseits und Lobpreis Gottes andererseits, wie sie in Ps. Sol. 3,1–2 zum Ausdruck kommt, findet sich in der frühjüdischen Literatur wohl am prägnantesten im äthiopischen Henochbuch ausgedrückt, wo die niemals schlafenden Engel Gott ohne Unterbrechung immerfort lobsingen (1 En. 39,12–13; vgl. auch 40,2; 61,12)[17]:

> Dich preisen die, die nicht schlafen, und sie stehen vor deiner Herrlichkeit und preisen, verherrlichen und erheben (dich), indem sie sprechen: ‚Heilig, heilig, heilig ist der Herr der Geister—er füllt die Erde mit Geistern!' und hier sahen meine Augen all die, die nicht schlafen; sie standen vor ihm, priesen (ihn) und sprachen: ‚Gepriesen seist du, und gepriesen sei der Name des Herrn immer und ewig!'[18]

---

16. Wörtlich: „und ich bin zerfallen durch das Herz vor Beunruhigung."—Zur Klage über die eigene Schlaflosigkeit vgl. auch Job 7,4.13–15. Dass die Frevler nicht zu Schlaf finden, lehrt auch Prov 4,16b LXX: „Ihr Schlaf ist hinweg genommen und sie schlafen nicht ein" (ἀφῄρηται ὁ ὕπνος αὐτῶν καὶ οὐ κοιμῶνται). Schlaflosigkeit bzw. unruhiger Schlaf werden innerhalb der Septuagintaliteratur besonders im Sirachbuch an verschiedenen Orten reflektiert und auf unterschiedliche Ursachen zurückgeführt: So nennt Sir 31[34],1–2 Reichtum und schwere Krankheit als Ursachen der Schlaflosigkeit, während nach Sir 31[34],19–20 „einem erzogenen Menschen" (ἀνθρώπῳ πεπαιδευμένῳ, V. 19) der „Schlaf der Gesundheit" (ὕπνος ὑγιείας, V. 20) widerfährt; nach Sir 40,5–7 findet der von Wut, Eifersucht, Verwirrung, Unruhe, Todesfurcht oder Zorn ergriffene nicht zur Nachtruhe, sondern wird „verwirrt beim Anblick/Traumbild seines Herzens" (τεθορυβημένος ἐν ὁράσει καρδίας αὐτου, V. 6) und schließlich kann die Sorge um die eigene Tochter dem Vater den Schlaf rauben (Sir 42,9).

17. Vgl. Balz, *TDNT* 8:552 (Anm. 51).

18. 1 En. 39,12–13 nach der Übersetzung von Siegbert Uhlig, „Das äthiopische Henochbuch," *JSHRZ* 5:461–780.

Je weiter wir in der jüdisch-christlichen Literatur- und Religionsgeschichte fortfahren, desto deutlicher wird die Wertschätzung des Ideals der Wachsamkeit. Breit entfaltet ist das Motiv der Wachsamkeit nicht zuletzt in der neutestamentlichen Literatur, die an dieser Stelle nur schlaglichtartig beleuchtet werden kann.[19] Wie schon im frühjüdischen Schrifttum so lässt sich auch in den Texten des Neuen Testaments keine einheitliche Redeweise von Schlaf und Wachsamkeit feststellen. So bemerkt Evald Lövestam in seiner Studie zum Motiv der Wachsamkeit im Neuen Testament:

> Representing the opposite to the passive and unconscious condition of sleep, the motifs of awakening and wakefulness vary considerably in their use. They can be used as expressions for entering into animation and activity or function, being liberated from the aberration and the imprisonment in the material world; arising from the dead; being watchful and on one's guard; and being intent on something; etc.[20]

Das breite Spektrum der Rede vom Wachen bzw. von der Wachsamkeit im Neuen Testament erstreckt sich sowohl über die Brief- als auch die Evangelienliteratur. In Röm 13,11–14 nutzt Paulus die gegensätzlichen Bilder von Tag (ἡμέρα) und Nacht (νύξ) sowie Licht (φῶς) und Finsternis (σκότος),[21] um angesichts der nahenden Parusie die Christusgläubigen zur Wachsamkeit und einem neuen Leben zu rufen: „denn die Stunde ist da, dass ihr aus dem Schlaf erwacht" (ὅτι ὥρα ἤδη ὑμᾶς ἐξ ὕπνου ἐγερθῆναι) (Röm 13,11). Auch in 1 Thess 5,1–11 spielen die Opposita von Licht und Finsternis eine zentrale Rolle, wenn der Apostel den Christusgläubigen versichert, dass sie als „Söhne des Lichtes und des Tages" (V. 5) nicht der lebensfeindlichen Sphäre der Finsternis angehören. Aus dieser Erkenntnis ergibt sich für Paulus der Aufruf an die Gemeinde: „Also lasst uns nun nicht schlafen (καθεύδω) wie die übrigen, sondern wachen (γρηγορέω) und nüchtern (νήφω) sein!" (V. 6).[22] Paulus bezeichnet mit καθεύδω („schlafen")

---

19. Einen guten Überblick zum Motiv der Wachsamkeit im Neuen Testament bietet Evald Lövestam, *Spiritual Wakefulness in the New Testament*, trans. W. F. Salisbury, LUÅ NS 55/3 (Lund: Gleerup, 1963).

20. Lövestam, *Spiritual Wakefulness*, 6.

21. Zur Bedeutung dieser Kontrastbilder in der alttestamentlichen, frühjüdischen und rabbinischen Literatur vgl. Aalen, *„Licht" und „Finsternis"* und für das johanneische Schrifttum Otto Schwankl, *Licht und Finsternis: Ein metaphorisches Paradigma in den johanneischen Schriften*, HBS 5 (Freiburg: Herder, 1995).

22. Vgl. auch 1 Thess 5,10 und zur Stelle John Paul Heil, „Those Now 'Asleep'

in 1 Thess 5,6.10 „eine geistliche oder vielmehr ungeistliche Haltung, die im Gegensatz steht zu der Sammlung und Energie des Glaubenslebens"[23]. Die Haltung der Wachsamkeit wird „im Glauben" (ἐν τῇ πίστει) eingenommen wie der Appell in 1 Kor 16,13 verrät: „Wachet, steht fest im Glauben, seid tapfer, seid stark!"[24] So hat die Rede von der Wachsamkeit im Neuen Testament einen stark ethischen Akzent, und das Verb γρηγορέω „hat offenbar schon früh Eingang in die allgemeine Paränese gefunden als Ausdruck der spezifischen Haltung wacher Bereitschaft, die den Christen auszeichnen soll."[25]

Die Stellen Lk 6,12 und Mk 1,35 bezeugen, dass Jesus in der Nacht bzw. am frühen Morgen zu seinem himmlischen Vater betete. Eindringlich ist Jesu Ermahnung seiner Jünger zur Wachsamkeit in der Gethsemane-Perikope (Mt 26,41–46 par.), in der zugleich von den folgenschweren Konsequenzen des Schlafes der Jünger erzählt wird (Mt 26,47–56 par.).

Grundlegend für das Verständnis des Wachsamkeitsideals im Neuen Testament erscheint nicht nur hier, sondern auch andernorts im Neuen Testament der Zusammenhang zwischen Wachen und Beten.[26] Daneben begegnet der Ruf zur Wachsamkeit im eschatologischen Kontext im Zusammenhang mit der Ankündigung der Parusie: „Wacht (γρηγορεῖτε)

(not dead) Must be 'Awakened' for the Day of the Lord in 1 Thess 5.9-10," NTS 46 (2000): 470-71: „In conclusion, 'whether we may be awake or whether we may be asleep' in [1 Thess] 5.10 does not mean whether we may be physically alive or dead as in 4.13-18, but whether we may be ethically or spiritually 'awake' or 'asleep' as in 5.6-8. A consideration of the overall hortatory and parenetic character of the context of 5.9-10 indicates that if some Thessalonian Christians may presently be 'asleep', they must be 'awakened' to a life of holiness before living with the Lord Jesus Christ in the future after he comes again." Vgl. auch Markus Lautenschlager, „Εἴτε γρηγορῶμεν εἴτε καθεύδωμεν: Zum Verhältnis von Heiligung und Heil in 1Thess 5,10," ZNW 81 (1990): 39-59. Lautenschlager ermittelt, dass das Verb καθεύδω (anders als κοιμάομαι) nirgends in der griechischen Literatur die Bedeutung ‚tot sein' oder ‚entschlafen' trägt, vgl. ad loc., 49.

23. Albrecht Oepke, „καθεύδω," TDNT 3:436.

24. Vgl. auch den Appell zur Achtsamkeit im Glauben in 1 Petr 5,8: „Seid nüchtern, wacht [γρηγορήσατε]! Euer Widersacher, der Teufel, geht umher wie ein brüllender Löwe und sucht, wen er verschlingen kann."

25. Traugott Holtz, Der erste Brief des Paulus an die Thessalonicher, 3rd ed., EKKNT 13 (Zürich: Benziger, 1998), 223.

26. Vgl. Eph 6,18; Kol 4,2; 1 Petr 4,7 und zu den genannten Stellen ausführlich Lövestam, Spiritual Wakefulness, 64-77.

nun, denn ihr wisst nicht, wann der Herr des Hauses kommt..." (Mk 13,35; vgl. auch V. 37 und Mt 24,42; 25,13).

2.2. Die Vorstellung vom Todesschlaf und die Auferstehungshoffnung

Wie wir sahen, steht die Vorstellung vom Todesschlaf deutlich im Hintergrund von Ps. Sol. 16,1–4. Nicht unbedingt eine entfaltete Vorstellung vom Todesschlaf, aber zumindest die euphemistische Rede vom Tod als Schlaf begegnet in Ps. Sol. 2,31, wo die mit κοιμάομαι gebildete euphemistische Rede das Sterben bedeutet.

Die visuelle Ähnlichkeit zwischen einem Schlafenden und einem Toten führte offenbar schon früh zu einer Identifikation des Schlafes mit dem Tod. So kennt die griechische Mythologie den Gott Hypnos nicht nur als Bruder, sondern auch als Zwillingsbruder (διδυμάων) des Thanatos (Homer, Il. 16,672). In einem Hesiod-Fragment begegnet die Rede vom ὕπνος θανάτοιο („Schlaf des Todes")[27], und kaum zu zählen sind die Belege in der griechisch-paganen Literatur, in denen vom ‚schlafen' im Sinne von ‚sterben' die Rede ist, „so daß man...von einer literarisch geläufigen Metapher sprechen kann."[28]

Xenophon (430–354 v. Chr.) lehrt in seiner Kyrupädie: „Bedenkt aber auch, daß unter allen menschlichen Dingen dem Tod nichts so ähnlich ist wie der Schlaf."[29] Spätestens ab dem dritten Jahrhundert v. Chr. begegnet „die Metapher vom Todesschlaf auch innerhalb literarischer bzw. nichtliterarischer, aber metrischer—im wesentlichen kaiserzeitlicher— Grabepigramme"[30]. Beispielhaft sei eine pagane Inschrift aus dem 1./2. Jh. n. Chr. erwähnt, die den um die Verstorbene Trauernden tröstend auffordert: καὶ λέγε Ποπιλίην εὕδειν... („und sage, dass Popilia schläft...") (IGUR 3,1310,7). Schließlich sei unter den vielen literarischen Zeugen für die Vorstellung vom Todesschlaf in der paganen Welt noch Ovid (43

---

27. Hesiod, *fr.* 278,6 (*Fragmenta Hesiodea*, ed. Reinhold Merkelbach und Martin L. West [Oxford: Clarendon, 1967]) *apud* Strabo, *Geogr.* 14,1,27.

28. Wöhrle, *Hypnos*, 24.

29. Xenophon, *Cyr.* 8,7,21 (Übersetzung Rainer Nickel, ed., *Kyrupädie: Die Erziehung des Kyros, griechisch–deutsch*, Sammlung Tusculum [Munich: Artemis & Winkler, 1992]).

30. Wöhrle, *Hypnos*, 27.

v. Chr. – 17 n. Chr.) genannt, der im Schlaf „ein Abbild des Todes" (*mortis imago*) erkennt (Ovid, Am. 2,9,41).[31]

Auch wenn die Rede vom Schlaf als Sinnbild für den Tod bereits in der klassischen Gräzität nachweisbar ist, so scheint der metaphorische Gebrauch des Verbs κοιμάομαι im Sinne von „sterben" in einem breiteren Kontext erst in hellenistisch-römischer Zeit gebräuchlich zu sein.[32] Mit Marbury B. Ogle lässt sich feststellen:

> The conclusion [is] unavoidable that the conception of death as sleep was not a natural one to the Greek folk, nor ... to the Roman. It may not be going to far to say that the sudden appearance of references to the sleep of death in the literary epitaphs of the Hellenistic period was due to the syncretism of Greeks with peoples of Phoenician stock to whom, if we may trust the evidence of art, the idea was familiar.[33]

Auch im Alten Testament finden sich Belege, in denen euphemistisch vom Tod als Schlaf gesprochen wird (vgl. etwa 1 Kön 1,21; 2,10; Ez 31,18 u.a.m.). Eine besondere Entfaltung findet die Vorstellung vom Todesschlaf in Jer 51[28],39: „Wenn sie erhitzt sind, richte ich ihnen ein Trinkgelage an und mache sie betrunken, so dass sie frohlocken und entschlafen zu ewigem Schlaf und nicht mehr erwachen, spricht der HERR."

Ebenfalls in eschatologischer Rede begegnet die Vorstellung vom Todesschlaf in Ijob 14,12^{MT}: „Und ein Mensch legt sich hin und steht nicht wieder auf. Bis der Himmel nicht mehr ist, werden sie nicht erwachen und erweckt werden aus ihrem Schlaf." Der Todesschlaf erscheint an dieser Stelle als ein immerwährender, nicht endender Zustand. Der Gedanke einer Totenauferstehung findet sich hier nicht.

---

31. Vgl. Ovid, Am. 2,9,39–42 (Übersetzung *Ovid: Die Liebeselegien: lateinisch und deutsch*, ed. Friedrich Walter Lenz, 3rd ed., SQAW 15 [Berlin: Akademie, 1976]): „Unglücklich ist, wer es vermag, die ganze Nacht zu ruhen, / und den Schlaf einen großen Segen nennt. / Tor, was ist denn der Schlaf wenn nicht ein Abbild des kalten Todes? / Lange Zeit zum Ruhen wird das Geschick dir geben."

32. Marbury B. Ogle, "The Sleep of Death," MAAR 11 (1933): 98.

33. Ibid., 87.

Eine breite Weiterentwicklung findet die Vorstellung vom Todesschlaf schließlich in der Apokalyptik[34] (vgl. etwa 1 En. 49,3; 91,10; 92,3; 100,5; 2 Bar. 30,1; 36,11).[35]

Der Glaube an eine Auferstehung der Toten, gedanklich vorbereitet durch Texte wie Ez 37,1–14; Jes 53,10; Ijob 19,25–27 oder Ps 73[72][36], findet sich in 2 Makk 12,43–45 ausgedrückt und ist hier eng mit der Vorstellung vom Todesschlaf verknüpft: Im Gedanken an die „Auferstehung" (ἀνάστασις) und angesichts der Zuversicht, dass „die mit Frömmigkeit schlafenden" (οἱ μετ' εὐσεβείας κοιμώμενοι, V. 45) Gefallenen einst „aufstehen" (ἀνίστημι, V. 44) werden, sammelt Judas Makkabäus in seinen Reihen eine Kollekte zugunsten eines Sühnopfers für die Toten.

Im Zuge der Herausbildung des Glaubens an eine leibliche Auferstehung erweist sich das Bild vom Tod als Schlaf besonders tragfähig: „Judaism did come to a belief in the resurrection of the body, and made it one of her cardinal doctrines, but the view of sleep which is now seen to presuppose resurrection helped to formulate that belief."[37]

Für die Aufnahme der bildhaften Rede vom Todesschlaf im Neuen Testament sei exemplarisch auf die Erzählung von der Auferweckung der Tochter des Jairus (Mk 5,35–43 par.) sowie die Lazarus-Perikope (Joh 11,11–14) hingewiesen. Besonders Mk 5,39 verdeutlicht, dass sich der Anblick eines Toten und eines Schlafenden stark ähneln können: „Was lärmt und weint ihr? Das Kind ist nicht gestorben, sondern es schläft." (Mk 5,39)

Gerade die neutestamentlichen Texte zeigen besonders gut, wie eng die Rede vom Todesschlaf mit dem Auferweckungsgedanken verbunden ist. Traditionsgeschichtlich ist die neutestamentliche Rede von einzelnen Totenerweckungen (vgl. 1 Kön 17,17–24; 2 Kön 4,18–37; 13,20–21) ebenso wie die Darstellung der Hoffnung auf eine allgemeine Auferstehung durch das Alte Testament (vgl. Ez 37,1–14; Jes 26,19; 53,10; Ijob 19,25–27; Ps

---

34. Vgl. dazu Otto Michel, „Zur Lehre vom Todesschlaf," *ZNW* 35 (1936): 287: „In der Apokalyptik ist das Bild vom ‚Schlafen' oft anzutreffen, in den meisten Fällen ist es auf den Gerechten bezogen und unter der Voraussetzung der Auferstehung angewandt. Es...kann sowohl von der Seele wie auch vom Körper, aber auch vom Menschen schlechthin ausgesagt sein (*Jub.* 23,31)."

35. Vgl. Balz, *TDNT* 8:551.

36. Vgl. Albrecht Oepke, „ἀνίστημι κτλ," *TDNT* 1:369.

37. James G. S. S. Thomson, "Sleep: An Aspect of Jewish Anthropology," *VT* 5 (1955): 431.

73[72]) vorbereitet: „Und viele von denen, die im Land des Staubes schlafen, werden aufwachen: die einen zu ewigem Leben und die anderen zur Schande, zu ewigem Abscheu." (Dan 12,2)

Zuletzt sei noch auf die immense Bedeutung der Metapher vom Todesschlaf in jüdischen Grabinschriften aus dem dritten bis fünften nachchristlichen Jahrhundert hingewiesen: "The wish ἐν εἰρήνη ἡ κοίμησις αὐτοῦ/αὐτῆς/σοῦ (henceforth ε.ε.η.κ.α.), 'in peace be his/her/your sleep,' seems to be the single most numerous funerary salutation occuring in Jewish inscriptions from Rome."[38]

Die jüdischen Grabinschriften aus nachchristlicher Zeit sind Zeugen für die weite Verbreitung der euphemistischen Redeweise vom Tod als Schlaf im spätantiken Judentum. Dabei ist die Idee vom Todesschlaf eng mit dem tröstenden Gedanken verbunden,

> that death brings one rest from the labours of life. This is, strictly speaking, compatible with both a belief in a blessed afterlife, and an unending rest in the grave.[39]

3. Zusammenfassung und Gedanken zur theologischen Leistungsfähigkeit der Rede vom Schlaf in den Psalmen Salomos

1. Die in Hinsicht auf Begriffe und Inhalt durchaus divergierende Rede vom Schlaf in den Psalmen Salomos knüpft durchgängig an Traditionen an, die sich auch andernorts in jüdischer und paganer Literatur finden lassen und auf deren Popularität Texte späterer Zeit (z.B. aus dem Neuen Testament) hindeuten.
2. Bemerkenswert ist, dass sich innerhalb der Psalmen Salomos eine durchgängig negative Betrachtung des Phänomens Schlaf findet. Eine positive Beschreibung des Schlafes, wie sie sich etwa in Jer 31[38],26 (ὁ ὕπνος μου ἡδύς μοι ἐγενήθη) oder Prov 3,24 zeigt, findet sich nicht.
3. Inhaltlich erscheint die Rede vom Schlaf in den Psalmen Salomos in dreierlei Hinsicht bedeutsam:

---

38. Joseph S. Park, *Conceptions of Afterlife in Jewish Inscriptions: With Special Reference to Pauline Literature*, WUNT 2/121 (Tübingen: Mohr Siebeck, 2000), 98 (und Anm. 49).

39. Ibid., 112.

3.1. Die Rede vom Schlaf dient der typologischen und zugleich polarisierenden Darstellung des Frommen und des Sünders: Während der Sünder zu keinem sorgenfreien Schlaf findet, können den Frommen selbst böse Träume nicht schrecken.

3.2. Die negative Zeichnung des Schlafens oder Einschlummerns verweist auf das Konzept der Wachsamkeit, das seinerseits wiederum eng mit dem Ruf zum Lobpreis Gottes verknüpft ist.

3.3. Die Rede vom Schlaf ist in besonderer Weise mit der Darstellung der Gottesferne und Todesnähe einerseits und der Hoffnung auf Auferstehung andererseits verbunden.

Die Leistungsfähigkeit der metaphorischen Rede vom Schlaf in den Psalmen Salomos besteht also primär darin, dass sie an allgemeinmenschliche Erfahrungen (Schlaf/Schlaflosigkeit/Aufstehen etc.) anknüpfen kann und sie für die Beschreibung theologisch zentraler Themen wie Gottesferne oder Wachsamkeit sowie Tod und Auferstehung fruchtbar zu machen vermag.

Prayers for Being Disciplined: Notes on ΠΑΙΔΕΥΩ and ΠΑΙΔΕΙΑ in the Psalms of Solomon

Patrick Pouchelle

1. Introduction

It is commonly said of the Psalms of Solomon that their usage of παιδεύω (Pss. Sol. 3:4; 7:3; 13:8; 16:11; 17:42), παιδεία (7:9; 8:26; 10:2, 3; 13:7, 9, 10; 14:1; 16:13; 18:4, 7), and παιδευτής (8:29) means that the community that wrote this corpus suffered badly. In a recent contribution, Atkinson wrote that "the pious must not consider their present misfortune and suffering as a sign of God's neglect, but as a form of divine chastisement that will lead to salvation."[1] This opinion has not really evolved since Ryle and James. For them, the author of the Psalms of Solomon considered "the extinction of the Jewish dynasty and the overthrow of hopes for Jewish independence" as "necessary discipline (παιδεία) for the offences of his [God's] people."[2]

Kaiser and Werline offered slightly different ideas. For them, the divine discipline should be interpreted in the context of contemporary education. Werline compared παιδεία to a "struggle" due "to the rise of the Roman era" which included "the loss of influence of the community." According to him the community interpreted these events "within their habitus," that is to say, within their environment of scribes for whom education is related to correction.[3] As for Kaiser, he divided the corpus into two parts: the first

---

1. Kenneth Atkinson, "Enduring the Lord's Discipline: Soteriology in the *Psalms of Solomon*," in *This World and the World to Come: Soteriology in Early Judaism*, ed. Daniel M. Gurtner, LSTS 74 (London: T&T Clark, 2011), 155.

2. Herbert R. Ryle, and Montague R. James, *ΨΑΛΜΟΙ ΣΟΛΟΜΩΝΤΟΣ: Psalms of the Pharisees, Commonly Called the Psalms of Solomon* (Cambridge: Cambridge University Press, 1891), xlix.

3. Rodney A. Werline, "The Experience of God's *Paideia* in the *Psalms of Solo-*

contains texts with historical allusions, and the second includes texts with theological ideas about divine παιδεία. He concluded that this construction leads the reader to create a synthesis through the concept of divine discipline between an ethical way of life and historical events.[4]

Winninge seems to disconnect completely divine discipline from historical events.[5] For him, divine discipline is a central tenant of the Psalms of Solomon. By divine discipline, the righteous one is allowed to move from sinfulness to righteousness. Indeed, the righteous one is made aware of sins, and, thus, can confess sin and endure trials which provide atonement for sin. The discipline is also what distinguishes the wicked from the righteous, "the former receive ἀπώλεια, whereas the latter only encounter παιδεία."[6]

However, the concept that lies behind the words παιδεύω (Pss. Sol. 3:4; 7:3; 13:8; 16:11; 17:42), παιδεία (Pss. Sol. 7:9; 8:26; 10:2, 3; 13:7, 9, 10; 14:1; 16:13; 18:4, 7), and παιδευτής (Ps. Sol. 8:29) is not as clear as several scholars imagine, and the texts from the Psalms of Solomon in which those words are found deserve further attention. This paper will examine each occurrence of these words in the Psalms of Solomon along with the immediate context in which they appear, and will then conclude with a short summary.

2. Analysis

2.1. Ps. Sol. 3

Ps. Sol. 3 begins with a call to the reader to wake up and praise God (vv. 1–2), for God should be on the mind of the righteous (v. 3). In v. 4, we find the first occurrence of παιδεύω in the entire corpus:

---

mon," in *Experientia, Volume 2: Linking Text and Experience*, ed. Colleen Shantz and Rodney A. Werline, EJL 35 (Atlanta: Society of Biblical Literature, 2012).

4. Otto Kaiser, "Tradition und Gegenwart in den Psalmen Salomos," in *Prayer from Tobit to Qumran*, ed. Renate Egger-Wenzel and Jeremy Corley, DCLY 2004 (Berlin: de Gruyter, 2004), 352–53; and idem, *Gott, Mensch und Geschichte: Studien zum Verständnis des Menschen und seiner Geschichte in der klassischen, biblischen und nachbiblischen Literatur*, BZAW 413 (Berlin: de Gruyter, 2010), 128–29.

5. Mikael Winninge, *Sinners and the Righteous: A Comparative Study of the Psalms of Solomon and Paul's Letters*, ConBNT 26 (Stockholm: Almqvist & Wiksell, 1995), 137–40.

6. Winninge, *Sinners and the Righteous*, 68–69.

οὐκ ὀλιγωρήσει δίκαιος παιδευόμενος ὑπὸ κυρίου.

The use of ὀλιγωρέω is a clear allusion to the Septuagint of Prov 3:11:

Υἱέ, μὴ ὀλιγώρει παιδείας κυρίου.
My son, do not belittle the Lord's discipline. (NETS)

Indeed, ὀλιγωρέω is never used elsewhere in the Septuagint. Hence, its association in Ps. Sol. 3:4 with the verb παιδεύω is hardly a coincidence. Why, therefore, did the Greek text use here παιδευόμενος ὑπὸ κυρίου and not παιδείας κυρίου?

Some scholars believe that it is due to a misreading of the Hebrew text.[7] The translator may have read מִיסַר, a participle form of יָסַר, instead of מוּסָר.[8] The suggestion is unlikely because the translator probably noticed an allusion to Prov 3:11, since he used ὀλιγωρέω.[9] Why then did he suddenly decide to depart from the Septuagint of Proverbs? Further, the translator may have intentionally altered Prov 3:11 LXX so as to transform the transitive verb ὀλιγωρέω into an intransitive one.[10]

The righteous one who is disciplined by the Lord will not be negligent.
(author's own translation)

By this modification, the text prepares its reader to consider how one can avoid being negligent and how one should take into account the disciplinary process of God. Indeed, the next verse explains that the good will of the righteous one should be oriented toward God.[11] The structure that fol-

---

7. It is beyond this contribution to deal with the issue of the *Vorlage*. It could be similar to Prov 3:11 MT, but this verse may well have been directly written in Greek; see Jan Joosten in the present volume for a new approach to the original language of the Psalms of Solomon.

8. See George B. Gray, "The *Psalms of Solomon*," APOT 2:635; Wilhelm Frankenberg, *Die Datierung der Psalmen Salomos: Ein Beitrag zur jüdischen Geschichte*, BZAW 1 (Giessen: Ricker, 1896), 87–88; and Joseph L. Trafton, *The Syriac Version of the Psalms of Solomon: A Critical Evaluation*, SCS 11 (Atlanta: Scholars Press, 1985), 54.

9. This verb is used in Prov 3:11 only. It corresponds to מאס, "to despise." This Hebrew verb is associated with מוּסָר in Prov 15:32 and Job 5:17.

10. *Pace* NETS, see LSJ for this usage. See also, e.g., Isocrates, *Evag.* 41.

11. ἡ εὐδοκία αὐτοῦ διὰ παντὸς ἔναντι κυρίου. Gottlob Schrenk, "εὐδοκέω, εὐδοκία," TDNT 2:744, argues that εὐδοκία has God as subject. This is ambiguous, however, Ryle and James, *Psalms of the Pharisees*, 33 presents both explanations without decisively

lows in vv. 5–11 is very interesting, for it states that both the righteous and the wicked person stumble and fall. There is, however, a key difference. In regards to the righteous one, the text uses προσκόπτω and πίπτω in parallel lines (Ps. Sol. 3:5), which leads to a discussion about the development and the behavior of the righteous one's relationship with God.[12]

The section dedicated to the wicked begins in v. 9 with προσκόπτω and it ends with πίπτω in v. 10 in a reference to the end of the sinners:

ἔπεσεν, ὅτι πονηρὸν τὸ πτῶμα αὐτοῦ καὶ οὐκ ἀναστήσεται.
[H]e fell, because his fall is evil, and he shall not rise up. (NETS)

The discussion between these terms in the psalm focuses on the sinner as one who curses his life. This is definitely a harsh punishment.[13] It signals that the fate of the sinner is irreversible and leads to a final fall.[14]

The behavior of the righteous one and that of the sinner is also contrasted. This is emphasized by use of the common expression ἁμαρτία ἐφ' ἁμαρτίαν, resp. ἁμαρτίας ἐφ' ἁμαρτίας.[15] Ps. Sol. 3:10 is a probable allusion to Isa 30:1 or Sir 3:27; 5:5, which describe how sinners accumulate sins over sins.[16] In contrast, the righteous one does not permit even one single

---

choosing between the two. For Joseph Viteau, *Les Psaumes de Solomon: Introduction, texte grec et traduction, avec les principales variantes de la version syriaque par François Martin*, Documents pour l'étude de la Bible (Paris: Letouzey et Ané, 1911), 268, this is the goodwill of the righteous one.

12. See Dan 11:19 LXX or Isa 8:5 Sym. In accordance with Winninge, *Sinners and the Righteous*, 39, this does not refer to moral failure but to misfortune.

13. Some scholars have compared this with Job 3:1–3; 19:25–29, and Jer 20:14; see Dieter Lührmann, "Paul and the Pharisaic Tradition," *JSNT* 36 (1989): 81. For Winninge, *Sinners and the Righteous*, 40 these parallels are not relevant as these formulas are, for him, too common. Lührmann, however, is right in stating that the author of the Psalms of Solomon is close to the opinion of some friends of Job (Lührmann, "Paul and the Pharisaic Tradition," 82): one cannot affirm that one is free from sins.

14. This is close to the signification of Prov 24:16 (see Winninge, *Sinners and the Righteous*, 39): ἑπτάκι γὰρ πεσεῖται ὁ δίκαιος καὶ ἀναστήσεται, οἱ δὲ ἀσεβεῖς ἀσθενήσουσιν ἐν κακοῖς. See Ryle and James, *Psalms of the Pharisees*, 37.

15. Winninge, *Sinners and the Righteous*, 42 rightly stated that the expression is in the singular for the righteous.

16. All these occurrences use this expression with the verb προστίθημι "to add, to accumulate."

sin to stay (αὐλίζομαι) in his house. Ps. Sol. 3:7–8 explains how the righteous one can remove his sins by examining his life and by fasting.¹⁷

To summarize, Ps. Sol. 3 shows that with the divine discipline, the righteous one avoids multiplying his sins. In contrast, without divine discipline, the sinner is fated to complete destruction.

2.2. Ps. Sol. 7

Ps. Sol. 7:2 juxtaposes God's discipline to God's abandonment of his people to the nations:

σὺ ἐν θελήματί σου παίδευσον ἡμᾶς, καὶ μὴ δῷς ἔθνεσιν.
Discipline us by your will, and do not give us to the nations. (NETS)

This probably alludes to Hos 10:10 MT:

בְּאַוָּתִי וְאֶסֳּרֵם וְאֻסְּפוּ עֲלֵיהֶם עַמִּים בְּאָסְרָם
It is my desire to discipline them and nations shall be gathered against them. (NRSV, slightly modified)

The author seems to fear that the prophecy of Hos 10:10 is coming true. If this allusion is correct, the author departs from the LXX, as the LXX renders Hos 10:10 in the following manner: ἦλθεν παιδεῦσαι αὐτούς, καὶ συναχθήσονται ἐπ' αὐτοὺς λαοὶ ἐν τῷ παιδεύεσθαι αὐτοὺς ἐν ταῖς δυσὶν ἀδικίαις αὐτῶν. As one can see, the translator in the LXX has confused בְּאַוָּתִי with a form of the verb בוא, "to go."

I understand the reference to God's discipline and punishment by the nations to be standing in an antithetical poetic relationship. That is, in Ps. Sol. 7:2 divine discipline and the invasion of a foreign army stand as opposites of one another. This event could well be interpreted as the ultimate punishment of a wicked people.

---

17. ἐπισκέπτεται διὰ παντὸς τὸν οἶκον αὐτοῦ ὁ δίκαιος τοῦ ἐξᾶραι ἀδικίαν ἐν παραπτώματι αὐτοῦ, ἐξιλάσατο περὶ ἀγνοίας ἐν νηστείᾳ καὶ ταπεινώσει ψυχῆς αὐτοῦ, καὶ ὁ κύριος καθαρίζει πᾶν ἄνδρα ὅσιον καὶ τὸν οἶκον αὐτοῦ. For Winninge, as well as Lührmann, "Paul and the Pharisaic Tradition," 84, it is a possible argument for a pharisaic provenance of the Psalms of Solomon (Winninge, *Sinners and the Righteous*, 41), especially because fasting points back to Lev 16:29 without any reference to offerings. Therefore, it is atonement through a daily life of piety.

Furthermore, in Ps. Sol. 7:9, the text rejoices about the fact that the people are under the whip of his discipline forever:

καὶ ἡμεῖς ὑπὸ ζυγόν σου τὸν αἰῶνα καὶ μάστιγα παιδείας σου.
And we are under your yoke forever, and the whip of your discipline. (NETS)

The association of ζυγός and παιδεία also occurs in Sir 51:26. In Ps. Sol.7, it is the result of God's kindness for disciplining his people: he will not reject his people (see Ps. Sol. 7:6, 8). In essence, divine discipline in Ps. Sol. 7 allows the righteous to avoid being severely punished.

2.3. Ps. Sol. 8

Ps. Sol. 8:26 connects παιδεία with God's judgment:

κρίνων τὸν Ισραηλ ἐν παιδείᾳ.
Judging Israel with discipline. (NETS)

The construction of κρίνω with ἐν means "to judge someone" in the Septuagint (see, e.g., 2 Sam [2 Kgdms] 19:10; 2 Chr 20:12; Ps 109[108]:6; Isa 5:3). Therefore, in Ps. Sol. 8:26, ἐν παιδείᾳ should probably be understood in an instrumental sense in connection with the verb, much like δικαιοσύνῃ in Ps. Sol. 8:24 (see Rev 19:11). In fact, the whole of Ps. Sol. 8 is a reflection on the divine judgment.[18] However, should one understand the fall of Jerusalem as the manifestation of the judgment of God or in some other sense? A parallel phrase in Ps. Sol. 8:24 complicates the traditional interpretation that the fall is simply punishment:

Κύριος ὁ κρίνων πᾶσαν τὴν γῆν ἐν δικαιοσύνῃ αὐτοῦ. (Ps. Sol. 8:24)
The Lord who judges all the earth in his righteousness. (NETS)

One should especially note that God judges Israel with παιδεία while judging the earth with righteousness. It shows that παιδεία is a specificity for Israel. God's people are disciplined whereas the other peoples are judged.

---

18. With twelve occurrences of either κρῖμα or κρίνω among the thirty-six occurrences in the Psalms of Solomon.

PRAYERS FOR BEING DISCIPLINED 121

The expression καὶ σὺ παιδευτὴς ἡμῶν εἶ, (Ps. Sol. 8:29)[19] seems to be an allusion to Hos 5:2 LXX.[20] In our text, this phrase follows the expression καὶ ἡμεῖς ἐσκληρύναμεν τὸν τράχηλον ἡμῶν, which occurs most notably in Jer 17:23:

> καὶ ἐσκλήρυναν τὸν τράχηλον αὐτῶν ὑπὲρ τοὺς πατέρας αὐτῶν τοῦ μὴ ἀκοῦσαί μου καὶ τοῦ μὴ δέξασθαι παιδείαν.
> and they stiffened their neck more than their fathers so as not to hear me and not to receive instruction. (NETS)

Therefore, the discipline is presented as the consequence of the stubbornness of the people as well as a measure of kindness from God. To summarize, Ps. Sol. 8 presents a harsh discipline resulting from the sin of the people, which is part of God's justice. This discipline is only endured by Israel.

2.4. Ps. Sol. 10

Ps. Sol. 10 displays a pattern similar to that of Ps. Sol. 3:

> Μακάριος ἀνήρ, οὗ ὁ κύριος ἐμνήσθη ἐν ἐλεγμῷ,
> καὶ ἐκυκλώθη ἀπὸ ὁδοῦ πονηρᾶς ἐν μάστιγι
> καθαρισθῆναι ἀπὸ ἁμαρτίας τοῦ μὴ πληθῦναι.
> ὁ ἑτοιμάζων νῶτον εἰς μάστιγας καθαρισθήσεται
> χρηστὸς γὰρ ὁ κύριος τοῖς ὑπομένουσιν παιδείαν. (Ps. Sol. 10:1–2)
>
> Happy is the man whom the Lord remembers with reproving
> and who is fenced from the evil road by a whip,
> that he may be cleansed from sin, that it may not increase.
> He who prepares his back for lashes shall be cleansed,
> for the Lord is kind to those who endure discipline. (NETS)

This psalm begins with an odd paradox. The one who is "blessed" is the person whom God "remembers" through "reproving." In contrast, the

---

19. Winninge, *Sinners and the Righteous*, 62, this title mingles the notion of correction, salvation, and ruling.

20. For the expression ἐγὼ δὲ παιδευτὴς ὑμῶν, which does not correspond to the MT, see Eberhard Bons, "'Je suis votre éducateur' (Os 5,2LXX)—Un titre divin et son contexte littéraire," in *Le Jugement dans l'un et l'autre Testament I: Mélanges offerts à Raymond Kuntzmann*, ed. Eberhard Bons, Lectio Divina 197 (Paris: Cerf, 2004), 192–206.

wicked, who are spared God's rebuke, are, in the end, facing a much worse destiny—ultimate destruction. The author of the psalm may have in mind Job 5:17 (which uses νουθετέω) and Ps 94[93]:12.[21] Further, a similar paradox appears in Prov 3:12, which also employs the term μάστιξ. The verb κυκλόω is strange here and probably means "to protect from."[22] Holm-Nielsen suggests a comparison with Ps 114[113]:5, in which one finds סבב in the MT with the meaning "to withdraw, to depart." Indeed, κυκλόω usually corresponds to this Hebrew root. However, Ps 114[113]:5 LXX renders סבב with ἀναχωρέω when speaking of seas and rivers. More convincing is the parallel with Exod 13:18:

καὶ ἐκύκλωσεν ὁ θεὸς τὸν λαὸν ὁδὸν τὴν εἰς τὴν ἔρημον εἰς τὴν ἐρυθρὰν θάλασσαν.
And God led the people a roundabout way towards the wilderness towards the Red Sea. (NETS)

In this verse, the verb κυκλόω is used in relation with ὁδόν and refers to God departing from a predefined way, that of the Philistine, and leading the people in a different direction.[23]

"To purify," καθαρίζω, is mainly used in Leviticus to express cleansing from sin through sacrifice (e.g., Lev 13:6, 7, 13, 17, 23). In Ps. Sol. 10:1–2, the verb occurs twice, first, to declare that the purpose of cleansing is to avoid the sin multiplying, and, second, to express the fact that it is the whipping that cleanses the believer. The expression ὁ ἑτοιμάζων νῶτον εἰς μάστιγας καθαρισθήσεται could be an allusion to both Isa 50:6 (τὸν νῶτόν μου ἡτοίμασα[24] εἰς μάστιγας) and Isa 53:10 (καὶ κύριος βούλεται καθαρίσαι

---

21. Svend Holm-Nielsen, "Die Psalmen Salomos," *JSHRZ* 4:84.
22. According to BDAG, the verb has three meanings: to move around, to surround, and to protect. Only the meaning "to protect" matches the context, although the association of the verb with the preposition ἀπό is unique to the Septuagint and the Greek literature (it seldom occurs in some Christian authors). Holm-Nielsen, "Die Psalmen Salomos," 4:84, compares it with Ps 32[31]:10 and Deut 32:10.
23. Therefore Holm-Nielsen ("Die Psalmen Salomos," 4:84) is probably right in rejecting the conjecture of Fritzsche (*LAVTG*, 580, ἐκωλύθη), However, the sentence could have been influenced by Ps 119[118]:101: ἐκ πάσης ὁδοῦ πονηρᾶς ἐκώλυσα τοὺς πόδας μου. This reading is somewhat confirmed by the Syriac version, even if in Syriac the verb is in the active voice (see Trafton, *The Syriac Version*, 106).
24. According to Ryle and James, *Psalms of the Pharisees*, 98 this is "modeled on Is l.6." Indeed, in the LXX, according to Rahlfs and Joseph Ziegler (*Isaiah*, SVTG 14,

αὐτὸν τῆς πληγῆς). It means that the one who endures the Lord's discipline will be cleansed.

Enduring the Lord's discipline is precisely what the unique colocation ὑπομένω παιδείαν means.[25] Indeed, ὑπομένω means basically "to be patient." It is used to mean "to endure bad feeling," but also "to wait for God," as in Nah 1:7 (χρηστὸς κύριος τοῖς ὑπομένουσιν αὐτὸν ἐν ἡμέρᾳ θλίψεως); Ps 145[144]:9;[26] and Lam 3:25. In the Psalms of Solomon, the nuance of "awaiting" is present in Ps. Sol. 2:36.[27] Therefore, this colocation means that the psalmist willingly accepts the regular discipline of God (see Isa 53:4 Sym).

Ps. Sol. 10 continues with the following statement in v. 3:

ὀρθώσει γὰρ ὁδοὺς δικαίων.
For he will straighten the ways of the Righteous. (NETS)

This sentence finds a parallel in Prov 3:6 LXX:[28]

ἐν πάσαις ὁδοῖς σου γνώριζε αὐτήν, ἵνα ὀρθοτομῇ τὰς ὁδούς σου, [ὁ δὲ πούς σου οὐ μὴ προσκόπτῃ].
In all your ways make her [i.e., Wisdom] know, that she may make straight your ways [and your foot will not stumble]. (NETS)

2nd ed. [Göttingen: Vandenhoeck & Ruprecht, 1967]), it is δέδωκα. However, there are a few witnesses with ἑτοιμάζω (e.g., Acts Phil. 78.8; Nilus Ancyranus, *Ep.* 4.31.2). It is hard to say whether it is a unique witness for the Old Greek of Isaiah or if it is a Hexaplaric revision. Such reading, whether modeled by the author of the Psalms of Solomon or borrowed by him, may well have been influenced by Ps 38[37]:18 (see Ryle and James, *Psalms of the Pharisees*, 98 and Winninge, *Sinners and the Righteous*, 81). I think the influence of Prov 19:29: ἑτοιμάζονται ἀκολάστοις μάστιγες, is less convincing, contra Holm-Nielsen, "Die Psalmen Salomos," 4:84, since the verb is used in the middle voice: this is the whips which are prepared and not the back.

25. This collocation cannot be found elsewhere in the Septuagint. However, Heb 12:7 offers εἰς παιδείαν ὑπομένετε in a similar context.

26. See Rahlfs's *apparatus criticus*. See Marguerite Harl, "Naoum," in *Les douze prophètes: Joël, Abdiou, Jonas, Naoum, Ambakoum, Sophonie*, La Bible d'Alexandrie 23.4–9 (Paris: Cerf, 1999), 201–2, n. 1,7.

27. ὅτι χρηστὸς ὁ κύριος τοῖς ἐπικαλουμένοις αὐτὸν ἐν ὑπομονῇ. But cf. Ps. Sol. 16:15: ἐν τῷ ὑπομεῖναι δίκαιον ἐν τούτοις ἐλεηθήσεται ὑπὸ κυρίου.

28. Ryle and James, *Psalms of the Pharisees*, 98.

The sentence, ὁ δὲ πούς σου οὐ μὴ προσκόπτῃ, does not appear in all the witness of Prov 3:6 LXX. However, having been probably borrowed from Ps 91[90]:12, it shows that a clear connection exists between a straight path and the fact that somebody will not fall.

Finally, Ps. Sol. 10:3 contains the idea of straightness:

καὶ οὐ διαστρέψει ἐν παιδείᾳ.
and will not turn them aside by discipline. (NETS)

Whether the verb requires "the righteous" or "the path" as its object is not so important.[29] More important is that the discipline of Lord does not lead the righteous astray;[30] it will not cause him to sin.[31]

As this overview emphasizes, Ps. Sol. 10:1–3 has several features in common with Ps. Sol. 3. Both these psalms claim that divine discipline is a blessing and that it avoids the multiplication of sins. However, Ps. Sol. 10 does not explicitly speak about the fall of the sinner; rather, the wicked person's future exists only implicitly in the text.

2.5. Ps. Sol. 13

Ps. Sol. 13:1–3 describes how the sinner has been destroyed by "sword, famine, and pestilence" and how God spared the righteous from suffering the same punishments. Most important for this discussion, vv. 7–8 establish a key distinction between discipline and judgment; the discipline of the righteous is not the same as the fate of the sinners:

ὅτι οὐχ ὁμοία ἡ παιδεία τῶν δικαίων ἐν ἀγνοίᾳ καὶ ἡ καταστροφὴ τῶν ἁμαρτωλῶν.
For not the same is the discipline of the righteous in ignorance and the destruction of the sinners. (NETS)

The text continues with the description of the function of the discipline:

ἐν περιστολῇ παιδεύεται δίκαιος, ἵνα μὴ ἐπιχαρῇ ὁ ἁμαρτωλὸς τῷ δικαίῳ.

---

29. As observed by Viteau, *Les Psaumes de Solomon*, 309.
30. Contrary to Wisdom as described by Sirach (Sir 4:17).
31. This could be understood as discipline is enough to maintain the righteous in the correct path. One could also understand that the discipline is not so harsh that the righteous will despair and sin (see particularly Ps. Sol. 5:6).

The righteous is disciplined with distinctness so that the sinner may not rejoice over the righteous. (NETS)

The word περιστολή is notoriously difficult to interpret.[32] In agreement with the majority of scholars,[33] I translated it elsewhere by "quietly" or "sparingly."[34] Others suggest "secretly."[35] However, none of these translations is completely convincing. These translators assume that ἐν περιστολῇ must qualify παιδεύεται, unless the syntax of the verse is awkward, as Winninge has stated.[36] However, if ἐν περιστολῇ meant "secretly," then it means that the righteous one was afraid to experience "public" discipline. This is strange, as the author of this text seems to be very proud of being disciplined by God. The nuance "sparingly" would fit the context better, but this qualification of the discipline is, in my opinion, superfluous. Indeed, the righteous one is disciplined so that the sinners will not laugh at him. The parallelism with Sir 23:2–3 is quite convincing:

τίς ἐπιστήσει ἐπὶ τοῦ διανοήματός μου μάστιγας
καὶ ἐπὶ τῆς καρδίας μου παιδείαν σοφίας
ἵνα ἐπὶ τοῖς ἀγνοήμασίν μου μὴ φείσωνται
καὶ οὐ μὴ παρῇ τὰ ἁμαρτήματα αὐτῶν,
ὅπως μὴ πληθυνθῶσιν αἱ ἄγνοιαί μου
καὶ αἱ ἁμαρτίαι μου πλεονάσωσιν
καὶ πεσοῦμαι ἔναντι τῶν ὑπεναντίων
καὶ ἐπιχαρεῖταί μοι ὁ ἐχθρός μου;

---

32. For a synthesis of the different interpretations of that difficult word, see Patrick Pouchelle, "Critique textuelle et traduction du treizième *Psaume de Salomon*," *JSJ* 42 (2011), 529–30.

33. "With Regard," Ryle and James, *Psalms of the Pharisees*, 109–10 n. 7; "Avec discrétion," Viteau, *Les Psaumes de Salomon*, 321; "with distinctness," Kenneth Atkinson, *I Cried to the Lord: A Study of the Psalms of Solomon's Historical Background and Social Setting*, JSJSup 84 (Leiden: Brill, 2004), 116; "quietly," Robert B. Wright, *The Psalms of Solomon: A Critical Edition of the Greek Text*, JCTC 1 (New York: T&T Clark, 2007), 151.

34. Pouchelle, "Critique textuelle et traduction," 528.

35. "In secret," Winninge, *Sinners and the Righteous*, 83, 138; "Secretly (?)," George B. Gray, "The *Psalms of Solomon*," 2:645, "insgeheim," Eduard Ephraem Geiger, *Der Psalter Salomo's herausgegeben und erklärt* (Augsburg: Wolff, 1871), 61; "Im Verborgenen," *LXX-D* and Holm-Nielsen, "Die Psalmen Salomos," 90.

36. Winninge, *Sinners and the Righteous*, 83.

Who will set whips upon my thought
and discipline of wisdom upon my heart
so that they might not spare my faults of ignorance
and he shall not let their sins go,
that my acts of ignorance may not be multiplied,
and my sins may increase,
and I will fall before my adversaries,
and my enemy will rejoice over me? (NETS, slightly modified)

This text is a call for the divine discipline (v. 2). Without this discipline, one will accumulate sins. Hence one's enemy will rejoice (ἐπιχαίρω[37]) because one will be judged by God and then fall. Therefore, παιδεύεται δίκαιος, ἵνα μὴ ἐπιχαρῇ ὁ ἁμαρτωλὸς τῷ δικαίῳ is a kind of summary of the idea expressed by Sir 23:2–3:[38] the righteous is disciplined so that the sinner may not rejoice over the righteous, implicitly because the sin of the righteous will not increase so he will not be ruined. Hence, I disagree with Winninge that the isolation of ἐν περιστολῇ from παιδεύεται is awkward. However, we have to explain ἐν περιστολῇ.

One could suggest adding the expression ἐν περιστολῇ to the preceding verse, as the Syriac version does, as well as some Greek manuscripts.[39] This would provide a balanced structure in which the phrase ἡ παιδεία τῶν δικαίων ἐν ἀγνοίᾳ parallels ἡ καταστροφὴ τῶν ἁμαρτωλῶν ἐν περιστολῇ. This interpretation would also require understanding περιστολή as a "shroud" for a corpse, as it does in several Greek papyri.[40] In this case, it may mean that the fate of the sinner is in the shroud, that is to say the death.[41] However, one could argue against this understanding by claiming that a shroud

---

37. This verb is specifically used to describe the bad joy one could feel when seeing the fall of somebody else (see LEH).

38. See also, Winninge, *Sinners and the Righteous*, 89. Although I have found other similarities between Sirach and Psalms of Solomon (Ps. Sol. 3:10 and Sir 3:27 or 5:5, Ps. Sol. 7:9 and Sir 51:26), the problem of dependence or independence of Psalms of Solomon with Sirach is beyond the scope of this article.

39. Oscar von Gebhardt, ed., ΨΑΛΜΟΙ ΣΟΛΟΜΩΝΤΟΣ: *Die Psalmen Salomo's zum ersten Male mit Benutzung der Athoshandschriften und des Codex Casanatensis*, TUGAL 13/2 (Leipzig: Hinrichs, 1895), 121.

40. This word is remarkably associated with κηδεία, "funeral," (see P. Oslo 3.130.12, Oxynrhinchos, first century CE or P. Mich. 5.322a.34, Tebtynis, first century CE; cf. Dionysus Halicarnassus, *Ant. Rom.* 3.21). To author's knowledge there is no attestation in Greek inscriptions.

41. See, e.g., this astrologer of the fourth century CE, Paulus Alexandrinus,

could not belong to a sinner who has been eaten by wild beasts. Further, the corpse of the sinner is forgotten, according to the text (e.g., 2:17; 3:11; 13:11).

Another possibility is to take into account the Syriac translation "in knowledge" (ܒܝܕܥܬܐ) and to suggest either a misreading of the Hebrew *Vorlage* or a corruption in the inner Greek transmission. In this case, the original reading could have been ἐπιστήμη.[42] Without any other material such as another Greek manuscript, it is doubtful that a convincing solution will soon be found.

Verse 9 is an allusion to Deut 8:5:

ὅτι νουθετήσει δίκαιον ὡς υἱὸν ἀγαπήσεως,
καὶ ἡ παιδεία αὐτοῦ ὡς πρωτοτόκου.

For he will admonish the righteous as beloved son,
and his discipline is as that of a firstborn. (NETS)

The verb νουθετέω is here a synonym for παιδεύω.[43]

Finally, the last occurrence of παιδεία in this text explains that the discipline of God is expiatory:

ὅτι φείσεται κύριος τῶν ὁσίων αὐτοῦ καὶ τὰ παραπτώματα αὐτῶν ἐξαλείψει ἐν παιδείᾳ.
For the Lord will spare his devout and will wipe away their transgressions with discipline. (NETS)

The verb ἐξαλείφω has the meaning of "to plaster, to wash." With these meanings, the expression could metaphorically refer to erasing the sinner from the earth (see Exod 17:17), or, perhaps, to erase the memory of a person's sin (Isa 43:25).

To conclude, the analysis of Ps. Sol. 13 shows that the discipline of God is a "benediction" that brings forgiveness of sins to the righteous. As a result, they avoid destruction that comes from the judgment of God.

Elem. Apo., 56, line 4 (ed. Boer [Leipzig: Teubner, 1958]), who uses τὴν τοῦ σώματος περιστολήν as a manifestation of death.

42. Corresponding to דַּעַת, e.g., in Exod 31:3; Num 24:16; Isa 33:6.

43. νουθετέω corresponds to יָסַר in Job 5:17. Both verbs are used synonymously in Wis 11:9–10.

2.6. Ps. Sol. 16

Ps. Sol. 16:11 describes how the righteous one should not grumble and despise being disciplined:

> γογγυσμὸν καὶ ὀλιγοψυχίαν ἐν θλίψει μάκρυνον ἀπ' ἐμοῦ, ἐὰν ἁμαρτήσω ἐν τῷ σε παιδεύειν εἰς ἐπιστροφήν.
> Grumbling and faint-heartedness in affliction keep far from me, when, if I sin, you discipline me to return me. (NETS)

The terms γογγυσμός and ὀλιγοψυχία seem to allude to the people in the wilderness (Exod 16:9 and 6:9, respectively). This is the sole attestation in Psalms of Solomon that God's discipline could be an "affliction" (θλῖψις), or something quite difficult, like Israel's stay in Egypt (Exod 4:31). Even if θλῖψις does not usually appear in texts that describe the journey into the wilderness, discipline is compared to the exodus in a possible reinterpretation of Deut 8:5.[44]

Further, Ps. Sol. 16:13 explains that God gives strength to the righteous in order to support them through the moment of παιδεία:

> ὅτι ἐὰν μὴ σὺ ἐνισχύσῃς, τίς ὑφέξεται παιδείαν ἐν πενίᾳ;
> For if you do not give strength, who will endure discipline in poverty?

The verb ὑπέχω is mainly used as a "legal *terminus technicus*" to say "to undergo punishment."[45] The collocation ὑπέχω παιδείαν is unique to this sentence. More than ὑπομένω, ὑπέχω conveys a legal nuance to the παιδείαν as a judiciary action following a transgression. The expression ἐν πενίᾳ, "in poverty," is only here associated with παιδεία.[46] All of this assumes that God's discipline is the result of sin and that it is difficult to endure. Thus, Ps. Sol. 16 emphasizes the severity of discipline that follows the transgression of the righteous. God receives praise because he gives strength to support the righteous during their punishment instead of for punishment itself.

---

44. However, the verse could also allude to Isa 26:16 LXX (κύριε, ἐν θλίψει ἐμνήσθην σου, ἐν θλίψει μικρᾷ ἡ παιδεία σου ἡμῖν—O Lord, in affliction I remembered you, with small affliction your chastening was on us. [NETS])

45. BDAG.

46. Except Prov 13:18, which says precisely the opposite: the παιδεία takes away poverty.

2.7. Ps. Sol. 17

Ps. Sol. 17:42 describe God's messiah disciplining or educating his people:

ἀναστῆσαι αὐτὸν ἐπ' οἶκον Ισραηλ παιδεῦσαι αὐτόν.
To raise him up over the house of Israel to discipline it. (NETS)

That the messiah is here presented only as a chastiser seems unlikely.[47] Of course, the text may allude to the schism of Israel, in which Rehoboam is described as a harsher chastiser than his father Solomon (1 Kgs [3 Kgdms] 12:11, 14, and 2 Chr 10:11, 14). If this allusion is correct, the messiah described here is presented as an ideal king. Thus, the author of the psalm may be comparing the current king (a Hasmonean? Herod?) to Rehoboam. This implies that the verb παιδεύω conveys here a nuance of ruling. Such a nuance could be found in Sir 10:1:

Κριτὴς σοφὸς παιδεύσει τὸν λαὸν αὐτοῦ.
A wise judge will educate his people. (NETS)

The description of the action of a messianic king suggests that παιδεύω not only means "to discipline" or "to chastise," but also somewhat "to rule."

2.8. Ps. Sol. 18

Ps. Sol. 18:4 recalls Ps. Sol. 13:7–9.

ἡ παιδεία σου ἐφ' ἡμᾶς ὡς υἱὸν πρωτότοκον μονογενῆ
ἀποστρέψαι ψυχὴν εὐήκοον ἀπὸ ἀμαθίας ἐν ἀγνοίᾳ.

Your discipline is upon us as on a firstborn, an only son,
to turn back the obedient soul from ignorant stupidity. (NETS)

The expression υἱὸν πρωτότοκον μονογενῆ alludes to Ps. Sol. 13:9, whereas ἐν ἀγνοίᾳ recalls Ps. Sol. 13:7. The rare word εὐήκοος is used in Prov 25:12, but might also evoke Prov 13:1:

υἱὸς πανοῦργος ὑπήκοος πατρί, υἱὸς δὲ ἀνήκοος ἐν ἀπωλείᾳ.

---

47. See the contribution of Joseph L. Trafton in the present volume.

A smart son is obedient to his father, but a disobedient son is on course to destruction. (NETS)

The substantive ἀμαθία, which is used nowhere else in the Septuagint, means "stupidity" (LSJ). This verse, therefore, emphasizes the fact that discipline is given to the righteous so as to avoid committing even the slightest sin of ignorance.

Finally, Ps. Sol. 18:7 seems to allude to Ps. Sol. 17:42:

ὑπὸ ῥάβδον παιδείας χριστοῦ κυρίου.
Under the rod of discipline of the Lord's anointed. (NETS)

As in Ps. Sol. 17:42, the final psalm imagines that the days of the messiah will be good because the people will be directed by him.

3. Summary: Toward a Definition of God's Discipline in Psalms of Solomon

This examination of the Psalms of Solomon now permits a final assessment of the word παιδεία and its relationship to the concept of discipline. I agree with Winninge that divine discipline is essentially a topos with the following characteristics:

(1) The divine παιδεία functions to avoid the accumulation of sins.

(2) The accumulation of sin would lead to a fall.

(3) The fall occurs at a specific occasion, at which time it is revealed who is righteous and who is sinner.

Thus, God uses παιδεία to assist the righteous in avoiding sin so that they do not cross over into the category of "sinner." Behind this Greek word stands the Hebrew מוּסָר/יָסַר as it is used in the MT, and particularly in Proverbs: a harsh action taken by a master/father to obtain obedience from his disciple/son. However, the notion is slightly modified here.

The purpose of discipline is to control or to limit the sins of the righteous. Indeed, the pious person should be able to recognize God's discipline and then readjust accordingly. If one knows that one has sinned, then the person should repent. However, if the righteous person cannot recall the sin, then the sin must have been inadvertent. Nevertheless, the righteous person must still uncover the sin and repent in order to be forgiven. Therefore, this system intends to control sin and hold it to the lowest possible level.

Two more things are important. First, the one who is not disciplined will accumulate sins and will then fall. However, the righteous does not need to suffer badly to examine his life and to change his behavior. More than the gravity of the discipline, what is important is that the righteous has to consider the rebuke as a sign of election, a witness to the kindness of God. The righteous person has to take these rebukes into account and change behavior.

Second, the one who is not disciplined lives quite well before the fall. This means that the traditional notion of retribution is modified; having good life or significant wealth is not an assurance that God looks upon the person with favor and blessing. Ironically, if someone is living perfectly well, assuming that no rebukes have come, the person is in danger of becoming a great sinner.[48]

This concept of discipline can be found in other texts: for example, the prayer of Sir 23:2–3,[49] and 2 Macc 6:12 exhibits this same nuance in interpreting historical events:

Παρακαλῶ οὖν τοὺς ἐντυγχάνοντας τῇδε τῇ βίβλῳ μὴ συστέλλεσθαι διὰ τὰς συμφοράς, λογίζεσθαι δὲ τὰς τιμωρίας μὴ πρὸς ὄλεθρον, ἀλλὰ πρὸς παιδείαν τοῦ γένους ἡμῶν εἶναι
καὶ γὰρ τὸ μὴ πολὺν χρόνον ἐᾶσθαι τοὺς δυσσεβοῦντας, ἀλλ' εὐθέως περιπίπτειν ἐπιτίμοις, μεγάλης εὐεργεσίας σημεῖόν ἐστιν.
οὐ γὰρ καθάπερ καὶ ἐπὶ τῶν ἄλλων ἐθνῶν ἀναμένει μακροθυμῶν ὁ δεσπότης μέχρι τοῦ καταντήσαντας αὐτοὺς πρὸς ἐκπλήρωσιν ἁμαρτιῶν κολάσαι, οὕτως καὶ ἐφ' ἡμῶν ἔκρινεν εἶναι,
ἵνα μὴ πρὸς τέλος ἀφικομένων ἡμῶν τῶν ἁμαρτιῶν ὕστερον ἡμᾶς ἐκδικᾷ.
διόπερ οὐδέποτε μὲν τὸν ἔλεον ἀφ' ἡμῶν ἀφίστησιν, παιδεύων δὲ μετὰ συμφορᾶς οὐκ ἐγκαταλείπει τὸν ἑαυτοῦ λαόν.

---

48. Is this one of the meanings of the metaphor of sleep? (Ps 16:1–3), see the contribution of Sven Behnke in the present volume.
49. See above, the analysis of Ps. Sol. 13.

> Now I urged those who read this book not to be depressed by such calamities, but to recognize that these punishments were designed not to destroy but to discipline our people.
> In fact, it is a sign of great kindness not to let the impious alone for long but to punish them immediately.
> For in the case of the other nations the Lord waits patiently to punish them until they have reached the full measure of their sins, but he does not deal in this way with us
> in order that he may not take vengeance on us afterward, when our sins have reached their height.
> Therefore he never withdraws his mercy from us. While he disciplines us with calamities, he does not forsake his own people. (NETS)

Later, this notion appears in rabbinic thoughts:

> If a man sees suffering coming upon him, let him scrutinize his actions. (b. Ber. 5a)

This concept was probably coined sometime before the writing of the Psalms of Solomon. It provides a better understanding of the traditional notion that retribution does not match the reality: sinners are wealthy and righteous poor. The Israelite righteous person is rebuked on the basis of God's paternal kindness. Such a rebuke is profitable. For this reason, the Psalms of Solomon contain so many "prayers for being disciplined."

The Formation of the Pious Person in the Psalms of Solomon

Rodney A. Werline

1. Introduction

The determination of the identity and social location of the authors of the Psalms of Solomon has proven to be notoriously difficult.[1] Two possibilities became especially attractive to some scholars. First, following Wellhausen, several generations of scholars saw the psalms as the product of Pharisaic circles.[2] As critical scholarship began to establish how little can be known about the Pharisees because of the numerous methodological pitfalls in using rabbinic sayings, the New Testament, and Josephus to reconstruct the group, this position began to lose proponents.[3] The discovery of the Qumran scrolls invited comparisons between the scrolls and the

---

1. For a brief summary of various positions, see Kenneth Atkinson, *I Cried to the Lord: A Study of the Psalms of Solomon's Historical Background and Social Setting*, JSJSup 84 (Leiden: Brill, 2004), 8.

2. For a summary of this history of interpretation, see Dieter Lührmann, "Paul and the Pharisaic Tradition," *JSNT* 36 (1989): 75–94. Lührmann believes that some stream of theological tradition exists between the Psalms of Solomon, Pharisaism, and Paul. For another example, see William L. Lane, "Paul's Legacy from Pharisaic Tradition: Light from the *Psalms of Solomon*," *Concordia Journal* 8 (1982): 130–38. Ryle and James refer to Pharisees as the authors of the Psalms of Solomon throughout their commentary (Herbert R. Ryle, and Montague R. James, ΨΑΛΜΟΙ ΣΟΛΟΜΩΝΤΟΣ: *Psalms of the Pharisees, Commonly Called the Psalms of Solomon* [Cambridge: Cambridge University Press, 1891]). Indeed, they attempt to reconstruct Pharisaical piety in their interpretation of the text.

3. Lührmann ("Paul and the Pharisaic Tradition," 76–78) discusses the methodological issues related to reconstructing the Pharisees at the turn of the era, but nevertheless thinks that the Psalms of Solomon represent a Judaism related to Pharisaism.

Psalms of Solomon, with some scholars proposing that the psalms were of Essene origins.[4] This position also fell on hard times, as no manuscripts of the collection surfaced at Qumran. Further, Psalms of Solomon lacked any of the sectarian features that one finds in some Qumran scrolls, and the psalms' most likely relative, the Hodayot, exhibits many features that hold no place in the Psalms of Solomon.[5] While many prayers at Qumran lack sectarian language and may have originated before the founding of the community, no evidence points to a direct link between the Psalms of Solomon and Qumran prayer texts.

Kenneth Atkinson's work on the Psalms of Solomon provides a valuable way forward.[6] Based on his careful analysis of the psalms, he proposes that the authors of the psalms belonged to a group of pious Jews who had fallen into dispute with the Jerusalem priesthood over various halakic issues. The group decided that the behavior of the priests had profaned the temple. So, they resorted to worshiping in synagogues and relying on prayer and fasting as a means for atonement and maintenance of their relationship with God. The level of their protest did not quite rise to that of those who founded the Qumran community; thus, the authors of the Psalms of Solomon did not completely withdraw from society. Atkinson's assessment of the historical references and allusions in the text also puts Psalms of Solomon studies on a surer footing in regard to dating. He exhibits a welcomed caution in assigning specific dates to individual psalms, as several psalms do not contain enough information to support a date. As a result of Atkinson's historical methodology, the era of dating individual psalms based upon isolated ambiguous phrases, as one sees in Ryle and James, most likely has come to an end.

Drawing on the work and theories of Richard Horsley, who grounds his research in James Scott,[7] I have argued that the authors of the Psalms

---

4. See, e.g., André Dupont-Sommer, *The Essene Writings from Qumran*, trans. Géza Vermès (Oxford: Blackwell, 1961), 296. Robert R. Hann, "The Community of the Pious: The Social Setting of the *Psalms of Solomon*," SR 17 (1988): 169–89.

5. Paul N. Franklyn ("The Cultic and Pious Climax of Eschatology in the *Psalms of Solomon*," *JSJ* 18 [1987]: 17) notes that, while there are some similarities between these texts and the Psalms of Solomon, the evidence is too meager to connect the Psalms of Solomon to these two groups.

6. Atkinson, *I Cried to the Lord*. See especially his conclusion (211–22); idem, "On the Herodian Origins of the Militant Davidic Messianism at Qumran: New Light from *Psalms of Solomon* 17," *JBL* 118 (1999): 435–60.

7. See, e.g., Richard A. Horsley, *Scribes, Visionaries, and Politics of Second Temple*

of Solomon were scribes, a social class that often provided various kinds of bureaucratic functions for ruling elites, and this would include the priestly elite in Judea at the beginning of the Roman era.[8] People in such positions often become embroiled in the politics of the era, and this would certainly be true for a period of shifting politics like that at the beginning of Roman rule, a time of internal instability when people jockeyed for the most powerful positions. Scribes might suffer if their patron fell from power, because their fate was often tied to the fortunes of these figures. Several passages in the Psalms of Solomon suggest that the authors occasionally suffered at the hands of powerful leaders and that they apparently knew of people whose property had been confiscated through the courts (Ps. Sol. 4:9–22). Beyond these rather broad statements, pinpointing the exact social location and function for these scribes in Judean society remains impossible. As Schams has shown, data from around this era reveal that scribes held a wide variety of positions at many levels of society—from personal service to rulers to drawing up documents for the general public.[9] For the moment, this line of inquiry may be at an impasse in regards to the Psalms of Solomon.

However, analysis that relies more on anthropology or social anthropology may open a pathway to new understandings about the authors of the Psalms of Solomon. My investigation into the use of παιδεία in the Psalms of Solomon drew on anthropological methods and combined this with what others have discovered about the education of scribes in the Hellenistic and Roman periods.[10] In an attempt to endure their personal suffering and struggles, both on an individual level and as part of the

---

Judea (Louisville: Westminster John Knox, 2007), 1–51. Anathea E. Portier-Young (*Apocalypse against Empire: Theologies of Resistance in Early Judaism* [Grand Rapids: Eerdmans, 2011], 31–42) also draws on James Scott in her examination of apocalyptic literature and movements that are historically located around the time of Antiochus IV and the Maccabean revolt. See James C. Scott, *Weapons of the Weak: Everyday Forms of Peasant Resistance* (New Haven: Yale University Press, 1985).

8. Rodney A. Werline, "The *Psalms of Solomon* and the Ideology of Rule," in *Conflicted Boundaries in Wisdom and Apocalypticism*, ed. Lawrence M. Wills and Benjamin G. Wright III, SBLSymS 35 (Atlanta: Society of Biblical Literature, 2005), 69–87.

9. Christina Schams, *Jewish Scribes in the Second-Temple Period*, JSOTSup 291 (Sheffield: Sheffield Academic Press, 1998).

10. Rodney A. Werline, "The Experience of God's *Paideia* in the *Psalms of Solomon*," in *Experientia, Volume 2: Linking Text and Experience*, ed. Colleen Shantz and Rodney A. Werline, EJL 35 (Atlanta: Society of Biblical Literature, 2012), 17–44.

Jewish people,[11] the authors drew on the embodied experience of παιδεία from their habitus. Reaching into these experiences of their own formation within scribal social traditions, the authors transformed the world into a classroom in which God occupied the role of παιδευτής and they became students who faced the sufferings of that age as God's discipline. In other words, their strategy for survival consisted of calling on their learned dispositions as students and living out of that.

The examination of παιδεία from this approach invites further questions about and investigations into community formation and the way in which this would have and continued to shape the individual members. How does the community shape the individual and by what means and methods? Answers to questions like this one can begin to fill in some of the gaps in the knowledge about those who produced the psalms and provide a better picture of the lived experiences of people from this era.

2. Methodology

Anthropological studies into the way in which communities shape the individual already exist. In his work *Genealogies of Religion*, Talal Asad explores the role of the community and monastic rule in the formation of the medieval monk.[12] Asad presumes "that communicative discourse is involved in learning, performing, and commenting upon rites."[13] However, he expresses skepticism about anthropological theories that tout "ritual as object of a general theory." By rejecting the "idea that ritual itself encodes some special meaning," Asad instead argues for "a specific historical analysis" in which "[m]onastic rites are analyzed in relation to programs for forming or reforming moral dispositions (that is, for organizing the physical and verbal practices that constitute a virtuous Christian self), in particular, the disposition to true obedience."[14]

---

11. These two levels of suffering correspond to what most agree comprise the basic forms of the psalms: psalms of the nation, and psalms of the individual. For a list, see George W. E. Nickelsburg, *Jewish Literature between the Bible and the Mishnah: A Historical and Literary Introduction*, 2nd ed. (Minneapolis: Augsburg Fortress, 2005), 238–48.

12. Talal Asad (*Genealogies of Religion: Discipline and Reasons of Power in Christianity and Islam* [Baltimore: Johns Hopkins University Press, 1993], 136–39) also situates his discussion within a longer general history of *paideia/disciplina*.

13. Ibid., 130.

14. Ibid.

At the foundation of Asad's approach lie the theories of Marcel Mauss. Asad singles out Mauss especially because Mauss emphasized ritual action as practice and the acquisition of "bodily aptitudes," moving away from ritual as only a conveyer of a symbolic message.[15] According to Asad, "Mauss sought to focus attention on the fact that if we were to conceptualize human behavior in terms of learned capabilities, we might see the need for investigating how these are linked to authoritative standards and regular practice."[16] Mauss used the term habitus to designate this "assemblage of embodied aptitudes," and these were not to be considered "as a medium of symbolic meanings."[17]

Strangely, Asad does not bring the theories of Pierre Bourdieu into his discussions; Asad wants to highlight how practice leads to the development of particular dispositions, exactly the point Bourdieu makes. Bourdieu claims that habitus, "which is constituted in practice is always oriented toward practical functions,"[18] and refers to "a system of durable, transposable dispositions, structured structures predisposed to function as structuring structures," and operates within the practical world as a "system of cognitive motivating structures."[19] Or, as Bourdieu later states, habitus is "a system of dispositions common to all products of the same conditionings."[20] In other words, practices within a society, or class, produce homogeneity among its members as they share a practical history that has become embodied in them over time.[21] As Bourdieu asserts, "What is 'learned in the body' is not something that one has, like knowledge that can be brandished, but something that one is."[22]

In his use of these theories when studying medieval monasticism, Asad narrows his focus on the role of penance in the development of proper dispositions and virtues in twelfth-century Cistercian monastic orders. Penance seems to function as a crucial linchpin in the system, where "punishment for disobedience and the creation of willing obedi-

---

15. Ibid., 75–77.
16. Ibid., 75.
17. Ibid.
18. Pierre Bourdieu, *The Logic of Practice*, trans. Richard Nice (Stanford, CA: Stanford University Press, 1990), 52.
19. Ibid., 53.
20. Ibid., 59.
21. Ibid., 58–59.
22. Ibid., 73.

ence are jointly managed."²³ This "disciplinary process depends on two functions: (a) continuous observations and (b) periodic correction."²⁴ This approach fits well with the medieval understanding of sacrament, and especially this particular sacrament, because it "belongs at once to both the disciplinary functions."²⁵

Carol Newsom applies similar methods in her analysis of the formation of the self among the Qumran sectarians.²⁶ She relies especially on Foucault's understanding of the self, Bakhtin's theories about discourse, and Dorothy Holland's understanding of cultural agency in culturally figured worlds, who builds on both Foucault and Bourdieu. The Qumran scrolls lend themselves quite well to such analysis. The sectarian writings present a somewhat clear outline of the initiation of new members into the group.²⁷ Further, the scrolls address the issues of ongoing evaluation and discipline of community members. The covenant renewal ceremony in 1QS provides an important ritual moment that shaped members and clearly defined those who stood on the inside and those on the outside. Finally, the texts include numerous sections that invite the kind of discourse analysis that Newsom employs.

The character and nature of the Psalms of Solomon, however, differ from these two studies. Obviously, the Psalms of Solomon does not reflect a sacramental communal structure, practice, and theology. The text contains no indication that members of this group confessed sins to one another. However, the members did confess to God, whom they considered their παιδευτής, and they believed that God administered correction through national disasters and the struggles of the micropolitics of daily life, and simply life in general. These features deserve careful examination in regard to how they formed the members of the community because details within the psalms suggest that the community developed and engaged in practices that would lead to the embodiment of dispositions appropriate to God's righteousness. What are these textual features, what were the practices, what was said, and what significance would these have? Also, the

---

23. Asad, *Genealogies of Religion*, 159.
24. Ibid.
25. Ibid., 160.
26. Carol A. Newsom, *The Self as Symbolic Space: Constructing Identity and Community at Qumran*, STDJ 52 (Leiden: Brill, 2004).
27. However, the scrolls do contain some inconsistencies about the initiation process.

Psalms of Solomon does not contain the amount of material and the kind of material found within the Qumran scrolls. They reveal no initiation process or rites, no ongoing disciplinary assessments and maintenance, and no annual covenant ceremony that contains blessings for those inside the group and curses for those who stand on the outside. Thus, despite the few characteristics Psalms of Solomon shares with these two different collections of texts, the particular contextual features of all these texts must remain in focus and must exert a methodological regulatory function.

Since no clear and relatively certain theory has been established for determining the order in which the entire collection of the Psalms of Solomon historically emerged, only a synchronic treatment is available. Unfortunately, this approach produces only a snapshot of the community's entire history frozen in a single frame. However, the overarching concerns, ideology, and values of the group through the span of their production become visible.

3. Forming Dispositions in the Psalms of Solomon

3.1. Gerichtsdoxologie

The theme of God's righteousness dominates these psalms.[28] This applies to both of the basic divisions in the collection—the psalms of the nation and the psalms of the individual. From a traditio-historical perspective, the psalms' authors developed their ideas within the stream of Deuteronomic thought. However, these themes did not simply function as ideas held by the pious group, just as they did not work that way in the communities related to the production of Deuteronomy and other texts that show heavy influence from it.[29] Rather, these traditions arose in practice in such

---

28. All English translations come from Robert B. Wright, *OTP* 2:636–79. For the Greek text, see Alfred Rahlfs and Robert Hanhart, eds., *Septuaginta: Id est Vetus Testamentum graece iuxta LXX interpretes*, rev. ed. (Stuttgart: Deutsche Bibelgesellschaft, 2006). Translations of the Bible are the NSRV and are taken from BibleWorks 9.

29. See, e.g., Steven Weitzmann, "Sensory Reform in Deuteronomy," in *The Formation of the Self in Antiquity*, ed. David Brakke, Michael L. Satlow, and Steven Weitzman (Bloomington: University of Indiana Press, 2005), 123–39. While his study does not specifically focus on the pronouncement of God's righteousness in Deuteronomy, Weitzman shows how Deuteronomy served to form the self, including the emotions, in such a way as to devalue the role of the senses. For Deuteronomy, tradition trumps the senses.

a way that they formed the adherents' dispositions and, thus, shaped their lived experiences as well. The basic structure of Deuteronomic theology assumes that God rewards righteousness and punishes disobedience in Israel. The most serious forms of punishment in this scheme include invasion from foreign armies, occupation, and exile (see Deut 28 and 1 Kgs 8). Ironically, through time, as authors adjusted the Deuteronomic tradition, they concluded that God must eventually drive out the nations in order to protect God's righteousness among all peoples (see, e.g., Bar 2:15; Isa 49:26; Ezek 26:6, 9, 16, 21; 30:8, 19, 25, 26) and fulfill God's promises made to the patriarchs and through Israel's prophets (see, e.g., Pr Azar 12–14; 4Q504 fr.1–2, V, 6b–11a). The Psalms of Solomon exhibits all these variations on this theme.

The penitential prayer tradition grew, in part, out of Deuteronomic ideology,[30] and the Psalms of Solomon shares several characteristics with these prayers. Like the Psalms of Solomon, these prayers drew on and variously developed these themes. These prayers frequently included a statement that declared God's righteousness in bringing punishment upon the people, what von Rad labeled the *Gerichtsdoxologie*. The following list provides examples of the form:

O Lord, God of Israel, you are just. (Ezra 9:15)

Righteousness is on your side. (Dan 9:7)

You are righteous, O Lord, and all your deeds are just. (Tob 3:2)

For you are just in all you have done;
    all your works are true and your ways right,
    and all your judgments are true. (Pr Azar 4)

---

30. See Rodney A. Werline, *Penitential Prayer in Second Temple Judaism: The Development of a Religious Institution*, EJL 13 (Atlanta: Scholars Press, 1998); Mark J. Boda, *Praying the Tradition: The Origin and Use of Tradition in Nehemiah 9*, BZAW 277 (Berlin: de Gruyter, 1999); Richard Bautch, *Developments in Genre between Postexilic Penitential Prayers and the Psalms of Communal Lament*, SBLAB 7 (Atlanta: Society of Biblical Literature, 2003); Judith H. Newman, *Praying by the Book: The Scripturalization of Prayer in Second Temple Judaism*, EJL 14 (Atlanta: Scholars Press, 1999); more recently, Michael D. Mattlock, *Discovering the Traditions of Prose Prayer in Early Jewish Literature*, LSTS 81 (London: T&T Clark, 2012).

The Lord our God is in the right. (Bar 1:15)

The Lord our God is in the right. (Bar 2:6)

True and righteous is God in sending his judgments against our ancestors. (1QS I, 25b–26)

To you, to you, Lord, belongs righteousness. (4Q504 fr. 1–2, VI, 3)

The Psalms of Solomon makes special use of this form. In fact, as the discussion below demonstrates, references to making such a declaration and the actual action of annunciating God's righteousness occur with enough frequency in the Psalms of Solomon to suggest that this constituted an actual practice within the community; that is, the members performed the declaration. Following the theories of Asad, this practice would have become a way in which the worshipers embodied these Deuteronomic ideals, for they announced them through their bodies and then were expected to live according to the affirmations with their bodies. Further, Roy Rappaport has argued that a primary task of ritual is to establish moral obligation. Rituals enacted within or before a community through their unique formal features and performative sequence produce an atmosphere of weightiness that thoughts or directives standing on their own may not achieve.[31] Statements that include performatives have a way of becoming fact to the participants: "Ritual's words do, after all, bring conventional states of affairs, or 'institutional facts' into being, and having been brought into being they are as real as 'brute facts.'"[32] Rappaport believes that such practices reach beyond discursive logic and into the more intuitive and unconscious aspects of the human.[33] Especially with this last statement, Rappaport comes quite close to the concepts in Asad, Mauss, and Bourdieu. Further, since performance of a ritual action has a way of bringing it into being—making real (*res*)—only through its execution, ritual possesses other cultural powers. As he continues, Rappaport asserts:

---

31. Roy A. Rappaport, *Ritual and Religion in the Making of Humanity*, CSSCA 110 (Cambridge: Cambridge University Press, 1999), 116.
32. Ibid., 117. Here Rappaport draws his language from Searle.
33. Ibid.

> This relationship between the act of performance to that which is being performed—that it brings into being—cannot help but specify as well the relationship of the performer to that which he is performing. He is not merely transmitting messages he finds encoded in the liturgy. He is participating in—that is, *becoming part of*—the order to which his own body and breath give life.
>
> To *perform* a liturgical order, which is by definition a more or less invariant sequence of formal acts and utterances *encoded by someone other than the performer* himself is *necessarily to conform to it.... To say that performers participate in or become parts of the orders they are realizing is to say that transmitter-receivers become fused with the messages they are transmitting and receiving. In conforming to the orders that their performances bring into being, and that come alive in their performance, performers become indistinguishable from those orders, parts of them, for the time being.... Therefore, by performing a liturgical order the participants accept, and indicate to themselves and to others that they accept whatever is encoded in the canon of that order.*[34]

Rappaport's theories prove especially helpful in understanding the power of the Psalms of Solomon in forming the pious person. The psalms provide a form for performing a key part of the community's ideology—God's righteousness. They also model the practice and demand the practice. Through such practice, according to Rappaport's theories, the participant becomes fused with the community's discourse. Such public performance and participation establish cultural demands upon the participants and a moral expectation. Through the ritual they feel the weight of the community's moral expectation upon them, which should cause them to hesitate before violating what they have publically affirmed. Thus, ritual provides a way to become fused with discourse, participate in the reality of that discourse, and establish cultural expectations.

This matches well with Asad's claims about the sacrament of penance within medieval monastic communities. The discipline was intended to give shape to the virtuous life, and it arose through the practice. Similarly, the Psalms of Solomon understood practice as the path toward the model pious person, and the texts contain unambiguous models for achieving this.

The discourse of Ps. Sol. 1 indicates the way in which the community understood a proper disposition and shaped this in its members. The

---

34. Ibid., 118–19 (all emphasis original).

model for this comes in the form of Mother Zion, who is most likely the referent of the "I" in the hymn. Her disposition demonstrates the proper response to disastrous events. The assault of the sinners, presumably the Romans, first takes Mother Zion by surprise, because she assumes that the city is full of righteousness (1:2–3). The false indication of righteousness has resulted from the prosperity of the people in the form of progeny, wealth, and renown (vv. 3b–4).[35] Society often understands these three types of success as signs of righteousness. However, looks are deceiving. Unbeknown to Mother Zion, the people have filled the city with their arrogance and their wickedness (vv. 5–8); their deeds had been in secret (v. 7). Upon learning this, Mother Zion holds back from a petitionary prayer or complaint. Indeed, vv. 2–3 sound as if she is about to voice a complaint, a feature Schüpphaus also recognizes, but she quickly changes course once she learns the causes of the assault on the city.[36] This knowledge shuts down any notion of lament. This movement in the emotional state of the character from near indignation, shock, and preparation for lament to recognition and then realization of God's rightful judgment becomes a model "of and for" the members of this community, to borrow and adapt language from Clifford Geertz.[37] The movement toward emotional acceptance of the disaster lies in the admission of the people's sins in 1:6–8, and the continued description of their sins and their punishment in Ps. Sol. 2, which now almost certainly forms a unity with Ps. Sol. 1. The final emotional resolution comes in the declaration of God's righteousness in 2:7, 15–21. Ps. Sol. 2 encourages those "who fear the Lord with understanding" to arrive at this same emotional disposition by joining in blessing God (2:33–37).

Similarly, Ps. Sol. 8 gives shape to the visceral response to invasion and destruction from a foreign invader:

And I said to my heart: "Where, then, will God judge it?"
I heard a sound in Jerusalem, the holy city.

---

35. Ryle and James (*Psalms of the Pharisees*, 4) recognize that the law promised children as a blessing and lists Exod 23:25, 26; Deut 7:13.

36. Joachim Schüpphaus, *Die Psalmen Solomos: Ein Zeugnis Jerusalemer Theologie und Frömmigkeit in der Mitte des Vorchristlichen Jahrunderts*, ALGHJ 7 (Leiden: Brill, 1977), 22–23.

37. Clifford Geertz, *The Interpretation of Cultures: Selected Essays* (New York: Basic Books, 1973), 93–94.

> My stomach was crushed at what I heard,
>> my knees were weak, my heart was afraid,
>> my bones shook like reeds.
> I said: "They directed their ways in righteousness… (Ps. Sol. 8:3-6)

However, by v. 7 the psalmist has begun to accept and proclaim that the disaster reveals God's righteousness because the people sinned in secret; the disaster has brought this into the light of day:

> I thought about the judgments of God since the creation of the heaven and the earth
>> I proved God right in his judgments in ages past. [ἐδικαίωσα τὸν θεὸν ἐν τοῖς κρίμασιν αὐτοῦ]
> God exposed their sins in the full light of day
>> the whole earth knew the righteous judgments of God. (vv. 7-8)

In vv. 23-26, the psalmist has arrived at acceptance and reaffirms that God's actions among the nations are justified—a *Gerichtsdoxologie*:

> God was proven right [ἐδικαιώθη ὁ θεὸς] in his condemnation of the nations of the earth,
>> and the devout of God are like innocent lambs among them.
> Worthy of praise is the Lord, who judges the whole earth in his righteousness.
> See, now, God, you have shown us how you rightly judge;
>> our eyes have seen your judgments, O God.
> We have proven your name right [ἐδικαιώσαμεν τὸ ὄνομά σου], which is honored forever,
>> for you are the God of righteousness [σὺ ὁ θεὸς τῆς δικαιοσύνης],
>> judging Israel in discipline [ἐν παιδείᾳ].

If the current order of the psalms obtained in the early versions of this collection, Ps. Sol. 9 continues the calmer acceptance of Israel's situation, but with an appeal for God to activate the promises given to Abraham and delivered through the prophets (Ps. Sol. 9:8-11).

The contents of 8:27-32 and 9:1-11 show that the community did not ban petitionary prayer and expressions of hope for God to act in a way that ends suffering and commences a new era. A psalmist may request that God reconsider what seems to be impending judgment (Ps. Sol. 7). The psalmists, however, do not base the petitions on their own righteous complaint, but upon God's honoring of the promises made to the patriarchs and to the prophets. Thus, even petition bows to the practice of acclamation of God's righteousness. As a result, the petitionary disposition has been shaped and regulated by the *Gerichtsdoxologie*. To follow the theories of Asad and Mauss, this means that the petitionary prayers require from the practitioner a specialized cultural aptitude that almost intuitively considers all these elements. This becomes possible for a practitioner who has embodied the proper disposition by being shaped through cultural practices.

The same disposition established in the psalms of the nation applies to the psalms of the individual. Ps. Sol. 3 provides an example of this. The psalmist demands a "new song" from himself. This designation sometimes refers to a psalm that celebrates salvation (see Pss 32[33]:3; 40[39]:3; 96[95]:1; 98[97]:1; 144[143]:9; 149:1; Isa 42:10; Rev 5:9; 14:3).[38] The initial motivation in this psalm seems to be the waning of the proper disposition within the writer who seeks to return to a proper state:

> Why do you sleep, O my soul, and do not praise the Lord?
> > Sing a new song to God, who is worthy to be praised.
> Sing and be aware of how he is aware of you;
> > for a good psalm to God is from a glad heart. (Ps. Sol. 3:1–2)

"Remembering God" (v. 3) is accomplished in confession of sins, declaring God's righteousness, and singing from the heart. These constitute real practices and do not operate as simple metaphors. Through this process, the ideals of the community become embodied. By the end of this description of the disposition of the righteous, the text depicts them living in confidence because they know the hardships they suffer come as God's discipline.[39] They know how to respond and what God's response will be (3:5–6). The psalm also places other ritual practices within this process of acknowledging God's righteousness and dealing with one's own unrighteousness—"fasting and humbling of his soul" (v. 8). The confident life as a result of practice also emerges, for example, in Pss. Sol. 6:1–6; 10:1–4; 13:1–5; 14:1–5; 15:1–9. By contrast, the wicked live with constant anxiety, or the righteous wish it upon them (Pss. Sol. 3:6; 4:13; 13:5).

---

38. Werline, "The Experience of God's *Paideia*," 34.
39. There is a translation problem in 3:6 in regards to the word "confidence." Nevertheless of the emotion of the text remains the same.

The difference between the disposition of the righteous and the wicked becomes clearly evident in Ps. Sol. 3. When difficulties come upon the sinner, the sinner curses life for its problems, which apparently involves some culturally classic objects for the curse—at least according to what the authors of the text consider the objects for the impious: cursing the person's day of birth and his mother's pains (3:9). While the righteous "remember" (v. 3), the sinners will "not be remembered" (οὐ μνησθήσεται) (v. 11). The one not remembering may be God, as Wright translates the passage, or the phrase may allude to culturally erasing the memory of a despised, wicked person upon that person's death.

Ps. Sol. 15 especially expresses this same type of confidence found in Ps. Sol. 3. Again, confidence springs from action:

> For who, O God, is strong except the person who confesses you in truth [εἰ μὴ ἐξομολογήσασθαί σοι ἐν ἀληθείᾳ];
> and what person is powerful except he who confesses your name [εἰ μὴ ἐξομολογήσασθαι τῷ ὀνόματί σου]?
> A new psalm with song with a happy heart,
> the fruit of the lips with the tuned instrument of the tongue
> the first fruits of the lips from a devout and righteous heart.
> The one who does these things [ὁ ποιῶν ταῦτα] will never be disturbed by evil. (Ps. Sol. 15:2–4a)

With the phrase "the one who does these things," the psalmist emphasizes that a person is shaped through practice; a good song coming from a good heart produces confidence.

Sometimes a psalmist claims to be awakened through an action by God, as in Ps. Sol. 16. If one applies the logic of God's discipline from several psalms, perhaps some difficult moments came upon this near apostate, and, thus, the person returned to God. Or, perhaps the person observed the discipline that occurred within the life of another person. Whichever the case, or something else altogether, the psalm imagines the person as falling away, which means that this person had at one time engaged in the kinds of practices mentioned above. Such practices remain in a person's memory and may reactivate an earlier disposition if the right conditions arise. The psalmist describes the situation as follows:

> When my soul slumbered, (I was far away) from the Lord, wretched for a time
> I sank into sleep, far from God

For a moment my soul was poured out to death;
   (I was) near the gates of Hades with the sinner.
Thus my soul was drawn away from the Lord God of Israel,
   unless the Lord had come to my aid with his everlasting mercy.
He jabbed me as a horse is goaded to keep it awake;
   my savior and protector at all times saves me. (16:1–4)

In vv. 5–11 the psalmist says that he will "give thanks to God" (ἐξομολογήσομαί σοι ὁ θεός), and then the psalm contains several lines about returning to the disciplined, virtuous life.[40] Thus, through practice the psalmist wishes to recover the disposition appropriate to life in this group.

3.2. Blessings and Curses

Blessings and curses clearly demarcate social boundaries; those pronouncing and receiving blessings and curses know exactly where they stand with one another. However, blessings and curses play a greater role than simple social identification. They establish relationships and in the process may also negotiate power between parties.[41] Further, blessings and curses invoke a reality and, indeed, create a reality in their performance.[42] Within many religious settings, the spoken word carries a kind of magical property, and once it has been performed it is let loose in the world. The Hebrew Bible contains multiple examples of blessings and curses, and the practice certainly continued into the Second Temple period. The members of the Qumran sect in their covenant renewal ceremony annually blessed those inside the group and cursed all of those on the outside:

---

40. Notice that Wright's translation tends to obscure the Greek. Because "I will confess" (ἐξομολογήσομαι) has such an important function within the culture represented in these psalms, Wright should have been more consistent in his translation of this verb. A similar problem sometimes arises in his translation of δικαιόω.

41. See the theories of Catherine Bell. For an accessible summary, see Nathan D. Mitchell, *Liturgy and the Social Sciences* (Collegeville, MN: Liturgical Press, 1999). See Rodney A. Werline, "Prayer, Power and Politics in the Hebrew Bible," *Interpretation* 68 (2014): 5–16.

42. Applicable here is John L. Austin's understanding of speech acts; see his *How to Do Things with Words*, ed. J. O. Urmson and M. Sbisà (Cambridge: Harvard University Press, 1975).

> And the priests shall bless all the men of God's lot who walk unblemished in all his paths and they shall say: "May he bless you with everything good, and may he protect you from everything bad. May he illuminate your heart with the discernment of life and grace you with eternal knowledge. May he lift upon you the countenance of favour for eternal peace." And the levites shall curse all the men of the lot of Belial. They shall begin to speak and shall say: "Accursed are you for all your wicked, blameworthy deeds. May God hand you over to terror by the hand of all those carry out acts of vengeance. May he bring upon you destruction without mercy according to the darkness of your deeds..." (1 QS II, 1b–9)[43]

The opening chapters of 1 Enoch also contain the language of blessing for the righteous and cursing for all those who have rebelled against God (e.g., 1 En 1:8; 5:5–9).[44]

The statements in the Psalms of Solomon that most closely resemble the blessing and curse form use the optative mode. General petitions in the Psalms of Solomon, like other prayers, are formed with the imperative. Ps. Sol. 4 contains several of these curse-like lines in the optative as the author rails against hypocrites who sit in the council:[45]

> May God remove [ἐξάραι] from the devout those who live in hypocrisy;
>   may his flesh decay and his life be impoverished.
> May God expose [ἀνακαλύψαι] the deeds of those who try to impress people;
>   (and expose) their deeds with ridicule and contempt. (Ps. Sol. 4:6–7)

More curse-like lines continue in vv. 14–22. A few of the harsher examples are as follows:

> May the flesh of those who try to impress people be scattered by wild animals,

---

43. Quotes of the Dead Sea Scrolls are from Florentino García Martínez and Eibert J. C. Tigchelaar, eds., *The Dead Sea Scrolls Study Edition: Volume One, 1Q1–4Q273* (Leiden: Brill, 1997). The few Hebrew words have been taken from BibleWorks 9.

44. See the woes in the Epistle of Enoch.

45. For a possible reference to a member of the Sanhedrin in this passage, see Kenneth Atkinson, *An Intertextual Study of the Psalms of Solomon: Pseudepigrapha*, SBEC 49 (Lewiston, NY: Mellen, 2001), 76–77.

and the bones of the criminals dishonored out in the sun... (v. 19)
Let the crows peck out the eyes of the hypocrites. (v. 22a)

In a psalm that petitions God for protection against the "criminal and wicked man," the author includes this imprecatory language:

> May God remove the lips of the criminals in confusion far from the innocent,
> and (may) the bones of the slanderers be scattered far from those who fear the Lord.
> May he destroy the slanderous tongue in flaming fire far from the devout. (12:4)

The blessing form in the Psalms of Solomon may also occur in the optative, but appears in other forms, as the following sample demonstrates. They also tend to be placed at the end of psalms:

> May the mercy of the Lord be upon the house of Israel forever.
> τοῦ κυρίου ἡ ἐλεημοσύνη ἐπὶ οἶκον Ισραηλ εἰς τὸν αἰῶνα καὶ ἔτι. (9:11)

> The Lord's salvation be upon the house of Israel,
>   (that they may be) happy forever.
> τοῦ κυρίου ἡ σωτηρία ἐπὶ οἶκον Ισραηλ
> εἰς εὐφροσύνην αἰώνιον. (10:8)

> May the Lord do what he has spoken about Israel and Jerusalem;
> May the Lord lift up Israel in the name of his glory
> May the mercy of the Lord be upon Israel forevermore
> ποιήσαι κύριος ἃ ἐλάλησεν ἐπὶ Ισραηλ καὶ Ιερουσαλημ
> ἀναστήσαι κύριος τὸν Ισραηλ ἐν ὀνόματι δόξης αὐτοῦ
> τοῦ κυρίου τὸ ἔλεος ἐπὶ τὸν Ισραηλ εἰς τὸν αἰῶνα καὶ ἔτι. (11:8–9)

> May the salvation of the Lord be upon Israel his servant forever...
> τοῦ κυρίου ἡ σωτηρία ἐπὶ Ισραηλ παῖδα αὐτοῦ εἰς τὸν αἰῶνα... (12:6a)

> And may the Lord's devout inherit the Lord's promises...
> καὶ ὅσιοι κυρίου κληρονομήσαισαν ἐπαγγελίας κυρίου... (12:6c)

> May God dispatch his mercy to Israel;
> May he deliver us from the pollution of profane enemies.
> ταχύναι ὁ θεὸς ἐπὶ Ισραηλ τὸ ἔλεος αὐτοῦ
> ῥύσαιτο ἡμᾶς ἀπὸ ἀκαθαρσίας ἐχθρῶν βεβήλων. (17:45)

Helpful for the current study, and for expanding an understanding of blessings and curses in the process of developing a particular disposition, are the following opening lines from 1QS which instruct the leaders and the members of the community what to love and what to hate:

> [A]s he commanded by the hand of Moses and by the hand of all his servants the Prophets; in order to love [ולאהוב] everything which he selects and hate [ולשנוא] everything that he rejects; in order to keep oneself at a distance from evil, and to become attached to all good works...in order to welcome all those who freely volunteer to carry out God's decrees into the covenant of all kindness...in order to love all the sons of light...and to detest [ולשנוא] all the sons of darkness, each one in accordance with his guilt in God's vindication. (1QS I, 2b–11a)

The annual covenant-renewal ceremony, using Asad's theories, did not simply send a message. Rather, in the ceremony the covenanters acted out their relationships with those inside and outside the group and by doing so they established through practice the proper dispositions toward these groups. The rule unambiguously states whom the sectarians should love and whom they should hate—love all that God has selected and hate all that God has rejected, especially the sons of darkness. Blessings and curses provide a very adequate way for expressing these dispositions and cultivating them. Thus, love and hate are culturally formed and expressed according to accepted cultural practices. To use Rappaport's concepts, in the ritual performance, the performer is "participating in—that is, *becoming part of*—the order to which his [*sic*] own body and breath give life."[46] As the congregation of the Psalms of Solomon enunciated their blessings and curses, the members were formed in whom to love and whom to hate. Further, in the performance of the blessings and curses, they enacted that disposition.

3.3. The Concluding Ideal: Psalm 18

As Franklyn notes, Ps. Sol. 18 offers a fitting conclusion to the collection, and from the perspective of this essay, sums up the proper disposition to be held by the righteous person.[47] While the psalm may not quite lead

---

46. Rappaport, *Ritual and Religion*, 119.
47. Franklyn, "The Cultic and Pious Climax," 4–5. He also suggests that Ps. Sol. 1

the collection to an eschatological climax as Franklyn asserts, it nevertheless contains the community's teleological vision.[48] Certainly, the final psalm draws together key themes from throughout the psalms. The opening lines, however, depict the current situation for Israel and the righteous. God's mercy rests upon all things (v. 1),[49] and the psalmist remains confident that God knows the needs of the righteous and provides and cares for them (vv. 2–3). Any hardship they face is the result of God's discipline (v. 4). However, the "cleansing" of Israel is yet to come (v. 5). In vv. 5–9, the author longs for the arrival of a messiah, who will embody—as this term has been used in this essay—the ideals of the community and bodily administer God's discipline in the world:

> Blessed are those born in those days,
>   to see the good things of the Lord
>   which he will do for the coming generation;
> (which will be) under the rod of discipline of the Lord messiah. (see 17:32)[50] (vv. 6–7a)

Under a messiah, the community's formation will continue and be maintained in discipline. The psalm ends with a description of the dependability of the heavenly bodies (vv. 10–12). While these final lines appear somewhat out of place in comparison to the other psalms—creation themes do not dominate the corpus—the author introduces this in the conclusion in order to emphasize the importance of discipline and obedience. The heavenly bodies manifest the community's ideal:

---

introduces the entire collection by establishing the themes of "the comfortable pious one" (Ps. Sol. 4), "historical chaos" (Ps. Sol. 2; 8), and the "hidden sins of foreign rulers as well as local Jews" (Pss. Sol. 4 and 12).

48. The use of the word eschatological seems somewhat strong, unless Franklyn simply means that the psalm hopes for the advent of a new era in which a messiah reigns and establishes a just society. The psalm does not seem to imagine the consummation of all things.

49. For an examination of the balance of God's righteousness and mercy, see Schüpphaus, *Die Psalmen Solomos*, 83–115. However, Schüpphaus's treatment of these topics is quite theological, as the title of this section suggests. The influence of methods and topics from "Old Testament" theology that were en vogue at the time shaped his presentation and perhaps obscures the particular aspects of these elements in the Psalms of Solomon.

50. For the problematic aspects of this phrase, see Wright, *OTP* 2:667 n. z, 669 n. f.

Their course each day is in the fear of God,
> from the day God created them forever.
And they have not wandered
> from the day he created them, from ancient generations.
They have not veered off their course. (vv. 11–12a)

The use of the heavenly bodies as a way to emphasize obedience appears in several texts from the Second Temple period.[51] From an anthropological perspective, this particular kind of invocation of creation has profound meaning and effects. For the authors of these texts, which the author of Ps. Sol. 18 joins, obedience becomes part of the very fabric of the universe. In regards to the Psalms of Solomon, then, obeying God means coming into alignment with this order, in a way, to embody this order. The proper disposition aligns one with all creation.

4. Conclusions, Observations, and Proposals

Most likely these psalms were performed, whether by an individual in communal gatherings or the entire community seems unclear. However, either way, these psalms become communal property and a communal expression. The performance of a psalm required an engaged body, with the mind, the voice, the ears, and the positioned body in action. Even if individuals performed the psalms before an audience in the "synagogues of the pious," the audience members also became engaged. Their minds, ears, and positioned bodies also made them active participants, and the experience of the setting would have formed them—not simply intellectually, but as social bodies. As Catherine Bell makes clear:

> [T]he power of performance lies in great part in the effect of the heightened multisensory experience it affords: one is not being told or shown something so much as one is led to experience something. And according to the anthropologist Barbara Myerhoff, in ritual-like behavior "not only is seeing believing, doing is believing."[52]

---

51. See Michael E. Stone, "The Parabolic Use of Natural Order in Judaism of the Second Temple Age," in *Gilgul: Essays on Transformation, Revolution and Permanence in the History of Religions*, ed. Shaul Shaked, David Shulman, and Guy G. Stroumsa (Leiden: Brill, 1987), 298–308.

52. Catherine Bell, *Ritual: Perspectives and Dimensions* (Oxford: Oxford University Press, 1997), 160.

The performed psalm also heightened the emotional state of the individuals, as they either listened to the psalm performed or joined in its performance.[53] Either way, the action within this setting would encourage the people to take on the emotions of the psalm and the effect of this is quite powerful. Angela Kim Harkins has explored this phenomenon in her book on the Hodayot.[54] Important for this current essay, Kim Harkins notes that current work on emotions has emphasized the social aspect of this human trait, which much of western tradition since the Enlightenment has deemed personal and isolated to the experience of the individual. However, communities form emotions in individuals by indicating what emotions are appropriate for any particular setting and by modeling them. Colleen Shantz in her recent work on Paul notes similar aspects of emotions.[55] Talal Asad also makes comparable claims in his treatment of medieval monasticism:

> This point must be stressed, because the emotions mentioned here [those required for model monks] are not universal human feelings, not "powerful drives and emotions associated with human physiology."... They are historically specific emotions that are structured internally and related to each other in historically determined ways. And they are the product not of mere readings of symbols but of processes of power.[56]

Further, societies develop various ritualized behaviors, especially if one includes speech within these practices, as ways to trigger the collective emotion of a community. The result is quite powerful and becomes another way in which the community morally shapes and forms its members.[57]

---

53. Franklyn ("The Cultic and Pious Climax," 5–6) believes that the psalms most likely did have a communal setting within a synagogue.

54. Angela Kim Harkins, *Reading with an "I" to the Heavens: Looking at the Qumran Hodayot through the Lens of Visionary Traditions*, Ekstasis 3 (Berlin: de Gruyter, 2012), 91–113.

55. Colleen Shantz, "Emotion, Cognition, and Social Change: A Consideration of Galatians 3:28," in *Mind, Morality and Magic: Cognitive Science Approaches in Biblical Studies*, ed. István Czachesz and Risto Uro (Durham: Acumen, 2013), 251–70.

56. Asad, *Genealogies of Religion*, 134.

57. Though he is making a slightly different argument, Asad also emphasizes the place of words written within the monastic regulations in the performance. The words do not simply regulate; rather, "[t]hey are also literally part of the performance: written words to be variously changed, recited, read, attended to, meditated on by the monks" (ibid., 140).

The Psalms of Solomon reveals a community that understood how practice shapes the dispositions of individuals and communities. The centerpiece of the life of practice was the declaration of God's righteousness. With this, they embodied the heart of their community's ideology. The performance of this liturgical ritual produced confidence and calm within the individual. By contrast, the wicked always lived on the edge of disaster, and some psalmists believed that the practices of the wicked could only produce anxiety. On occasion, they cursed the wicked with the hope that they would experience sleeplessness and dread. But, for the members of the community related to the Psalms of Solomon, practice produced the disposition out of which one lived the righteous life.

What Would David Do? Messianic Expectation and Surprise in Ps. Sol. 17

Joseph L. Trafton

1. Introduction

In the introduction to their 1891 commentary on the Psalms of Solomon, Herbert E. Ryle and Montague R. James addressed all of the areas that one would expect to find in the introduction to a commentary—editions, manuscripts, date, authorship, place of writing, original language, purpose, parallels with other literature—but with two significant additions: they included a section on Jewish parties and the religious thought of the document, and a section on the idea of the messiah in the document.[1]

Indeed, it is probably fair to say that it is precisely these two features of the Psalms of Solomon—their "group" perspective and their messianism—that placed them on the radar of scholars during the second half of the nineteenth and the first half of the twentieth centuries.

My own introduction to the Psalms of Solomon came in a graduate course taught by William L. Lane on the life and teachings of Paul. Like most scholars coming out of that era, Professor Lane viewed the Psalms of Solomon as a product of the Pharisees. As such, he emphasized to his students that it is the *only* source that we have for pre-Christian Pharisaism and is therefore of unique importance for understanding the Pharisee-turned-Christian Paul.[2] But there was more, Professor Lane pointed out. This Pharisaic document contained the most extensively drawn portrait

---

1. Herbert R. Ryle, and Montague R. James, *ΨΑΛΜΟΙ ΣΟΛΟΜΩΝΤΟΣ: Psalms of the Pharisees, Commonly Called the Psalms of Solomon* (Cambridge: Cambridge University Press, 1891), xliv–lii, lii–lviii.

2. William L. Lane, "Paul's Legacy from Pharisaic Tradition: Light from the Psalms of Solomon," *Concordia Journal* 8 (1982): 130–38.

of the messiah that we have from pre-Christian Judaism, with all that that implies for shedding light on Paul's view of Jesus.

I was hooked.

Yet, we gather here in Strasbourg in 2013—some four decades after my Paul class and over one hundred years after Ryle and James published their influential[3] commentary—for the *first—the first*—international meeting on the Psalms of Solomon.

What happened?

Many answers to this question could be given, but I would like to suggest that one of the most important was the discovery of the Dead Sea Scrolls.

First, the fascinating—and sometimes scandalous—story of the discovery, identification, and (decades-long) publication—or lack thereof—of the Scrolls naturally drew major attention to the Scrolls themselves, and rightly so. None of us would want to go back in time and try to conduct our research without all that we have learned—and are continuing to learn—from the Scrolls. But, as anyone who has a younger brother or sister can attest, attention to the new can easily eclipse attention to the old.

Second, among the Scroll manuscripts scholars found previously known Jewish writings, such as Tobit and Jubilees and the books that make up the better part of 1 Enoch. But they did *not* find the Psalms of Solomon. To modify the analogy of the older brother or sister, the Psalms of Solomon were therefore relegated to the lesser status of stepbrother or stepsister. After all, surely the most *important* Second Temple Jewish documents would have had a place in the library of those folks who lived and studied at Qumran!

Not that study of the Psalms of Solomon has fallen into oblivion.

First, the recognition of parallels between the Scrolls and the Psalms of Solomon almost immediately led some scholars to challenge the traditional association of the Psalms of Solomon with the Pharisees. The question of who wrote the Psalms of Solomon—Pharisees? Qumran Essenes? non-Qumranic Essenes? Hasidim? Some other group that cannot be named?—remains with us.[4]

---

3. At least for the English-speaking world. There was, of course, a longstanding interest in the Psalms of Solomon on the Continent prior to Ryle and James's commentary. See, e.g., the important contribution of Benedikt Eckhardt in this volume.

4. See, e.g., Joseph L. Trafton, "The *Psalms of Solomon* in Recent Research," *JSP* 12 (1994): 3–19; Mikael Winninge, *Sinners and the Righteous: A Comparative Study of the*

Second, the indefatigable Robert B. Wright devoted virtually his entire professional career to tracking down and examining all of the extant manuscripts of the Psalms of Solomon, which culminated in the 2007 publication of his critical text of the Greek version, with Syriac variants, along with digitalized copies of the manuscripts themselves.[5]

Third, the Scrolls have shed new light on pre-Christian Jewish messianism. But look at what has happened in this regard. Let me give two examples.

The subtitle of John Collins's influential 1995 monograph, entitled *The Scepter and the Star*, is *The Messiahs of the Dead Sea Scrolls and Other Ancient Literature*. Alas, poor Psalms of Solomon! You are now "other." But, to be fair, I should note that Collins *does* give the Psalms of Solomon eight pages out of his 214 pages of text.[6] Eight out of 214!

Similarly, Joseph Fitzmyer, in *The One Who Is to Come*, published in 2007, allots *three* pages to the Psalms of Solomon out of his fifty-two-page chapter entitled "Extrabiblical Jewish Writings of the Second Temple Period."[7] The Dead Sea Scrolls, by the way, get twenty-seven.[8]

Now, I am not trying to denigrate the importance of the messianic material in the Scrolls—I have *written* on these texts.[9]

But here is the thing: when all is said and done with our messiahs of Aaron and Israel, our Star arising out of Jacob, our explicitly Davidic interpretation of Gen 49:10, and *whatever* is going on in 4Q246—Ps. Sol. 17

Psalms of Solomon and Paul's Letters, ConBNT 26 (Stockholm: Almqvist & Wiksell, 1995), 141–80; Kenneth Atkinson, *I Cried to the Lord: A Study of the Psalms of Solomon's Historical Background and Social Setting*, JSJSup 84 (Leiden: Brill, 2004), 211–22.

5. Robert B. Wright, *The Psalms of Solomon: A Critical Edition of the Greek Text*, JCTC 1 (New York: T&T Clark, 2007).

6. John J. Collins, *The Scepter and the Star: The Messiahs of the Dead Sea Scrolls and Other Ancient Literature*, ABRL (New York: Doubleday, 1995), 49–56.

7. Joseph A. Fitzmyer, *The One Who Is to Come* (Grand Rapids: Eerdmans, 2007), 115–17.

8. Ibid., 88–115.

9. Joseph L. Trafton, "Commentary on Genesis (4Q252)," in *Pesharim, Other Commentaries, and Related Documents*, vol. 6b of *The Dead Sea Scrolls*, ed. James H. Charlesworth, PTSDSSP (Tübingen: Mohr Siebeck, 2002), 203–19; and idem, "The Bible, the *Psalms of Solomon*, and Qumran," in *The Dead Sea Scrolls and the Qumran Community*, vol. 2 of *The Bible and the Dead Sea Scrolls*, ed. James H. Charlesworth (Waco, TX: Baylor University Press, 2006), 427–46.

remains the longest, continuous description of the messiah that we possess from pre-Christian Judaism.[10]

I believe that it is time to rehabilitate Ps. Sol. 17.

But first, a word of clarification. To this point in my paper I have, for the most part, been using the expression "pre-Christian Judaism." That has been deliberate. To read Ryle and James's treatment of the messiah in the Psalms of Solomon is to get an eye-opener about the way in which scholars of an earlier period tended to view the value of Jewish writings primarily in terms of how they set up the coming of Jesus.[11] Today we speak of Second Temple Judaism and study it for its own value, a view that I happily adopt. And so I will shift my language accordingly. Yet exploring how Ps. Sol. 17 portrays the messiah within its larger Second Temple Jewish context does not render *unimportant* the question of how a better understanding of messianic expectations in Second Temple Jewish thought might shed light on what the earliest Christians meant when they claimed that Jesus of Nazareth was the Messiah.

2. The Question

Several issues have been at the forefront of the study of Ps. Sol. 17. For example, an earlier view held that the concept of a Davidic messiah was distinctive of the Pharisees;[12] hence, Ps. Sol. 17 was used as evidence that

---

10. The Temple Scroll contains an even longer section on the king (11Q19 LVI, 12–LIX, 21). While a detailed comparison between this section and Ps. Sol. 17 is beyond the scope of this article, is must be pointed out that (1) this king is never connected with David, (2) this king is never identified as messiah, and (3) the orientation of the Temple Scroll is different: like Deuteronomy it is focused on the Israelites coming into the land after the Exodus, while Ps. Sol. 17 hopes for a coming king who will deal with the present calamities that have befallen the people. See the brief comments of Collins, *The Scepter and the Star*, 110. Fitzmyer, *The One Who is To Come*, ignores the Temple Scroll completely.

11. E.g., Ryle and James, *Psalms of the Pharisees*, lvi–lvii: "The picture of the Messiah in our xviith Psalm marks the most notable advance in the conception of the Messianic expectation.... In this representation of the human Messiah, perfect in holiness and taught of God, free from sin and wielding only the weapons of spiritual power, we find ourselves brought more nearly than in any other extant pre-Christian writing to the idealization of 'the Christ' who was born into the world not half a century later than the time at which these Psalms were written."

12. See, e.g., Ryle and James, *Psalms of the Pharisees*, lvii–lviii; George B. Gray, "The *Psalms of Solomon*," APOT 2:630.

the Psalms of Solomon are Pharisaic. Some recent scholars have challenged that position,[13] while others have affirmed it in a more nuanced way.[14] Who is right?

Or, scholars have asked, which passages from the Hebrew Bible did the author use in constructing his picture of the messiah? Isaiah 11 and Psalm 2 are obvious choices, but what about others?[15]

One final example: Is the messiah depicted in Ps. Sol. 17 to be understood as "violent"? For some, the answer is an obvious yes; others would disagree.[16]

All of these questions are important, but I wish to propose that we take a look at Ps. Sol. 17 in a bit of a fresh way. I want to explore one fundamental question: Given the writings to which a group of Jews presumably had access, which we now call the Hebrew Bible,[17] what might these Jews have *expected* the future Davidic king to do, and how do these expectations line up with the portrayal of this king in Ps. Sol. 17? Are there any surprises? If so, what do we make of them?

2.1. The Hope for a King from the Line of David in the Hebrew Bible: Sources

When the idea of a future king from the line of David entered Jewish thought remains a matter of debate.[18] *That* such an idea is already present in various passages in the Hebrew Bible is clear.

By way of an aside, I should add that the question of *when* the idea of a future king from the line of David became associated with the concept of

---

13. See, e.g., Atkinson, *I Cried to the Lord*, 175–76.

14. See, e.g., Winninge, *Sinners and the Righteous*, 174.

15. See, e.g., Trafton, "The Bible," 435–42; Kenneth Atkinson, *An Intertextual Study of the Psalms of Solomon: Pseudepigrapha*, SBEC 49 (Lewiston, NY: Mellen, 2001), 329–78.

16. For yes, see, e.g., Atkinson, *I Cried to the Lord*, 141–44. On those who disagree, see, e.g., Trafton, "The Bible," 440–42.

17. Or, at least, to some of them. It is not necessary to get into the complex issue of the canonization of the Hebrew Bible here. The Dead Sea Scrolls provide ample evidence that books that eventually became a part of the Hebrew Bible, along with others, were being collected in this period. That is my only point.

18. This question is Fitzmyer's primary focus in *The One Who Is to Come* (see 1–7).

a coming "messiah" is controversial, as Joseph Fitzmyer points out.[19] But clearly in Ps. Sol. 17 such an identification is made, *however* we are to understand χριστὸς κύριος in 17:32—that is, as "the Lord messiah" or, if emended to χριστὸς κυρίου, "the messiah of the Lord."[20]

I have found it useful to divide passages from the Hebrew Bible into two categories: what I call "Davidic" passages and "non-Davidic" passages.

"Davidic" passages are those that can arguably be connected—usually explicitly, in fact—to a belief in God's enduring promise to the line of David: 2 Sam[2 Kgdms] 7:8–29, with its parallel in 1 Chr 17:7–27; Pss 18[17], 89[88], 101[100], 110[109], and 132[131]; Isa 9:6–7; 11:1–12:3; and 16:4–5; Jer 23:5–6; 30[37]:9; and 33:14–16 (although this passage is not in the Septuagint);[21] Ezek 34:20–31 and 37:21–28; Hos 3:4–5; Amos 9:11–15; Mic 5:2–4; the book of Haggai, especially 2:20–23[22]; and Zech 3:8–10; 6:12–15; and 12:7–13:1.[23]

---

19. After examining several scholarly definitions of "messiah," Fitzmyer observes: "All of this reveals, however, how in modern discussions 'messianism' or 'the messianic idea' has become 'a rubber-band concept' that is made to embrace far more than 'Messiah' was ever meant to denote when it first emerged and gradually developed in Palestinian Judaism" (ibid., 6).

20. This is, of course, a long-standing crux in Psalms of Solomon scholarship. See, e.g., Ryle and James, *Psalms of the Pharisees*, 141–43, and Atkinson, *I Cried to the Lord*, 131–32.

21. See, e.g., Jack R. Lundbom, *Jeremiah 21–36: A New Translation with Introduction and Commentary*, AB 21B (New York: Doubleday, 2004), 537–39, for discussion.

22. The "Davidic" element in Haggai refers, of course, to Zerubbabel, who is identified consistently as the son of Shealtiel (Hag 1:1, 12, 14; 2:2, 23; cf. Ezra 3:2; 5:2; Neh 12:1). According to 1 Chr 3:17, Shealtiel is the son of (the Davidic) King Jeconiah (see 1 Chr 3:1). First Chronicles 3:19 identifies Zerubbabel as the son of Pedaiah, the brother of Shealtiel (1 Chr 3:18), thus making Shealtiel Zerubbabel's uncle. Whatever the precise relationship between Zerubbabel and Shealtiel, it is clear that Zerubbabel was understood to be a member of the Davidic line. On all of this see, e.g., Carol L. Meyers and Eric M. Meyers, *Haggai and Zechariah 1–8: A New Translation with Introduction and Commentary*, AB 25B (New York: Doubleday, 1987), 9–13.

23. An excellent example of the "broad" approach to messianism in this period is the great Jewish scholar Joseph Klausner's classic monograph, *The Messianic Idea in Israel: From Its Beginning to the Completion of the Mishnah*, trans. William F. Stinespring (New York: Macmillan, 1955). On the Christian side, Justin Martyr's *Dialogus cum Tryphone* has had a lasting—even if largely unrecognized—effect on Christian messianic interpretation of the Hebrew Bible from the second century to the present. Once one has an idea of what the messiah—or the messianic age—is "supposed" to look like, it is easy find "messianic" passages just about anywhere in the Hebrew Bible.

"Non-Davidic" passages are those that are *not* connected with David as such, but *are* connected with the king: Deut 17:14–15; Pss 2, 45[44], and 72[71]; and Zech 9:9–13.[24] On the one hand, one could argue that these passages should not be included in this study at all, since they are not explicitly about David. If we are focusing on a *Davidic* king, then we should restrict our examination to *Davidic* sources. On the other hand, one could argue that *any* passage related to kingship should be fair game, since the coming figure in Ps. Sol. 17 is said to be, after all, a Davidic *king*. Indeed, one might press this argument further by saying that the kingship of David is so important in the Hebrew Bible, and the hope for a future king is so strong, that *any* king would naturally be understood in Davidic terms. Certainly the author of Ps. Sol. 17 had no qualms about *using* some "non-Davidic" passages in his description of a future *Davidic* king, as we shall see. Nonetheless, the very fact that he does so is *precisely* the reason why we should keep the two categories distinct, as I will suggest later.

2.2. The Hope for a King from the Line of David in the Hebrew Bible: Expectations

To a Jew in the middle of the first century BCE who had access to the books that now make up the Hebrew Bible, not to mention traditions of interpretation that might have grown up around certain passages in those books, what might a future king from the line of David have been expected to *do*?

If we focus on the "Davidic" passages, the answer seems to be pretty straightforward, if general. The king will (1) rule his people (2 Kgdms [2 Sam], 1 Chr, Isa, Jer, Ezek, Hos, Mic, and Zech), (2) engage in hostile activities against his enemies (Pss 2, 88[89], 100[101], and 131[132]; and Isa), and (3) judge—that is, dispense justice among—the people whom he rules (Isa and Jer). As such, he might be said (4) to be a "shepherd" for his people (Ezekiel and Micah; cf. 2 Sam [2 Kgdms] 5:2). He might also be expected (5) to build a temple for God (2 Samuel [2 Kingdoms], 1 Chron-

---

Like Fitzmyer, I have tried to limit my focus to passages in the Hebrew Bible that *in their own literary and historical contexts* seem to anticipate a future Davidic king.

24. Other non-Davidic passages that do not explicitly mention the "king," such as Gen 49:10 and Num 24:17, are certainly interpreted messianically in this period (see, e.g., 4Q252 VI, 1–3; CD VII, 18–21), but they are not used by the author of Ps. Sol. 17, hence they lie outside the scope of this paper.

icles, Haggai, and Zechariah).[25] Five activities: ruling, fighting enemies, judging, shepherding, and building. What is interesting is that while the "Davidic" passages in the Hebrew Bible do not get much more specific than this, Ps. Sol. 17 does, as we shall see.

2.3. The Hope for a King from the Line of David in Ps. Sol. 17: Some General Remarks

Ps. Sol. 17 is the longest psalm in the Psalms of Solomon. It also stands strategically as the next to the last. What has always fascinated scholars is that the author of the psalm not only places his hope in a coming king from the line of David but also *sets that hope over against recent political events*. After mentioning "sinners" who "rose up against us … set upon us and drove us out" (v. 5), to whom God "did not promise"—that is, Davidic kingship, of which the author has spoken in v. 4—but "took (it) away by force," the author goes on to explain: "In glory they established a kingdom in place of their pride;/ they laid waste to the throne of David in the arrogance of change" (v. 6). He then exults in the downfall of these sinners who have usurped, as it were, the promise to David: "But you, O God, overthrew them, and uprooted their descendants from the earth,/ when there rose up against them a man alien to their race" (v. 7), one whom he further characterizes as "the lawless one [who] laid waste to our land" (v. 11).

The consensus of scholarship today is that behind the "sinners" of Ps. Sol. 17 stand the Hasmoneans—a family whose kings were *not* Davidic— and that the "man alien to their race" refers to Pompey, who captured Jerusalem in 63 BCE and put an effective, if not immediate, end to the Hasmonean dynasty.[26]

For the psalmist, then, the expectation of a Davidic king is not merely a tradition; it is a central component in the psalmist's response to

---

25. The first two books speak, of course, of Solomon; the last two of Zerubbabel. Though not technically a "king," Zerubbabel was understood to be a descendent of David (see footnote 23) and, according to Ezra 3:8–11; 5:12, played a key role in rebuilding the temple after the exile. See 1 Esdras, where Zerubbabel's stature is enhanced (3:1–4:46; 5:66–70; 6:18–19, 27–31).

26. See, e.g., Trafton, "The *Psalms of Solomon* in Recent Research"; Atkinson, *I Cried to the Lord*, 135–39; Winninge, *Sinners and the Righteous*, 99–101. But see the important contribution of Benedikt Eckhardt in the present volume, who revives the notion that the "man alien to their race" is Herod the Great.

the complex web of calamities that have befallen the Jewish people and that stand behind the writing and collection of the Psalms of Solomon. Among many of their other failures—perhaps even at the root of them—the Hasmoneans established a kingship *from the wrong family*. But God has promised to "raise up" (v. 21: ἀνίστημι—the verb is found in this connection [Heb. קום] in 2 Sam [2 Kgdms] 7:12; 1 Chr 17:11; Jer 23:5; Ezek 34:23; and Amos 9:11) the son of David (v. 21; cf. v. 4: αἱρετίζω). When he comes, as Ps. Sol. 17 makes clear and as Ps. Sol. 18, which stands as a brief epilogue to the entire collection, confirms, everything will be made right.

But what will the son of David *do*?

The Greek version of Ps. Sol. 17 uses thirty-four verbs to characterize the Davidic king's actions. If we take into account that some verbs occur more than once, the number is reduced to twenty-eight. Some of the verbs are almost certainly alternate translations of the same Hebrew verb. For example, the Septuagint uses both κρίνω and διακρίνω, two verbs that are found in Ps. Sol. 17 (vv. 26, 29, and 43), and that correspond to the same Hebrew root—שפט—in Ezek 34:20-22. Given that fact, the number of actions could undoubtedly be reduced even further. This does even not take into account Hebrew synonyms.[27] By my count, there are about thirteen different actions ascribed to the Davidic king in Ps. Sol. 17, and four "nonactions"—that is, things that he will *not* do. The actual number could, of course, be debated and is not terribly significant to my argument. Below I will classify these actions into "expectations," "extended expectations," and "surprises."

2.4. The Hope for a King from the Line of David in Ps. Sol. 17: Expectations

Before proceeding any further, let us make clear that the expected figure in Ps. Sol. 17 is indeed identified as "king" (βασιλεύς) three times (17:32

---

27. E.g., שפט and דין. I am, of course, assuming the scholarly consensus that the Psalms of Solomon were composed in Hebrew. But see the important contribution in the present volume by Jan Joosten, who revives the theory of Greek as the original language. The Psalms of Solomon are extant today only in Greek and in Syriac. On the relationship between the Greek and the Syriac versions, see Joseph L. Trafton, *The Syriac Version of the Psalms of Solomon: A Critical Evaluation*, SCS 11 (Atlanta: Scholars Press, 1985) and idem, "The *Psalms of Solomon*: New Light From the Syriac Version?" *JBL* 105 (1986): 227–37.

[twice], 42).²⁸ Furthermore, the psalmist understands the establishment of this king to be in accordance with the promise that God gave to David (see 2 Sam [2 Kgdms] 7:8–29; 1 Chr 17:7–27): "You, O Lord, raised up David as king over Israel,/ And you swore to him concerning his seed forever,/ that his kingship would not cease before you" (17:4). Hence, it is legitimate to speak of a coming/expected Davidic king in Ps. Sol. 17.

On that basis, then, we can observe that of the five expected actions of the Davidic king found in the Hebrew Bible (see §2.2, above), Ps. Sol. 17 contains four of them.

(1) The king will rule (vv. 21, 26, 36). The Greek uses three different verbs to connote the idea of ruling, all of which overlap: βασιλεύω (v. 21), ἀφηγέομαι (v. 26²⁹), and ἄρχω ³⁰ (v. 36). βασιλεύω is, of course, what a βασιλεύς does. The fundamental Hebrew equivalent of βασιλεύω is מָלַךְ. The LXX uses ἄρχων to translate both מֶלֶךְ and נָשִׂיא. Similarly, ὁ ἀφηγούμενος is used frequently in the LXX to translate נָשִׂיא.

(2) The king will fight enemies (vv. 22, 23, 24, 35, 36). The Greek uses seven different verbs for this action: θραύω (v. 22), ἐξωθέω (v. 23; cf. v. 5), ἐκτρίβω (v. 23), συντρίβω (v. 24; cf. 8:5), ὀλεθρεύω (v. 24; cf. 4:12; 15:5), πατάσσω (v. 35), and ἐξαίρω (v. 36; cf. 3:7; 4:6, 8, 22, 24). While it would be interesting to elaborate upon the different connotations that these verbs bring to the concept of fighting enemies—for example, "smashing," "driving out"—to do so must be left to another occasion. That the king fights his enemies is sufficient to make that point that such an action would be "expected" of a Davidic king.

(3) The king will judge (vv. 25, 26, 29, 36, 43). The Greek uses three different verbs here: ἐλέγχω (vv. 25, 36; cf. 16:14), κρίνω (vv. 26, 29; cf. 2:30, 32; 4:11; 8:3, 15, 24, 26), and διακρίνω (v. 43). That the LXX uses both κρίνω and διακρίνω to translate both שפט and דין demonstrates the overlap of these verbs. As in the previous case, ἐλέγχω is close enough in meaning for our purposes to include it here.

(4) The king will shepherd (v. 40). The verb used is ποιμαίνω, which is the standard translation in the LXX for רָעָה. The use of ἄγω³¹ ("lead") in v. 41 continues this idea.

---

28. Elsewhere in the psalm God is called "king" (17:34, 36). The subtitle of the psalm—"To the King"—is ambiguous.

29. The Syriac has "which will boast"; see Trafton, *The Syriac Version*, 172 n. 89.

30. The Syriac has the noun: "ruler"; see ibid., 180 n. 136.

31. The Syriac has "gather" in v. 41; see ibid., 181 n. 156.

The only possible "surprise" here is the omission of the building of the temple. However, the "Davidic" passages in the Hebrew Bible that speak of that activity are connected specifically with Solomon (1 Kgs [3 Kgdms] 5:5, echoing 2 Sam [2 Kgdms] 7:12–13) and Zerubbabel (Hag 1:1, 12–15). Furthermore, the temple—desecrated though it may be from the psalmist's perspective—was at least in existence when Ps. Sol. 17 was composed. So perhaps this omission should not really come as a "surprise."

Finally, one "nonaction" on the part of the king should be noted here. Twice the psalmist says that the king will "not permit" (ἀφίημι; see v. 9) something: iniquity to dwell in the midst of his people[32] (v. 27) or any of them to stumble in their pasture (v. 40). The general idea, if not the specifics, is found in Ps 101[100], where the psalmist (ostensibly David), eschews the work of those who fall away, perverseness of heart, evil, as well as the one who slanders his neighbor secretly, is characterized by haughty looks and arrogant heart, practices deceit, or utters lies (Ps 101[100]:3–5, 7). While "permit" is not found in Ps 101[100], the sense is—for example, "shall not cleave to me," "will not endure," "no man ... shall dwell in my house," "no man ... shall continue in my presence" (NRSV). Hence, while the forbidden actions are not identical, the idea that the king will prohibit certain states of affairs can reasonably be understood as something to be "expected" of a future king.

In sum, we find in Ps. Sol. 17 four out of the five "expected" actions of the coming Davidic king and one "nonaction" that can reasonably be understood to have been expected.

2.5. The Hope for a King from the Line of David in Ps. Sol. 17: Extended Expectations

A second category of actions marks out those that, while not being specified of a future Davidic king in the Hebrew Bible, might be seen as "extensions" of what any king might reasonably be expected to do. Of course, one could be strict and argue that since none of these actions are specified of a future Davidic king, they should all fall under the category of "surprise." I will not insist upon such rigidity here.

Three kinds of these actions are positive actions.

---

32. Verse 27 goes on to add that no one who knows evil will dwell with them. Verse 32 adds that there will be no injustice in their midst.

(1) The king will "glorify"[33] (δοξάζω) the Lord in all the earth (v. 30). What else would we expect a godly Jewish king do?

(2) and (3) The king will "know" (γινώσκω) his people that they are all sons of their God (v. 27) and "bless" (εὐλογέω) them in wisdom and joy (v. 35). Knowing and blessing your people seem reasonable for a king.

(4) The king will "have" (ἔχω) the nations[34] "serve" (δουλεύω) him under his yoke (v. 30). Conquering other nations can certainly result in enslaving them.

One of the actions is negative.

Twice (vv. 37, 38) the psalmist says that the king will not "grow weak" (ἀσθενέω).[35] If a king is established by God in the first place, that God would continually strengthen him is reasonable; indeed, v. 37 goes on to say that God will make him powerful (ὁ θεὸς κατειργάσατο αὐτὸν δυνατὸν).

In sum, we find in Ps. Sol. 17 four actions and one "nonaction" that can be reasonably understood as extensions of what would be expected of a coming Davidic king.

2.6. The Hope for a King from the Line of David in Ps. Sol. 17: Surprises

But if there are actions ascribed in Ps. Sol. 17 to the coming Davidic king that have antecedents in the Hebrew Bible, and others that might be considered to be extensions of those expectations, there are others that are not. Hence, I call them "surprises."

(1) Twice the psalmist says that the coming Davidic king will "cleanse" (καθαρίζω) Jerusalem (vv. 22, 30). David conquered Jerusalem and made it his capital (2 Sam [2 Kgdms] 5:6–9), but he did not cleanse it, nor is such an activity associated in the Hebrew Bible with a coming Davidic king or messiah.

Now one might ask, what about Hezekiah and Josiah? Both were Davidic kings, and both participated in cleansing activities. Hezekiah directed the priests to "sanctify" (LXX: ἁγνίζω; MT: קדש) the temple (2 Chr 29:5); the result was that they "cleansed" (LXX: καθαρίζω; MT: טהר) it (2 Chr 29:15), which they then reported to Hezekiah (2 Chr 29:18; LXX:

---

33. Syriac MS 16h1 reads "they will glorify"; see Trafton, *The Syriac Version*, 175 n. 109.

34. Literally, "peoples of nations." The Syriac has "a nation from the nations"; see ibid., 175 n. 107.

35. In v. 37 the Syriac has "be diminished"; see ibid., 180 nn. 139, 145.

ἁγνίζω; MT: טהר). The context in the Hebrew suggests that the author viewed the priests' actions to accomplish what Hezekiah directed; the variation in the verbs in the LXX shows clearly the Greek translator understood it that way. Similarly, Josiah "cleansed" (LXX: καθαρίζω; MT: טהר) Judah and Jerusalem (2 Chr 34:3, 5, 8 ["the land and the house"]).

Two responses are in order. First, the cleansings in 2 Chronicles are different from the cleansing in Ps. Sol. 17. In Hezekiah's case, *the temple* is cleansed from the actions of *"our fathers"* (2 Chr 29:6). But in Ps. Sol. 17 the temple is not in view, which is quite surprising given all that the Psalms of Solomon says about the desecration of the temple by the priests (e.g., 1:8; 2:3; 8:12, 22). In addition, those who have brought about the need for cleansing are *the gentiles* (v. 22). For Josiah, *Judah and Jerusalem* are cleansed of *the high places, the Asherim, and the graven and the molten images* (2 Chr 34:3–7). Therefore, although the psalmist and the Chronicler agree that Jerusalem is cleansed, the agreement stops there. The psalmist says nothing about cleansing *Judah*; nor are "the high places, the Asherim, and the graven and molten images" in view. For the psalmist, the cause of Jerusalem's desecration is *the gentiles*, specifically the actions of "the lawless one" (v. 11), who is further identified as a "foreigner," that is, a gentile (vv. 13–14; cf. 2:2).[36] Thus, the differences between the "cleansings" as viewed by the psalmist and the Chronicler are profound.

But there is a second response as well. Even if one were to persist in arguing that the model(s) of the psalmist's statement about the king "cleansing" Jerusalem were Hezekiah and/or Josiah, such an argument would support the point of this article: how *did* Jews in the Second Temple period construct their portrayals of the coming Davidic king/messiah? If they did not use the "standard" passages in the Hebrew Bible, did they simply search for other passages that they could use? And why would they have mined the material in 2 Chronicles about Hezekiah and/or Josiah? Put differently, should we begin to talk about a coming *Josianic* (or Hezekian) king as a figure whom some Jews anticipated? If so, why did the psalmist not use the material in 2 Chronicles (or 2 Kings, for that matter) about Josiah finding and reading "the book of the covenant" (2 Kgs [4 Kgdms] 22:8–23:3; 2 Chr 34:14–32), something that certainly would have served the psalmist's purposes (e.g., vv. 14–15, 19–20)? Indeed, if the psalmist was going to write

---

36. One might observe further the linguistic connection between "the lawless one" (ὁ ἄνομος) and the expression "lawless gentiles" (ἔθνη παράνομα) in 17:24. Both are used to translate, for example, רשע, in the LXX.

"the king was in lawlessness" (v. 20), what better way to present his picture of the coming king than by painting him in Josianic colors!

No, it is certainly best to consider the psalmist's portrayal of the coming king as one who will "cleanse" Jerusalem as a "surprise."

(2) The coming Davidic king will "gather" (συνάγω) a holy people (v. 26). From where he will gather them is not made clear in this verse, but the psalmist speaks at several points about the scattering of at least some Jews (vv. 5, 12, 15–18). In v. 31 we read that nations will bring back the scattered exiles "from the ends of earth."[37] If this is how the king will indeed "gather" them, then such an action is certainly a surprise. While the future return of the exiles is a common theme in the Hebrew Bible (e.g., Isa 11:11–16; 49:8–13; 60:4; Jer 23:3; 31[38]:7–14; Ezek 34:13–14; 37:21–22; Zech 8:7–8; 9:6–12), the agent is always God (see v. 44), never the Davidic king or the messiah.

(3) The coming Davidic king will "distribute" (καταμερίζω) the people upon the land according to their tribes (v. 28). The original allotment of the land to the various tribes of Israel is set out in Num 34 and Josh 13–19, with one elder from each tribe functioning under the oversight of Eleazar the priest and Joshua son of Nun (Num 34:17 and Josh 19:51). Similarly, the end of the Book of Ezekiel depicts a future, idealized allotment of the land according to tribes (Ezek 47:13–48:29).[38] In neither instance is any messiah or king—Davidic or otherwise—involved.[39] Indeed, in a brief ref-

---

37. The Greek and the Syriac differ significantly in this verse in two ways. First, the Greek speaks of children "who had fainted," while the Syriac speaks of children "who were scattered." If the Syriac is to be preferred (so Wright, *The Psalms of Solomon*, 193), this is a clear reference to the return from exile. Second, the Greek has a double accusative: "bringing (as) gifts her children..." The gifts *are* the children, whom the nations bring. The Syriac has a preposition: "when they bring gifts to her children..." Since the nations bring gifts *to* the scattered children, the nations are not the agents of the return of those children. See Trafton, *The Syriac Version*, 176 nn. 118–119.

38. Both the Temple Scroll (11QT XXXIX,12–XL,11; 4Q365a fr. 2, II,1–4) and the New Jerusalem document from Qumran (4Q554 fr. 1–2, I,12–II,10) speak of the gates of the city being named for the twelve tribes of Israel in a manner that reflects Ezek 48:30–34. But the fragmentary nature of the MSS renders moot the question of who allots the land to the tribes. On the naming of the gates of (the new) Jerusalem, see Joseph L. Trafton, *Reading Revelation: A Literary and Theological Commentary*, Reading the New Testament (Macon, GA: Smyth & Helwys), 208.

39. The Book of Ezekiel contains references, of course, to a Davidic "prince" (נָשִׂיא) in 34:24 and 37:25. "The prince" (הַנָּשִׂיא) is mentioned sixteen times in the climactic vision of 41:1–48:35 (44:3; 45:7, 16, 22; 46:2, 4, 8, 10, 12, 16, 17, 18; 48:2

erence in Isaiah to the coming resettling of the tribes in the land, it is God who distributes the "desolate heritages" (Isa 49:8).⁴⁰

(4) The coming Davidic king will "discipline" (παιδεύω) the house of Israel (v. 42). Although this verb is used in connection with Rehoboam's threat to the Israelites following the death of his father Solomon (1 Kgs [3 Kgdms] 12:11, 14; and 2 Chr 10:11, 14), this instance hardly renders the idea of "discipline" as something to be desired in a future Davidic king! Apart from Rehoboam, παιδεύω is never found in association with a king or a messianic figure in the Hebrew Bible. Rather, it is God who disciplines (e.g., Lev 26:18; Deut 8:5; Ps 94[93]:12; Prov 3:12; Hos 10:10; Jer 10:24).

(5) While the coming Davidic king is expected to judge his people Israel, nowhere in the Hebrew Bible is he said to do so "in synagogues," as we find in v. 43. Now one could argue that since there are no synagogues in the Hebrew Bible, then of course the king would not be expected to judge Israel there. But why would the psalmist not have the king judge Israel in, say, in a purified temple (e.g. Deut 17:8–10), or at the city gate (e.g., Deut 21:18–20), or in his throne hall (e.g., 2 Kgs [4 Kgdms] 7:7, in reference to Solomon)? Why in synagogues?

(6) The coming Davidic king will "show mercy upon" (ἐλεέω) all the nations before him in fear (v. 34). Given the generally negative view of the nations in the psalm (vv. 3, 7, 11–15, 22, 24–25, 30), this action can only come as a surprise.

But is it really a surprise in terms of the expected Davidic king? The Hebrew Bible contains passages anticipating the nations coming to Jerusalem to worship the God of Israel (e.g., Isa 2:1–4; 60:1–3; Zech 8:20–22). Indeed, the psalmist himself echoes this hope in v. 31. But the antecedents in the Hebrew Bible are, with one notable exception, unconnected with a Davidic king. The exception is Isa 11:10, which speaks of a day upon which the nations will seek the root of Jesse. Thus, one could argue that, by extension, the root of Jesse—the coming Davidic king—will have mercy upon them, and that this action falls under the category of extended expectations.

[twice], 22 [twice]). There is no reason to identify the two with one another. But even if one chose to do so, the "prince" in this section is not engaged in apportioning the land among the tribes.

40. Despite all the Temple Scroll says about the organization of the king's rule, it says nothing about his apportioning the land among the tribes.

Fair enough. But it must not be overlooked that Isa 11:10 says nothing of the sort. Furthermore, in the Hebrew Bible, it is *God*—and never a coming Davidic king—who typically shows mercy (e.g., Gen 43:29; Exod 33:19; Num 6:25; Deut 13:17; 2 Sam [2 Kgdms] 12:22; 2 Kgs [4 Kgdms] 13:23; Ps 6:2; 9:13; 25[24]:16; 26[25]:11; Isa 14:1; Jer 12:15; Ezek 39:25; Hos 2:23; Amos 5:15; Zech 1:17).

(7) Finally, while the coming Davidic king is expected to engage in "hostile actions" against his enemies, in the Hebrew Bible these enemies are routinely identified as non-Israelites (e.g., Isa 11:4, 13–15). To be sure, that notion is found in Ps. Sol. 17:24 where the king is said to "destroy" (ὀλεθρεύω) lawless nations."[41] But elsewhere in Ps. Sol. 17, the king is expected to "destroy" (v. 22: θραύω) "rulers" (ἄρχων) and to "drive out" (v. 23: ἐξωθέω; v. 36: ἐξαιρέω) "sinners" (ἁμαρτωλός). He will further "smash" (ἐκτρίβω) the arrogance of the "sinner" (v. 23), and he will "rebuke" (ἐλέγχω) both groups: "sinners" in v. 25 and "rulers" in v. 36. Both ἄρχων and ἁμαρτωλός occur frequently throughout the Psalms of Solomon, and their meaning is not always consistent, but in Ps. Sol. 17 both terms refer to *Jews* (ἄρχων: vv. 12, 20, 22, 36; ἁμαρτωλός: vv. 23, 25, 36).[42] In the Hebrew Bible, the coming Davidic king and/or messiah is not portrayed as acting in such a hostile fashion against his own people.

Now for the one "non-Davidic" passage. As is well known, the psalmist seems to have used Deut 17:16–17 in v. 33. The psalmist says of the king that "He will not place his hope (ἐλπίζω) upon horse and rider and bow,/ nor will he multiply (πληθύνω) gold and silver for war." Indeed, he will not "gather" (συνάγω) hope for the day of war "by means of many people."[43] The Septuagint of Deut 17:16–17 reads: "He will not multiply (πληθύνω) for himself horses… / nor will he multiply (πληθύνω) for himself silver and gold." Are we not surprised that the psalmist has employed in his description of a *specific Davidic* king a passage that is nonspecific and does not mention, even implicitly, David?[44]

---

41. Indeed, the very next line says that they will "flee from his face" (Ps. Sol. 17:25).

42. It should be pointed out that in v. 35, the psalmist's observation that the king will "strike the earth with the word of his mouth," which is a virtual quotation of Isa 11:4, is followed by a comment on how he will drive out "sinners."

43. The Greek is garbled here. The Syriac is much clearer: the king "will not trust in many on the day of war"; see Trafton, *The Syriac Version*, 178 n. 129.

44. By contrast, the Temple Scroll echoes precisely this passage (11Q19 LVI, 15–19), which is to be expected of a book that is based upon Deuteronomy.

Thus, we find in Ps. Sol. 17 seven[45] actions of the coming Davidic king that turn out to be a "surprise," when viewed from the standpoint of the "Davidic" passages in the Hebrew Bible, and three further actions "non-actions" that fall into the same category in that they are found only in a "non-Davidic" passage in the Hebrew Bible.

2.7. The Hope for a King from the Line of David in Ps. Sol. 17: Other

Ps. Sol. 17 identifies a number of qualities of the anticipated king. In the category of "expected" one finds clear reflections of Isa 11:1–5.[46] The king is described in terms of "the fear of the Lord" (v. 40; Isa 11:3), "spirit" (v. 37; Isa 11:2), "wisdom" (vv. 23, 29, 35, 37; Isa 11:2), "understanding" (v. 37; Isa 11:2), "counsel" (v. 37; Isa 11:2), "strength" (vv. 22, 36, 37, 38, 40; Isa 11:2), "righteousness" (vv. 23, 26, 29, 37, 40; Isa 11:4 MT), and "faithfulness" (v. 40; Isa 11:5 MT).[47]

Other characteristics of the king may well fall under the category of "extended expectations": he will be taught by God (v. 32), the Lord will be his king (v. 34), the blessing of the Lord will be with him (v. 38), his hope will be upon the Lord (v. 39), and God will know him (v. 42). Twice the psalmist comments on the king's "words": they are refined beyond the purest gold, and they are like the words of the holy ones (v. 43). Such an interest is without parallel in the Hebrew Bible. On the other hand, if the king is going to judge (an expectation) with wisdom (v. 29), then perhaps an elaboration on the marvelous quality of his words is not really a surprise after all.

Likewise may be the case with certain conditions that will characterize the results of the king's rule: a lack of arrogance and oppressive behavior among the people (v. 41).

An oddity, however, is the idea that no alien or foreigner will dwell with the people during the coming king's reign (v. 28). This statement runs completely counter not only to the assumption in the Torah that the

---

45. For those who are keeping count, it is actually *five* actions, since judging and engaging in hostile actions also belong to the expectations category.

46. See Trafton, "The Bible," 437–40.

47. The psalmist has, of course, taken certain actions on the part of the king from Isa 11:1–5 as well: e.g., "judging" (17:26, 29, 43; Isa 11:3–4) and "smiting the earth with the word [Isa "rod"] of his mouth" (17:24, 35; Isa 11:4). Space limitations preclude a detailed analysis of the ways in which the psalmist has appropriated Isa 11:1–5.

presence of foreigners among the Israelites was to be expected, and their rights protected (e.g., Lev 19:10, 34; 23:22; Deut 10:19; 14:28–29; 24:19–21; 26:11–13; cf. Jer 7:6; Ezek 22:29; Mal 3:5), but also to Ezekiel's climactic vision, where aliens are to receive an allotment in the land amongst the twelve tribes (Ezek 47:22–23).

A final surprise is that the king will be "pure from sin" (v. 36). One might argue that in Ps 51[50] David cries out to God that he might be cleansed from his sin (Ps 51[50]:2 and passim). Hence, being pure from sin would be an obvious trait of the coming king. But such a trait is not found in the passages in the Hebrew Bible that speak of a coming king from the line of David. Indeed, the heading of Ps 51[50] explicitly relates the psalm to David's confrontation with the prophet Nathan following his sin with Bathsheba (see 2 Sam [2 Kgdms] 11:1–12:16). What would have made someone think of linking this very specific failing on David's part with a future Davidic king? Or does Ps 51[50] lie behind this passage at all?

3. Expectation and Surprise in Ps. Sol. 17: Some Observations and Questions

Given what was available in the Hebrew Bible, one encounters both expectation and surprise—with a good deal especially of the latter—in the depiction of the anticipated Davidic king in Ps. Sol. 17.[48] This study has focused on verbs; a literary analysis of the interplay between the "expected" and "surprise" actions of the Davidic king in Ps. Sol. 17 would be instructive, but must await another time.[49]

So what do we do with this combination of expectation and, especially, surprise in the messianic expectation of Ps. Sol. 17?

As one might have noted, several of what I call the "surprise" elements can be tied directly to the historical situation underlying the composition of the Psalms of Solomon, and the ensuing perspective of the group of Jews who produced them. As noted above, the anti-Hasmonean slant of the Psalms of Solomon is reflected in the emphasis on *Davidic* kingship in the psalm. Within this context, the idea that the king will

---

48. Technically, of the thirteen "actions" attributed to the coming Davidic king in this psalm, four are expectations, four are extended expectations, and five are surprises. Of the three "nonactions," one is an expectation and two are extended expectations.

49. In addition, it is striking that a psalm that devotes so much attention to the coming Davidic king begins and ends with a focus on God as King (Ps. Sol. 17:1, 46).

engage in "hostile activities" against Jewish "rulers" and "sinners"—that is, the Hasmoneans (or, at least, some of them)—makes sense. Similarly, various psalms within the collection (e.g., Pss. Sol. 1, 2, 8, and, of course, 17 itself) depict the effect of temple malpractices upon Jerusalem itself; hence, perhaps, the notion that the king will cleanse *Jerusalem*. The apparent association of the group with synagogues (see, e.g., 10:7; 17:16, 44) may well lie behind the notion of the king judging his people *in synagogues*. One can even note the centrality of the verb παιδεύω in the group's understanding of why God has allowed such calamities to befall the people (see 3:4; 7:3; 13:8; and 16:11); is there any wonder that the king will *discipline* the people? And if the author has indeed tailored at least *some* of the description to his historical situation, might this also explain why he would reach for a non-Davidic passage—Deut 17—to show that the king's "hostile activities" against the Jewish "rulers" and "sinners" are not, of course, to be construed literally?

And yet … unless we want to engage in a wooden "mirror reading" of Ps. Sol. 17, one wonders how many—if any—of the above questions should be pressed. One wonders how the king's distributing the tribes upon the land according to their tribes fits into this picture, or the king's "gathering" of the exiles, or his "showing mercy" upon the nations. Why these activities, and why here? Why will he be "pure from sin?" And why will no alien or foreigner dwell with the people?

4. Postscript

The issue of the developing messianic expectation in the Second Temple period is a fascinating one, and questions abound.

On what basis did Jews select certain passages from books that were later to make up the Hebrew Bible so that they could use those passages in their depictions of the coming Davidic king and/or messiah (or messiahs)?

Why would one group, such as the Essenes, use Gen 49:10 or Num 24:17—just to cite two examples—and another group, of which the author of Ps. Sol. 17 was a member, not?

On what basis were Jews, either individually or as members of a larger group, expanding their expectation *beyond* the basic elements already present in the Hebrew Bible?

How did these new elements make their way into the messianic hope? Were writers simply drawing a picture based on their current experiences— that is, *wishing* that the coming king would get them out of their difficulties?

Why would writers use *non-Davidic* passages to describe a *Davidic* king?

Indeed, were there *any* controls, biblical or otherwise, on their expectations? And if so, what were they?

Were Jews using "traditional" elements—that is, those that were *expected* of the coming king—alongside of what they considered to be the *more important* elements—that is, those that come as a "surprise"? If so, how do we know this?

However we are to answer such questions, as well as others that have nothing to do with messianic expectation at all, I would submit that it is time to give the Psalms of Solomon their due respect in our investigations into the fascinating world of Second Temple Judaism.

This is the *first* international meeting on the Psalms of Solomon. May it be the first of many more to come.

Responses

Kenneth Atkinson

Patrick Pouchelle and Sven Behnke had two goals in mind when they planned the first international conference devoted to the Psalms of Solomon: to reexamine established views and past studies and to develop new perspectives for future research. The two have succeeded in their goal. The present volume represents a significant advance in research on this valuable, but unfortunately neglected, corpus of poems that bear witness to some of the most significant historical events and theological developments of the Second Temple period that shaped Judaism and Christianity. The following responses highlight some of the major aspects of each contribution to the present volume, and conclude with a few observations on some unanswered questions regarding this unique text.

1. Benedikt Eckhardt

Eckhardt questions the traditional view that the Psalms of Solomon criticize the Hasmonean combination of kingship and high priesthood. He proposes this assumption is based largely on a misreading of Ps. Sol. 17:6[1] combined with a faulty use of Diodorus and Josephus.[2] Eckhardt rejects as unhistorical the story preserved by Diodorus Siculus (*Bibl.* 40.2; cf. Josephus *A.J.* 14.41–45) concerning the delegation of Jews that approached Pompey to demand the abolition of Hasmonean kingship and its replace-

---

1. "They set up in glory a palace corresponding to their loftiness" (NETS).
2. The Greek of this verse is, as Eckhardt notes, difficult to translate (ἔθεντο βασίλειον ἀντὶ ὕψους αὐτῶν) and has given rise to numerous conjectures, some of which are based on the Syriac; see Joachim Begrich, "Der Text der Psalmen Salomos," *ZNW* 38 (1939): 141–43; Joseph L. Trafton, *The Syriac Version of the Psalms of Solomon: A Critical Evaluation*, SCS 11 (Atlanta: Scholars Press, 1985), 161–62.

ment by priestly, non-Hasmonean rule. He proposes this narrative was intended to portray Pompey as a champion of Jewish traditional law since the Jews do not normally have kings. Although Eckhardt highlights some of the problems with Diodorus Siculus and his possible use of sources, some unacknowledged difficulties with Josephus's narrative of this event suggests the accounts of the delegation that met Pompey is historical.[3]

Josephus's account of this meeting is not in chronological order, but represents his thematic treatment of this time period.[4] Because the high priests had led Judea during the postexilic period, it is probable that some disaffected elements of the population wanted Pompey to restore the older theocratic form of government. In the early days of the Hasmonean dynasty, the high priest effectively ruled as a king. Hyrcanus I earlier sent envoys to the Seleucid monarch Antiochus VII Sidetes requesting that he allow him to keep this traditional form of Jewish government (*A.J.* 13.245). Pseudo-Hecataeus extols the leadership of the high priests and emphasizes that neither slander nor persecution can compel Jews to abandon their ancestral laws (Pseudo-Hecataeus, quoted in Diodorus Siculus, *Bibl.*, 40.3, 5–6). As the successor of the Seleucid monarchs, Pompey believed that he inherited the Seleucid's authority to appoint the high priest in Jerusalem. He not only did so in that city, but he also selected the high priest of the temple of the Great Mother at Comana in Syria when he annexed the province (Strabo, *Geogr.* 12.3.34). In light of these passages, there is no reason to doubt the existence of a faction that rejected the monarchy, especially since the Hasmoneans had no scriptural basis to reign as kings. The opposing delegation that met Pompey apparently wanted him to appoint a high priest of their choosing to rule them in lieu of a Hasmoenan monarch.

It is only because of Josephus that we can recognize many of the historical allusions in the Psalms of Solomon and the Dead Sea Scrolls. The

---

3. For a discussion of variants in the text of Diodorus pertaining to this event, see Thomas Fischer, "Zum jüdischen Verfassungsstreit vor Pompejus (Diodor 40,2)," *ZPE* 91 (1975): 46–49.

4. Josephus duplicates his account of Pompey's later arrival in Syria. Josephus, *A.J.* 14.34–36 dates to 63 BCE; Josephus, *A.J.* 14.37–40 documents the meeting of the autumn of 64 BCE when envoys from both brothers appeared before Pompey in Syria. For the misplacement of these sections, see Richard Laqueur, *Der jüdische Historiker Flavius Josephus: Ein biographischer Versuch auf neuer quellenkritischer Grundlage* (Giessen: Münchow Verlagsbuchhandlung, 1920), 153–54.

Dead Sea Scrolls, moreover, are often helpful for clarifying difficult passages in the *Jewish War* and the *Jewish Antiquities*.[5] But it is important not to accept Josephus's narratives of this time at face value. It is uncertain to what extent his accounts of the Hasmoneans should be viewed as historical sources for understanding pre-70 CE Judea or as historical sources for understanding the historical context of Josephus in Flavian Rome.[6] Because we have no complete and unbiased historical record from the Hasmonean period, we must use and compare all our extant sources to reconstruct the past. It is especially important to include the Psalms of Solomon in any study of Hasmonean history.

2. Jan Joosten

Jan Joosten challenges the consensus view that the eighteen Psalms of Solomon were originally written in Hebrew. He raises many methodological challenges that have been overlooked since the nineteenth century when Adolf Hilgenfeld proposed that Greek was the original language of the Psalms of Solomon based on its numerous allusions to the Septuagint.[7] Joosten adopts the view of Ryle and James that the Hebraisms of these poems are best referred to as "Septuagintisms."[8] He proposes that many grammatical features in the Psalms of Solomon are problematic in a text that is purportedly translated from the Hebrew. He concludes that the Psalms are "a text unique in its genre" whose Greek is at times difficult to understand, and that the composition is preserved in late manuscripts that do not always agree with one another.[9]

---

5. Cf. Kenneth Atkinson, "Historical References and Allusions to Foreigners in the Dead Sea Scrolls: Seleucids, Ptolemies, Nabateans, Itureans, and Romans in the Qumran Corpus," *QC* 21 (2013): 1–32.

6. Mladen Popović, "The Jewish Revolt against Rome: History, Sources and Perspectives," in *The Jewish Revolt Against Rome: Interdisciplinary Perspectives*, ed. Mladen Popović, JSJSup 154 (Leiden: Brill, 2011), 3. Cf. Eyal Regev, *The Hasmoneans. Ideology, Archaeology, Identity*, JAJSup 10 (Göttingen: Vandenhoeck & Ruprecht, 2013), 28–31.

7. Adolf Hilgenfeld, "Die Psalmen Salomo's und die Himmelfahrt des Moses, griechisch hergestellt und erklärt," *ZWT* 11 (1868): 133–68.

8. Herbert R. Ryle, and R. James Montague, *ΨΑΛΜΟΙ ΣΟΛΟΜΩΝΤΟΣ: Psalms of the Pharisees, Commonly Called the Psalms of Solomon* (Cambridge: Cambridge University Press, 1891), lxxxv.

9. This sentence is paraphrased from the discussion on page 32, particularly note 5, of the present volume.

The Greek text of the Psalms of Solomon often copies the exact wording of the Septuagint, but the words are often rearranged for poetic effect. However, the manuscripts suggest that the Greek of the Psalms of Solomon was sometimes revised to bring the text closer to the wording of the Septuagint. One example is the substitution in Ps. Sol. 3:2c of ἀγαθός[10] with ὅλης[11] to bring the text into conformity with the phrase ἐν ὅλῃ καρδίᾳ in the Septuagint Psalter (Pss 86[85]:12; 111[110]:1; 119[118]:2, 10, 34, 58, 69, 145; 138[137]:1). The 260 (MSS 260, 149, 471, 606, 3004) and 629 manuscript groups (MSS 629, 769) contain many substitutions, changes in word order, and omissions that make it difficult to determine the original Greek text. All the extant manuscripts of the Psalms of Solomon, moreover, contain improvements that were likely added by later scribes[12] such as the addition of complementary words[13] to clarify the meaning. The manuscripts also reflect Greek common to the tenth century CE as evident by the replacement of datives with accusatives as well as Atticizing corrections.[14] These features, and the many differences in the length of vowels and grammar, as well as the substitution of words, indicate that our extant manuscripts reflect a lengthy and as yet not fully understood period of extensive scribal changes to the text.

A Hebrew *Vorlage* perhaps best explains some features common in the Greek text of the Psalms of Solomon. Among these is the frequent change in tenses without any clear change implied in the action of the verbs (e.g., Pss. Sol. 2:9b–10; 3:7–8a; 4:12–13; 6:5b–6; 13:5–8; 17:6b–9). The use of the verb with a noun from the same root in some instances likely reflects an underlying Hebrew infinitive absolute (e.g., Pss. Sol. 1:8; 9:10). The relatively modest vocabulary suggests the Greek translator adhered to a fixed list of Hebrew-Greek equivalents. The frequent duplicate renderings of the same word, explanatory glosses, and difficult phrases (e.g., Pss. Sol. 1:6; 2:6; 6:3; 8:14; 9:6) suggest that the translator was often uncertain how to

---

10. 253 manuscript group and manuscript 336.

11. Remaining manuscript groups.

12. E.g., MS 655: 15:8d and 17:11; MS 659: 9:8h; 11:6; MSS 655 & 659: 4:12b; 8:19c, 8:20a; 9:1b.

13. E.g., MS 253 group at 2:25a, 32a; 3:11a, 12a; 17:30c; MS 260 group at 4:15b; 5:11a; 11:1c, 8; 14:5c; 15:12a.

14. For examples of these and other lexical features that suggest a Hebrew *Vorlage*, see Kenneth Atkinson, "Psalms of Solomon: Greek," in *The Textual History of the Bible Volume 2: Deutero-Canonical Scriptures*, ed. Matthias Henze (Leiden: Brill, forthcoming).

render the underlying Hebrew. It is also probable that in many instances the Greek of the Psalms of Solomon does not reflect the Semitic original, but the originality of the Greek translator(s) who sometimes added new material to the composition in a Septuagintal style. Our present Greek text, therefore, should be regarded as representing one period in the history of this document.

3. Eberhard Bons

Eberhard Bons also challenges the *opinion communis* that the Greek is a translation from a Hebrew text. He explores the use of ἐκλογή and ἐξουσία in Ps. Sol. 9:4 to illustrate this thesis and to demonstrate that both nouns are borrowed from contemporary philosophy, especially Stoicism.

Bons recognizes that many Stoic philosophers are extant only in documents that were written later, and are often preserved in summaries or quotations by Diogenes Laërtius, Stobaeus, and the church fathers. He accepts a likely date of Psalms of Solomon to the second half of the first century BCE or the first decades of the first century CE. Bons cautiously suggests that Jewish authors living in Jerusalem likely had some knowledge of contemporary Hellenistic philosophy. A recent literary discovery supports Bons's suggestion.

An examination of surviving scrolls from fifty literary collections and libraries from the second century BCE to the third century CE found that many of these manuscripts were used for 150–500 years. The average lifespan of these texts was between 200–300 years.[15] The recently discovered text of Περὶ Ἀλυπίας of Galen reveals that the libraries of the Palatine hill in Rome contained texts that were between 200 and 450 years old at the time of the fire in 192 CE.[16] Given the great age of some of the manuscripts in ancient libraries, it is probable that Jews living in Jerusalem or Egypt had access to collections with many ancient and now lost philosophical

---

15. George Houston, "Papyrological Evidence for Book Collections and Libraries in the Roman Empire," in *Ancient Literacies: The Culture of Reading in Greece and Rome*, ed. William A. Johnson and Holt N. Parker (Oxford: Oxford University Press, 2009), 233–67.

16. Galen, *On the Avoidance of Grief*, 13. For Galen's letter, see Clare K. Rothschild and Trevor W. Thompson, "Galen: 'On the Avoidance of Grief,'" *Early Christianity* 2 (2011): 110–29.

texts.[17] A look at some of the Hellenistic Jewish writers may provide further support for Bons's thesis that the author of Ps. Sol. 9:4 was influenced by Stoic philosophy.

The Jewish writer commonly known as Pseudo-Phocylides frequently uses the Septuagint and was influenced by Stoicism.[18] The mid-second-century BCE Jewish writer Aristobulus likewise used the Septuagint and shows the influence of Stoic philosophy.[19] Hellenistic Jews also wrote verses attributed to Greek poets such as Aeschylus, Sophocles, Euripides, Pythagoras, and others. Those attributed to Pseudo-Sophocles show the influence of Stoicism.[20] These few examples support the thesis of Bons that the writer (or perhaps translator) of Ps. Sol. 9:4 could have been influenced by Greek philosophy since many Jewish compositions that clearly predate the commonly accepted date of the Psalms of Solomon show the influence of Stoicism.

Bons notes that the closest parallel to Ps. Sol. 9:4 is the description of the Sadducees in Josephus *B.J.* 2.164-65. He proposes that only Josephus was familiar with the ethical use of ἐκλογή as found in Ps. Sol. 9:4. The famous passage on the three Jewish sects in Josephus (*B.J.* 2.119; cf. *A.J.* 13.171-73) clearly contains Stoic influence.[21] Because Josephus was not a native Greek speaker he used literary assistants to help him with his Greek style when he wrote his Jewish War.[22] The similarities between Josephus's description of the Essenes and the Dead Sea Scrolls make it likely that he

---

17. It has been suggested that the Psalms of Solomon was translated from Hebrew into Greek in Egypt between the late first century BCE to the mid-first century CE; Albert-Marie Denis, *Introduction aux pseudépigraphes grecs d'Ancien Testament*, SVTP 1 (Leiden: Brill, 1970), 63; Joseph Viteau, *Les Psaumes de Solomon: Introduction, texte grec et traduction, avec les principales variantes de la version syriaque par François Martin*, Documents pour l'étude de la Bible (Paris: Letouzey et Ané, 1911), 125-49.

18. The composition was likely written between 50 BCE to 100 CE. For its date, vocabulary, and content, see Pieter W. van der Horst, *The Sentences of Pseudo-Phocylides*, SVTP 4 (Leiden: Brill, 1978), 64-69, 81-83.

19. Carl R. Holladay, *Fragments From Hellenistic Jewish Authors Volume III; Aristobulus* (Atlanta: Scholars Press, 1995), 59, 73, 206-7.

20. For this literature, see Albert-Marie Denis, *Fragmenta Pseudepigraphorum quae supersunt Graeca: Una cum historicorum et auctorum Judaeorum Hellenistarum fragmentis*, PVTG 3 (Leiden: Brill, 1970), 161-74.

21. For examples, see Steve Mason, *Flavius Josephus Translation and Commentary, Volume 1B: Judean War 2* (Leiden: Brill, 2008), 131-35.

22. Henry St. John Thackeray, *Josephus, the Man and the Historian* (New York: Jewish Institute of Religion, 1929), 100-24. Elsewhere, Josephus acknowledges that his Greek was not impeccable (*A.J.* 2.262).

also had access to Semitic sources when he wrote his account of the three Jewish sects.[23] It cannot be excluded that Josephus or the other Hellenistic Greek authors could have obtained their knowledge of Greek philosopy from a Semitic source.

It is difficult to see how Ps. Sol. 9:4 could reflect a Hebrew text. It is possible that it is a loose translation or a paraphrase of a Semitic text that incorporates Greek thought. Although it is feasible that the paronomasia in the Syriac of this verse reflects a Hebrew *Vorlage*, it should likely be attributed to the Syriac translator's conscious imitation of Semitic style.[24] It is plausible that Ps. Sol. 9:4 and other portions of this composition were written in Greek.

4. Brad Embry

Brad Embry addresses the issue of the genre of the Psalms of Solomon to argue that the collection has more in common with biblical prophecy and Deuteronomic thought than with psalmic prayer or biblical wisdom. However, it is important to note that ancient authors did not write with our modern notions of genre in mind, and did not always separate history and poetry (Quintilian, *Inst.* 1.8–9). In terms of theology and style, the Psalms of Solomon is closest to Wisdom and Sirach. This is also demonstrated by the placement of these poems in the extant manuscripts and canon lists.[25] The manuscript 253 text that contains the Psalms of Solomon preserves the hexaplaric recension of the Wisdom of Solomon and Sirach. Manuscript 260 of the Psalms of Solomon, moreover, includes texts of Wisdom and Sirach that are related to the Lucianic recension. This does not mean that the manuscript 253 group text of the Psalms of Solomon should be identified as hexaplaric or the manuscript 260 group

---

23. For an extensive discussion of this issue and the relevant sources and texts, see Kenneth Atkinson, "Josephus the Essene at Qumran? An Example of the Intersection of the Dead Sea Scrolls and the Archaeological Evidence in Light of Josephus's Writings," *SJC* 10 (2012): 7–35.

24. Cf. Atkinson, "Psalms of Solomon: Syriac," in *The Textual History of the Bible Volume 2*.

25. Six of the eleven Greek manuscripts (MSS 149, 253, 260, 336, 471, 606) of the Psalms of Solomon contain the Wisdom of Solomon and Sirach; see Alfred Rahlfs, *Verzeichnis der griechischen Handschriften des Alten Testaments, für das Septuaginta-Unternehmen aufgestellt*, MSU 2 (Berlin: Weidmann, 1914), 13, 91, 145, 213, 249, 318.

as Lucianic.²⁶ Nevertheless, this evidence suggests that ancient readers and scribes viewed the Psalms of Solomon as not only related to the Wisdom of Solomon and Sirach, but to their textual traditions.

The earliest extant reference to the Psalms of Solomon in the fifth-century CE Christian Codex Alexandrinus contains the title "Psalms of Solomon" (Ψαλμοὶ Σολομῶντος).²⁷ The composition is included in numerous Christian canon lists and, according to the twelfth-century CE Christian writers Joannes Zonaras and Theodorus Balsamon, the Psalms of Solomon was included in the works prohibited for use in the church in the fifty-ninth canon of the Council of Laodicea (ca. 360 CE).²⁸ Although Embry claims that the Psalms of Solomon "was excised from the Christian codices" (78), the extant Christian references to the composition show that Christians used it for centuries. All the extant copies of the Psalms of Solomon are contained in manuscripts that appear to have been produced by Christians.²⁹ Among the most important is the manuscript of the Syriac Christian community, which may help us to understand more about the Christian reception of the Psalms of Solomon.

The "Odes and Psalms of Solomon" are listed in Pseudo-Athanasius's *Synopsis Scripturae Sacrae* and the ninth-century CE *Stichometria* of Patriarch Nicephorus among "those of the Old (Testament) that are spoken against and not accepted by the church."³⁰ In both lists the two compositions appear as a single book, and the Psalms of Solomon follow the Christian hymnbook known as the Odes of Solomon. Manuscripts of the two works exist only in Syriac. In manuscript 16h1 the combined collection is given the title "Ode," which suggests this was also a title for the Psalms of

---

26. Joseph Ziegler, "Die hexaplarische Bearbeitung des griechischen Sirach," *BZ* NS 4 (1960): 174–85; see idem, *Sapientia Salomonis*, SVTG 12/1, 2nd ed. (Göttingen: Vandenhoeck & Ruprecht, 1967), 48, 50–53, 61 and idem, *Sapientia Iesu Filii Sirach*, SVTG 12/2, 2nd ed. (Göttingen: Vandenhoeck & Ruprecht, 1965), 56–63, 70. Cf. Atkinson, "Psalms of Solomon: Greek."

27. Theodor Zahn, *Geschichte des Neutestamentlichen Kanons* (Erlangen: Deichert, 1890), 2/1:288–89.

28. For extant canon lists and Christian references to the Psalms of Solomon, see Kenneth Atkinson, *An Intertextual Study of the Psalms of Solomon: Pseudepigrapha*, SBEC 49 (Lewiston, NY: Mellen, 2001), 406–9.

29. For the most comprehension discussion and citation of literature on the extant manuscripts of the Psalms of Solomon, see Robert B. Wright, *The Psalms of Solomon: A Critical Edition of the Greek Text*, JCTC 1 (New York: T&T Clark, 2007), 13–25.

30. Zahn, *Geschichte des Neutestamentlichen Kanons*, 2/1:299, 317.

Solomon in the Syriac tradition.[31] The placement of the Psalms of Solomon with the Odes of Solomon suggests that some Christians either did not view the Psalms of Solomon as antithetical to the Christian message or perhaps thought both were Christian texts.

The debate whether the Psalms of Solomon had canonical status or not during the Second Temple is problematic. The absence of non-Masoretic manuscripts after 70 CE can be documented, and bears witness to the later growth of a fixed text of particular biblical books that eventually became authoritative and canonical. The canon itself, however, is the result of a long historical process. The listings of sacred books before 100 CE show that the semantic range of the collection designated "Prophets" was quite broad and often included all Scriptural writings not in the Torah.[32] The Qumran texts show that inspired prophetic writings were still written and that there was no widely accepted list of scriptural texts in the modern sense of a canon during the Second Temple period. However, Embry's proposal that the author of the Psalms of Solomon wrote in the prophetic tradition, and may have considered the collection to be inspired, is an important point that merits further study.

5. Sven Behnke

Sven Behnke engages in a detailed linguistic examination of all the relevant nouns and verbs that explicitly describe "sleep" in the Psalms of Solomon.[33] He notes that these lemma appear in five of the eighteen poems (Pss. Sol. 2:31; 3:1–2; 4:15–16; 6:3–4; 16:1–4). He comments that it is used in Ps. Sol. 4 to curse sinners and to praise the righteous. The emphasis on the righteous praising the Lord upon awakening in Ps. Sol. 4:15b may possibly have been a practice of the community behind these poems. This invites comparison with the corpus of penitential prayers, which frequently include statements of God's righteousness in bringing punishment upon the people.[34] The psalm is somewhat reminiscent of the theme of

---

31. Michael Lattke, *Odes of Solomon: A Commentary*, trans. Marianne Ehrhardt, Hermeneia (Minneapolis: Augsburg Fortress, 2009), 4.

32. Michael E Stone, *Ancient Judaism: New Visions and Views* (Grand Rapids: Eerdmans, 2011), 122–50.

33. See Behnke's list of terms on pages 97–98 in the present volume.

34. See Werline's essay, especially his discussion of *Gerichtsdoxologie* on pages 139–47 of the present volume.

wisdom and divine revelation found in 1 En. 61:12–13 and the Qumran Hodayot, which stresses praising God, the revelation of His mighty works, and wakefulness (1QH XXI, 4–7).

Behnke's discussion of sleep as a metaphor for death before resurrection in Ps. Sol. 2:30–33 is particularly relevant for understanding the theology of the collection as well as the community that produced and used these poems. He notes that sleep language in this particular psalm, especially the verbs κοιμίζω (v. 31b) and ἀνίστημι (v. 31a), suggests that the poet is referring to "death sleep" ("Todesschlafes"). In his discussion of this poem, Behnke explores how the author connects sleep with the concept of God's distance and the hope of resurrection. The replacement of "sleep" (ישׁן) with "lie" (שׁכב) in the quotation of Dan 12:2 in the Hodayot (1QH^a XIV, 37) invites comparison with Ps. Sol. 2:31. Because words related to sleep are found in five of the eighteen Psalms of Solomon, and other passages likely allude to it, it appears not only to have been an important theological concept for the community of the Psalms of Solomon, but an overlooked topic in need of additional study.

6. Patrick Pouchelle

Patrick Pouchelle examines the concept of discipline (παιδεία) in the Psalms of Solomon to suggest that the concept behind this word is theological and less connected to historical events than one would expect. He makes the important observation that discipline in the Psalms of Solomon is likely a theological concept that was probably coined sometime before the writing of this collection (132). If this concept predates the collection, it is plausible that some of the Psalms of Solomon were added, or possibly revised, to defend this earlier understanding of discipline in light of later historical events.

The Dead Sea Scrolls may offer a comparison that suggests the concept of discipline in the Psalms of Solomon likely predates the collection. In his discussion of Ps. Sol. 7:2, Pouchelle notes that the text not only alludes to Hos 10:10 MT, but also that the author apparently feared that this biblical prophecy was coming true. This poem reflects the historical background of an invasion that caused some to question God's justice and use of discipline.[35] The Nahum Pesher and the Habakkuk Pesher likewise contain

---

[35] Pouchelle comments that in Ps. Sol. 16:13 it appears the author emphasizes

interpretations of biblical texts that seek to explain God's discipline in light of the Roman conquest. Hanan Eshel has suggested that the second-century BCE author of the Habakkuk Pesher interpreted the phrase "the rest of the peoples" of Habakkuk 2:8 (1QpHab IX, 3-4) as a prediction that a number of nations will plunder the Hasmoneans. This passage, at first understood as a prediction of the Seleucids, was apparently updated to refer to the Romans following Pompey's conquest.[36] The author of the Habakkuk Pesher appears to display some of the discomfort shared by the Psalms of Solomon. The writers of both texts suggest that many Jews believed the Roman conquest was a sign that God no longer disciplines the righteous to protect them. Rather, God has abandoned the devout to the sinful nations. The author of the Habakkuk Pesher urges the righteous to be patient, and argues that scripture guarantees that God will protect them despite the Roman conquest (1QpHab VII, 9-14). Pouchelle's valuable insights concerning discipline may help us to understand the theological and historical development of the Psalms of Solomon, and strongly indicates that the present shaping of the collection may have been influenced by earlier beliefs about God's discipline.

7. Rodney A. Werline

Werline's study uses anthropological methods to propose that the Psalms of Solomon belongs to an emotional liturgy in which the community declares God's righteousness and his condemnation of the wicked. He recognizes that the identity and social location of the authors of the Psalms of Solomon are difficult to determine, and that we are also uncertain as to the order in which the individual poems emerged. Werline comments on the problems this poses: "Unfortunately, this approach produces only a snapshot of the community's entire history frozen in a single frame. However, the overarching concerns, ideology and values of the group through the span of their production become visible" (139). Werline also makes the important observation that the Psalms of Solomon emphasize confession

---

the severity of the discipline, which is less a benediction than a judiciary action. In this passage, moreover, the writer expresses his fear that his community is unable to endure their present calamity.

36. Hanan Eshel, "The Two Historical Layers of Pesher Habakkuk," in *Northern Lights on the Dead Sea Scrolls: Proceedings of the Nordic Qumran Network 2003-2006*, ed. Anders K. Petersen, STDJ 80 (Leiden: Brill, 2009), 107-17.

of sins to God but not to one another. He notes that the Qumran community, as evident throughout 1QS, also emphasized discipline and confession. However, the Qumran sect practiced discipline and confession through public rituals while the community of the Psalms of Solomon likely accomplished both through the public recitation of these poems.

Werline's comment that Ps. Sol. 15:2-4a emphasizes that a person is shaped through practice provides an important insight into the collection's theology and the community that produced and recited these poems. The authors of the Psalms of Solomon frequently appeal to the covenant to explain their present suffering. The poems proclaim that God's covenant with Israel is everlasting and guarantees the righteous will receive eternal life (Pss. Sol. 7.8-10; 9.1-2, 8-11; 11.7-11; 13.11; 14.2-5; 17.4). They acknowledge that no one is without sin (Pss. Sol. 3.7; 13.10). Although the authors regard themselves as members of the covenant community, they recognize that they are also sinners (Pss. Sol. 3.6-8; 5.6; 9.2, 6-7; 10.1; 13.7, 10; 16.11; 17.5). The poets show an understanding of the covenant similar to MMT and Galatians, namely, that the covenant does not guarantee that the righteous will be rewarded with prosperity. Rather, obedience to the law is understood as the consequence of being in the covenant and as a requirement for remaining in the covenant.[37] Werline notes that the declaration and act of proclaiming God's righteousness is frequent in the Psalms of Solomon, and suggests that it constituted an actual practice within the community (152-54). This is reminiscent of the Qumran sect as described in 1QS, which documents how members took oaths of admission to adhere to the laws of Moses and accepted public acts of rebuke, discipline, and correction.[38] Werline's examination on the role of ritual performance suggests that the community behind the Psalms of Solomon

---

37. See Kenneth Atkinson, "Enduring the Lord's Discipline: Soteriology in the *Psalms of Solomon*," in *This World and the World to Come: Soteriology in Early Judaism*, ed. Daniel M. Gurtner, LSTS 74 (London: T&T Clark, 2011), 151-55.

38. For oaths, see especially 1QS V, 7b-20 and 1QS VI, 13-23. For discipline, see especially CD XX, 1b-8a and 1QS VIII, 6b-9:2. The shorter version of 1QS V, 7b-20 in 4Q256 (4QS^b) and 4Q258 (4QS^d) shows that the oath underwent a lengthy process of change. Unfortunately, the lack of variant MSS of the Psalms of Solomon makes it impossible to determine whether there were comparable changes in the liturgy contained in the collection. Throughout his essay Werline correctly emphasizes that the extensive parallels between the Qumran texts and the Psalms of Solomon should not be taken to imply that the psalms were of Essene origins or directly connected to the community of the Dead Sea Scrolls (133-34).

helped to maintain their communal identity through the enunciation of their blessings and curses.

8. Joseph L. Trafton

Joseph L. Trafton examines the portrayal of the Davidic messiah in Ps. Sol. 17 in light of biblical and postbiblical texts that also describe this figure. He notes that the author of this psalm frequently used non-Davidic passages that are not connected with David, but which are associated with the king (Deut 17:14-15; Pss 2, 45[44], and 72[71]; and Zech 9:9-13). He also observes that these texts depict the king as performing five activities: ruling, fighting enemies, judging, shepherding, and building (164–65). He observes that Ps. Sol. 17 contains five expected actions of the Davidic king found in the Hebrew Bible—the only omission is the building of the temple. Trafton offers a plausible reason for the lack of this expectation, namely, that the temple was in existence when this poem was written.

Trafton observes that there is a second category of actions that, although not specified for a future Davidic king in the Hebrew Bible, are "extensions" of what a king would be expected to accomplish. These include glorifying God, knowing His people, dominating over the nations, and not growing weak (165–66). However, Trafton comments that there are seven unexpected elements in this poem, particularly the notion that the Davidic king will "cleanse" Jerusalem (Ps. Sol. 17:22, 30) and fight his enemies (Ps. Sol. 17:22-25, 36). Many of these features are also found in the Dead Sea Scrolls.

The author of Ps. Sol. 17 uses images of violence (Ps. Sol. 17:22-25, 36) and peace (Ps. Sol. 17:26-46) to describe the Davidic messiah. The Dead Sea Scrolls also contain texts that portray the Davidic messiah as a violent warrior (4Q161; 4Q285; 4Q246; 4Q252; 4Q174) and as a peaceful savior (4Q521). Other Dead Sea Scrolls contain passages that emphasize the messiah's role as a teacher, priest, and prophet (e.g., CD; 11Q19; 4Q174).[39] It may be that the events of the 63 BCE Roman conquest caused the community of the Psalms of Solomon to somewhat abandon their past expectation for traditional violent Davidic messiah and begin to emphasize the didactical qualities of this leader.

---

39. See John J. Collins, *The Scepter and the Star: The Messiahs of the Dead Sea Scrolls and Other Ancient Literature*, 2nd. ed.(Grand Rapids: Eerdmans, 2010), 110-48.

Trafton highlights some of the many similarities between Ps. Sol. 17 and the Qumran corpus. He notes that Ps. Sol. 17:33 used Deut 17:16–17. It is significant that the allusion to Deuteronomy in this verse includes the phrase εἰς πόλεμον that is not in the Masoretic Text. This same addition is in the Temple Scroll (11Q19 LVI, 15) and may either attest to the use of a Hebrew *Vorlage* that differed from the Masoretic Text, or the incorporation of a shared exegetical tradition.[40] Because an additional example of an exegetical tradition is also shared between Ps. Sol. 8:10-12 and CD IV, 15–18, it is plausible that the authors of the Psalms of Solomon were influenced by many of the same exegetical traditions as the writers of the Qumran texts. Although we should perhaps not expect a clear and coherent messianic picture from a text that is both polemical and dependent on diverse passages from the Hebrew Bible and possibly other exegetical traditions, Ps. Sol. 17 nevertheless suggests that pre-Christian Jewish messianic constructs were quite diverse. Trafton's review of scholarship on messianism demonstrates that many of the messianic features in of Ps. Sol. 17 are still neglected by scholars despite the publication of the complete Qumran corpus.[41]

9. Directions for Future Research

In his 1994 seminal review of scholarship on the Psalms of Solomon, Joseph L. Trafton outlined directions for future research.[42] The introduction to the present volume highlights a few of the items Trafton believed were in need of further study at the time of his article.[43] The following suggestions examine three of the most needed, and promising, directions for future research.

9.1. The Language of Composition

The studies of Joosten and Bons clearly demonstrate that the debate over the original language of the Psalms of Solomon has not been settled, as

---

40. See Debra Rosen and Alison Salvesen, "A Note on the Qumran Temple Scroll 56:15–18 and Psalm of Solomon 17:33," *Journal of Jewish Studies* 38 (1987): 99–101.

41. See especially his comments and citations on pages 156–58 of the present volume.

42. Joseph L. Trafton, "The *Psalms of Solomon* in Recent Research," *JSP* 12 (1994): 3–19.

43. Pages 173–74 of the present volume.

well as the relationship between the Greek and Syriac versions. The extensive studies of the Greek and Syriac texts and manuscripts by Hann and Trafton should provide a basis for all future work.[44] However, the issue of which dialect of Hebrew or Greek to compare with these poems has never been addressed. The Qumran corpus, for example, shows that there are differences between Qumran biblical-pastiche Hebrew or proto-Mishnaic Hebrew, and that dialect makes a difference. If we assume the Psalms of Solomon is a translation of a Semitic *Vorlage*, should we retrovert it as Hebrew or Aramaic?[45] Likewise, the versions and recensions of the Septuagint and the Hebrew Bible must be taken into consideration to determine whether citations and allusions to Scripture in the Psalms of Solomon reflect particular editions of biblical books. Because the translation of the Septuagint goes back to a Hebrew *Vorlage* that, with the occasional exception of *scriptio plena*, lacked vowels, it is also important to consider the possible role that the so-called parabiblical literature and traditions had upon the translation of these poems.[46]

9.2. The Literary Structure of the Psalms of Solomon

As the editors highlight in their introduction, few major monographs have been published on the Psalms of Solomon (3). None are devoted to the topic of the collection's literary style and structure in relation to both biblical and non-biblical texts.[47] This subject has important ramifi-

---

44. Robert R. Hann, *The Manuscript History of the Psalms of Solomon*, SCS 13 (Chico, CA: Scholars Press, 1982); Trafton, *The Syriac Version*.

45. For some of these issues in the study of Second Temple literature, see James R. Davila, "(How) Can We Tell If a Greek Apocryphon or Pseudepigraphon Has Been Translated from Hebrew or Aramaic?," *JSP* 15 (2005): 3–61. For a study that raises many of these issues, including the likely influence of Aramaic on the Septuagint translators, see further Jan Joosten, "On Aramaising Renderings in the Septuagint," in *Hamlet on a Hill: Semitic and Greek Studies Presented to Professor T. Muraoka on the Occasion of His Sixty-Fifth Birthday*, ed. M. F. J. Baasten and W. T. Van Peursen, OLA 118 (Leuven: Peeters, 2003), 587–600.

46. For this issue, see Stefan Schorch, "The Septuagint and the Vocalization of the Hebrew Text of the Torah," in *XII Congress of the International Organization for Septuagint and Cognate Studies, Leiden 2004*, ed. Melvin K. H. Peters (Atlanta: Society of Biblical Literature, 2006), 41–54.

47. This includes the new critical editions of many Qumran texts, particularly the Hodayot.

cations for understanding the nature and origin of the community that produced these poems, and possibly their transmission history. Any study of the composition's structure also needs to take into consideration the differences between the Greek and Syriac versions. This includes a detailed examination of features such as paronomasia which are sometimes shared in the Greek and Syriac versions (e.g., 1:8; 3:2, 5–6; 4:22–23; 8:4, 10, 23–25; 9:2, 10; 14:3; 17:5–6, 13, 31 [partial paronomasia in Greek 2:25–27), although it appears more frequently in the Syriac without a Greek parallel (e.g., 1:3–4; 2:1–3, 13, 21, 23, 34; 4:2–3, 9–10, 11–12, 15–17; 6:5; 7:7, 8–10; 8:12, 21–22; 9:4, 5, 8; 10:3–5, 6–7; 11:4, 5; 12:3; 13:10; 17:22–24).[48] Whether these are products of stylistic changes introduced by the communities that used these texts is uncertain. The placement of the Psalms of Solomon in the Syriac manuscripts may shed some light on the structure of the collection and needs to be explored in greater depth.[49]

9.3. Sectarian Background

Much work remains to be done on the sectarian background of the Psalms of Solomon. This issue affects how we date the composition, understand its theology, interpret its historical references, and view its use of Scripture and other Jewish traditions. The Psalms of Solomon needs to be compared with the recently completed official editions of the Dead Sea Scrolls as well critical editions of other Second Temple period texts. Available volumes of the *Flavius Josephus: Translation and Commentary* (ed. Steve Mason; Leiden: Brill, 2000–present) series should be brought into the discussion, not only for their historical and theological background, but also for the light they shed on the Jewish use of Greco-Roman philosophical traditions that may be reflected in the Psalms of Solomon.

Of all the issues related to the sectarian background of the Psalms of Solomon, perhaps none is still in need of greater study than messianism.

---

48. Trafton, *The Syriac Version*, 202–3, 233 (with the numbering of the Syriac version).

49. Syriac Manuscript "S" (Add. MS 17134) contains Ps. Sol. 3:1–6 in a marginal note in a manuscript of the Hymns of Severus (at hymn 277, fol. 62b) that was written by Jacob of Edessa, who misattributed the passage to the Wisdom of Solomon. This raises questions as to how later Christian readers of the Psalms of Solomon regarded its literary structure; see Ernest W. Brooks, "The Hymns of Severus and Others in the Syriac Version of Paul of Edessa as Revised by James of Edessa," *PO* 7 (1911): 726.

This is especially true now that the entire Qumran corpus is available. The observation of Trafton on the importance and continued neglect of the Psalms of Solomon for the study of messianism is worth quoting in full as a fitting conclusion to the present volume and as a plea for the importance of this valuable corpus:

> when all is said and done with our messiahs of Aaron and Israel, our Star arising out of Jacob, our explicitly Davidic interpretation of Gen 49:10, and *whatever* is going on in 4Q246—Ps. Sol. 17 remains the longest, continuous description of the messiah that we possess from pre-Christian Judaism. (157–58)

Bibliography

Aalen, Sverre. *Die Begriffe, "Licht" und "Finsternis" im Alten Testament, im Spätjudentum und im Rabbinismus*. SUNVA 1. Oslo: Dybwad, 1951.

Albrecht, Felix. "Zur Notwendigkeit einer Neuedition der Psalmen Salomos." Pages 110–23 in *Die Septuaginta: Text, Wirkung, Rezeption: 4. Internationale Fachtagung veranstaltet von Septuaginta Deutsch (LXX.D), Wuppertal 19.–22. Juli 2012*. Edited by Wolfgang Kraus and Siegfried Kreuzer. WUNT 1/325. Tübingen: Mohr Siebeck, 2014.

Asad, Talal. *Genealogies of Religion: Discipline and Reasons of Power in Christianity and Islam*. Baltimore: John Hopkins University Press, 1993.

Atkinson, Kenneth. *An Intertextual Study of The Psalms of Solomon: Pseudepigrapha*. SBEC 49. Lewiston, NY: Mellen, 2000.

———. "Enduring the Lord's Discipline: Soteriology in the *Psalms of Solomon*." Pages 145–66 in *This World and the World to Come: Soteriology in Early Judaism*. Edited by Daniel M. Gurtner. LSTS 74. London: T&T Clark, 2011.

———. "Historical References and Allusions to Foreigners in the Dead Sea Scrolls: Seleucids, Ptolemies, Nabateans, Itureans, and Romans in the Qumran Corpus." *QC* 21 (2013): 1–32.

———. *I Cried to the Lord: A Study of the Psalms of Solomon's Historical Background and Social Setting*. JSJSup 84. Leiden: Brill, 2004.

———. "Josephus the Essene at Qumran? An Example of the Intersection of the Dead Sea Scrolls and the Archaeological Evidence in Light of Josephus's Writings." *SJC* 10 (2012): 7–35.

———. "On the Herodian Origins of the Militant Davidic Messianism at Qumran: New Light from *Psalm of Solomon 17*." *JBL* 118 (1999): 435–60.

———. "Psalms of Salomon." Pages 763–76 in NETS.

———. "Psalms of Solomon: Greek." In *The Textual History of the Bible Volume 2: Deutero-Canonical Scriptures*. Edited by Matthias Henze. Leiden: Brill, forthcoming.

———. "Psalms of Solomon: Syriac." In *The Textual History of the Bible Volume 2: Deutero-Canonical Scriptures*. Edited by Matthias Henze. Leiden: Brill, forthcoming.

———. "Representations of History in 4Q331 (4QpapHistorical Text C), 4Q332 (4QHistorical Text D), 4Q333 (4QHistorical Text E), and 4Q468E (4QHistorical Text F): An Annalistic Calendar Documenting Portentous Events?" *DSD* 14 (2007): 125–51.

———. "Theodicy in the *Psalms of Solomon*." Pages 546–75 in *Theodicy in the World of the Bible*. Edited by Antti Laato and Johannes C. de Moor. Leiden: Brill, 2003.

———. "Toward a Redating of the *Psalms of Solomon*: Implications for Understanding the *Sitz im Leben* of an Unknown Jewish Sect." *JSP* 9 (1998): 95–112.

Atkinson, Kenneth and Jodi Magness. "Josephus's Essenes and the Qumran Community." *JBL* 129 (2010): 326–42.

Austin, John L. *How to Do Things with Words*. Edited by J. O. Urmson and M. Sbisà. Cambridge: Harvard University Press, 1975.

Baars, Willem. "Psalms of Solomon." Pages 1–27 in part 4.6 of *The Old Testament in Syriac according to the Peshiṭta Version*. Leiden: Brill, 1972.

Baltrusch, Ernst. *Herodes: König im Heiligen Land: Eine Biographie*. Munich: Beck, 2012.

Balz, Horst. "ὕπνος κτλ." *TDNT* 8:545–56.

Bar-Kochva, Bezalel. "Manpower, Economics, and Internal Strife in the Hasmonean State." Pages 167–96 in *Armées et fiscalité dans le monde antique: Actes du colloque national, Paris, 14–16 octobre 1976*. Edited by A. Chastagnol, C. Nicolet, and H. van Effenterre. Colloques nationaux du Centre national de la recherche scientifique 936. Paris: CNRS, 1977.

Barthélemy, Dominique. *Les devanciers d'Aquila: Première publication intégrale du texte des fragments du Dodécaprophéton trouvés dans le désert de Juda, précédée d'une étude sur les traductions et recensions grecques de la Bible réalisées au premier siècle de notre ère sous l'influence du rabbinat palestinien*. VTSup10. Leiden: Brill, 1963.

Baumgarten, Albert I. *The Flourishing of Jewish Sects in the Maccabean Era: An Interpretation*. JSJSup 55. Leiden: Brill, 1997.

Bautch, Richard. *Developments in Genre between Post-Exilic Penitential Prayers and the Psalms of Communal Lament*. SBLAB 7. Atlanta: Society of Biblical Literature, 2003.

Beentjes, Pancratius C. "'Full Wisdom is Fear of the Lord' Ben Sira 19,20–20,31: Context, Composition and Concept." Pages 87–106 in *"Happy is the One, who meditates on Wisdom" (Sir 14,20): Collected Essays on the Book of Ben Sira*. Edited by Pancratius C. Beentjes. CBET 43. Leuven: Peeters, 2006.

———. "Theodicy in the Wisdom of Ben Sira." Pages 265–79 in *"Happy is the One, who meditates on Wisdom" (Sir 14,20): Collected Essays on the Book of Ben Sira*. Edited by Pancratius C. Beentjes. CBET 43. Leuven: Peeters, 2006.

Begrich, Joachim. "Der Text der Psalmen Salomos." *ZNW* 38 (1939): 131–64.

Bell, Catherine. *Ritual: Perspectives and Dimensions*. Oxford: Oxford University Press, 1997.

Ben-Dov, Jonathan and Stéphane Saulnier. "Qumran Calendars: A Survey of Scholarship 1980–2007." *CurBR* 7 (2008): 124–68.

Berrin, Shani. "Pesher Nahum, *Psalms of Solomon* and Pompey." Pages 65–84 in *Reworking the Bible: Apocryphal and Related Texts at Qumran*. Edited by Esther G. Chazon, Devorah Dimant, and Ruth A. Clements. STDJ 58. Leiden: Brill, 2005.

Bevan, Edwyn R. *The House of Seleucus*. 2 vols. London: Arnold, 1902.

Blackburn, Rollin J. "Hebrew Poetic Devices in the Greek Text of the *Psalms of Solomon*." PhD diss., Temple University, 1995.

Boda, Mark J. *Praying the Tradition: The Origin and Use of Tradition in Nehemiah 9*. BZAW 277. Berlin: de Gruyter, 1999.

Boer, Emilie. *Pauli Alexandrini elementa apotelesmatica*. BSGRT 1533. Leipzig: Teubner, 1958.

Bonhöffer, Adolf. *Epictet und die Stoa: Untersuchungen zur stoischen Philosophie*. Stuttgart: Enke, 1890.

Bons, Eberhard. "'Je suis votre éducateur' (Os 5,2LXX)—Un titre divin et son contexte littéraire." Pages 191–206 in *Le Jugement dans l'un et l'autre Testament I: Mélanges offerts à Raymond Kuntzmann*. Edited by Eberhard Bons. Lectio Divina 197. Paris: Cerf, 2004.

———. "Rhetorical devices in the Septuagint Psalter." Pages 69–79 in *Et sapienter et eloquenter: Studies on Rhetorical and Stylistic Features of the Septuagint*. Edited by Eberhard Bons and Thomas J. Kraus. FRLANT 241. Göttingen: Vandenhoeck & Ruprecht, 2011.

Bourdieu, Pierre. *The Logic of Practice*. Translated by Richard Nice. Stanford: Stanford University Press, 1990.

Brandt, Ahasver von. *Werkzeug des Historikers: Eine Einführung in die Historischen Hilfswissenschaften.* 16th ed. Stuttgart: Kohlhammer, 2003.

Braun, Herbert. "Vom Erbarmen Gottes über den Gerechten: Zur Theologie der Psalmen Salomos." *ZNW* 43 (1950/51): 1–54.

Bringmann, Klaus. *Geschichte der Juden im Altertum: Vom babylonischen Exil bis zur arabischen Eroberung.* Stuttgart: Klett-Cotta, 2005.

Brooke, George J. "Authority and the Authoritativeness of Scripture: Some Clues from the Dead Sea Scrolls." *RevQ* 100 (2012): 507–23.

———. "Between Authority and Canon: The Significance of Reworking the Bible for Understanding the Canonical Process." Pages 85–104 in *Reworking the Bible: Apocryphal and Related Texts at Qumran: Proceedings of a Joint Symposium by the Orion Center for the Study of the Dead Sea Scrolls and Associated Literature and the Hebrew University Institute for Advanced Studies Research Group on Qumran, 15–17 January, 2002.* Edited by Esther G. Chazon, Devorah Dimant, and Ruth A. Clements. STDJ 58. Leiden: Brill, 2005.

Brooks, Ernest W. "The Hymns of Severus and Others in the Syriac Version of Paul of Edessa as Revised by James of Edessa." *PO* 6 (1911): 3–179; 7 (1911): 593–802.

Brueggemann, Walter. *The Message of the Psalms: A Theological Commentary.* OTS. Minneapolis: Augsburg, 1984.

Burr, Viktor. "Rom und Judäa im 1. Jahrhundert v. Chr. (Pompeius und die Juden)." *ANRW* 1:875–86. Part 1, *Von den Anfängen Roms bis zum Ausgang der Republik, 1.1.* Edited by H. Temporini. Berlin: de Gruyter, 1972.

Collins, John J. "Introduction: Towards the Morphology of a Genre." *Semeia* 14 (1979): 1–20.

———. *Jewish Cult and Hellenistic Culture: Essays on the Jewish Encounter with Hellenism and Roman Rule.* JSJSup 100. Leiden: Brill, 2005.

———. "Joseph and Aseneth: Jewish or Christian?" *JSP* 14 (2005): 97–112.

———. Review of *Studies on the Hasmonean Period* by Joshua Efron. *CBQ* 52 (1990): 372.

———. *The Apocalyptic Imagination: An Introduction to Jewish Apocalyptic Literature.* Grand Rapids: Eerdmans, 1998.

———. *The Scepter and the Star: The Messiahs of the Dead Sea Scrolls and Other Ancient Literature.* ABRL. New York: Doubleday, 1995. 2nd ed. Grand Rapids: Eerdmans, 2010.

———. "What Was Distinctive about Messianic Expectation at Qumran?" Pages 71–92 in *The Dead Sea Scrolls and the Qumran Community.* Vol.

2 of *The Bible and the Dead Sea Scrolls: The Second Princeton Symposium on Judaism and Christian Origins*. Edited by James H. Charlesworth. Waco, TX: Baylor University Press, 2006.

Crawford, Sidnie W. *Rewriting Scripture in Second Temple Times*. Grand Rapids: Eerdmans, 2008.

Curtis, Michael. *Orientalism and Islam: European Thinkers on Oriental Despotism in the Middle East and India*. Cambridge: Cambridge University Press, 2009.

Davies, Philip R. "Halakhah at Qumran." Pages 37–50 in *A Tribute to Geza Vermes: Essays on Jewish and Christian Literature and History*. Edited by Philip R. Davies and Richard T. White. Sheffield: JSOT Press, 1990.

Davila, James R. "(How) Can We Tell If a Greek Apocryphon or Pseudepigraphon Has Been Translated from Hebrew or Aramaic?" *JSP* 15 (2005): 3–61.

Delcor, Mathias. "Psaumes de Salomon." *DBSup* 9/48:214–45.

Denis, Albert-Marie. *Fragmenta Pseudepigraphorum quae supersunt Graeca: Una cum historicorum et auctorum Judaeorum Hellenistarum fragmentis*. PVTG 3. Leiden: Brill, 1970.

———. *Introduction aux pseudépigraphes grecs d'Ancien Testament*. SVTP 1. Leiden: Brill, 1970.

Denis, Albert-Marie and Jean-Claude Haelewyck. *Introduction à la littérature religieuse judéo-hellénistique*. 2 vols. Turnhout: Brepols, 2000.

Dobbin, Robert, ed. *Epictetus: Discourses Book 1*. Clarendon Later Ancient Philosophers. Oxford: Clarendon Press, 1998.

Dupont-Sommer, André. *The Essene Writings from Qumran*. Translated by Géza Vermès. Oxford: Blackwell, 1961.

Eckhardt, Benedikt. *Ethnos und Herrschaft: Politische Figurationen judäischer Identität von Antiochos III. bis Herodes I*. SJ 72. Berlin: de Gruyter, 2013.

———. "Die jüdischen Gesandtschaften an Pompeius (63 v. Chr.) bei Diodor und Josephus." *Klio* 92 (2010): 388–410.

———. "PsSal 17, die Hasmonäer und der Herodompeius." *JSJ* 40 (2009): 465–92.

———. "Vom Volk zur Stadt? Ethnos und Polis im hellenistischen Orient." *JSJ* 45 (2014): 199–228.

Efron, Joshua. *Studies on the Hasmonean Period*. SJLA 39. Leiden: Brill, 1987.

Embry, Bradley J. "Solomon's Name as a Prophetic Hallmark in Jewish and Christian Texts." *Henoch* 28 (2006): 47–62.

———. "The *Psalms of Solomon* and the New Testament: Intertextuality and the Need for a Re-Evaluation." *JSP* 13 (2002): 99–136.
Eshel, Hanan. *The Dead Sea Scrolls and the Hasmonean State*. Grand Rapids: Eerdmans, 2008.
———. "The Two Historical Layers of Pesher Habakkuk." Pages 107–17 In *Northern Lights on the Dead Sea Scrolls: Proceedings of the Nordic Qumran Network 2003–2006*. Edited by Anders K. Petersen. STDJ 80. Leiden: Brill, 2009.
Fernández Marcos, Natalio. *The Septuagint in Context: Introduction to the Greek Version of the Bible*. Translated by Wilfred G. E. Watson. Leiden: Brill, 2000.
Fischer, Thomas. "Zum jüdischen Verfassungsstreit vor Pompejus (Diodor 40,2)." *ZPE* 91 (1975): 46–49.
Fitzmyer, Joseph A. *The One Who Is to Come*. Grand Rapids: Eerdmans, 2007.
Frankenberg, Wilhelm. *Die Datierung der Psalmen Salomos: Ein Beitrag zur jüdischen Geschichte*. BZAW 1. Giessen: Ricker, 1896.
Franklyn, Paul N. "The Cultic and Pious Climax of Eschatology in the *Psalms of Solomon*." *JSJ* 18 (1987): 1–17.
Frede, Dorothea. "Schicksal." *DNP* 11:156–58.
Fritzsche, Otto Fridolin, ed. *Libri Apocryphi Veteris Testamenti Graece*. Leipzig: Brockhaus, 1871.
Fuentes González, Pedro Pablo. "Épictète." *DPA* 3:106–51.
García Martínez, Florentino. "Parabiblical Literature from Qumran and the Canonical Process." *RevQ* 100 (2012): 525–56.
García Martínez, Florentino and Eibert J. C. Tigchelaar, eds. *The Dead Sea Scrolls Study Edition*. 2 volumes. Leiden: Brill, 1999.
Gawantka, Wilfried. *Die sogenannte Polis: Entstehung, Geschichte und Kritik der modernen althistorischen Grundbegriffe der griechische Staat die griechische Staatsidee die Polis*. Stuttgart: Steiner, 1985.
Gebhardt, Oscar von, ed. ΨΑΛΜΟΙ ΣΟΛΟΜΩΝΤΟΣ: *Die Psalmen Salomo's zum ersten Male mit Benutzung der Athoshandschriften und des Codex Casanatensis*. TUGAL 13/2. Leipzig: Hinrichs, 1895.
Geertz, Clifford. *The Interpretation of Cultures: Selected Essays*. New York: Basic Books, 1973.
Geiger, Eduard Ephraem. *Der Psalter Salomo's herausgegeben und erklärt*. Augsburg: Wolff, 1871.
Gillingham, Susan E. *The Poems and Psalms of the Hebrew Bible*. Oxford Bible Series. Oxford: Oxford University Press, 1994.

Gold, Barbara K. "Pompey and Theophanes of Mytilene." *AJP* 106 (1985): 312–27.
Goodblatt, David. *The Monarchic Principle: Studies in Jewish Self-Government in Antiquity*. TSAJ 38. Tübingen: Mohr Siebeck, 1994.
Gray, George B. "The *Psalms of Solomon*." *APOT* 2:625–52.
Gunkel, Hermann. *The Psalms: A Form-critical Introduction*. Translated by Thomas M. Horner. FBBS 19. Philadelphia: Fortress Press, 1967.
Hann, Robert R. "The Community of the Pious: The Social Setting of the *Psalms of Solomon*." *SR* 17 (1988): 169–89.
———. *The Manuscript History of the Psalms of Solomon*. SCS 13. Chico, CA: Scholars Press, 1982.
Hanson, Paul D. *The Dawn of Apocalyptic: The Historical and Sociological Roots of Jewish Apocalyptic Eschatology*. Rev. ed. Philadelphia: Fortress Press, 1979.
Harl, Marguerite. "Naoum," in *Les douze prophètes: Joël, Abdiou, Jonas, Naoum, Ambakoum, Sophonie*. La Bible d'Alexandrie 23.4–9. Paris: Cerf, 1999.
Harrington, Hannah K. "Purity," Pages 724–28 in *Encyclopedia of the Dead Sea Scrolls*. Edited by Lawrence H. Schiffman and James C. VanderKam. Oxford: Oxford University Press, 2000.
Harris, Rendel, and Alphonse Mingana. *The Odes and Psalms of Solomon*. 2 vols. Manchester: Manchester University Press, 1916–1920.
Heil, John Paul. "Those Now 'Asleep' (Not Dead) Must Be 'Awakened' for the Day of the Lord in 1 Thess 5.9–10." *NTS* 46 (2000): 464–71.
Hengel, Martin. *Die Zeloten: Untersuchungen zur jüdischen Freiheitsbewegung in der Zeit von Herodes I. bis 70 n. Chr*. AGJU 1. 2nd ed. Leiden: Brill, 1976.
———. *Judaism and Hellenism: Studies in their Encounter in Palestine during the Early Hellenistic Period*. Translated by John Bowden. 2 vols. London: SCM Press, 1974.
———. *Judentum und Hellenismus: Studien zu ihrer Begegnung unter besonderer Berücksichtigung Palästinas bis zur Mitte des 2. Jh.s v. Chr*. 3rd ed. WUNT 1/10. Tübingen: Mohr Siebeck, 1988.
Hilgenfeld, Adolf. "Die Psalmen Salomo's und die Himmelfahrt des Moses, griechisch hergestellt und erklärt." *ZWT* 11 (1868): 133–68.
Hoffmann, Christhard. *Juden und Judentum im Werk deutscher Althistoriker des 19. und 20. Jahrhunderts*. SJMT 9. Leiden: Brill, 1988.
Holladay, Carl R. *Fragments From Hellenistic Jewish Authors, Volume III, Aristobulus*. Atlanta: Scholars Press, 1995.

Holm-Nielsen, Svend. "Die Psalmen Salomos." *JSHRZ* 4:51–112.

———. "Religiöse Poesie des Spätjudentums." *ANRW* 19.1:152–86. Part 2, *Principat*, 19.1. Edited by W. Haase. Berlin: de Gruyter, 1979.

Holtz, Traugott. *Der erste Brief des Paulus an die Thessalonicher*. 3rd ed. EKKNT 13. Zürich: Benziger, 1998.

Horbury, William. "The Remembrance of God in the *Psalms of Solomon*." Pages 111–28 in *Memory in the Bible and Antiquity: The Fifth Durham-Tübingen Research Symposium (Durham, September 2004)*. Edited by Steven C. Barton, Loren T. Stuckenbruck, and Benjamin G. Wold. WUNT 1/212. Tübingen: Mohr Siebeck, 2007.

Horsley, Richard A. *Scribes, Visionaries, and Politics of Second Temple Judea*. Louisville: Westminster John Knox, 2007.

Horst, Pieter W. van der. *The Sentences of Pseudo-Phocylides*. SVTP 4. Leiden: Brill, 1978.

Houston, George. "Papyrological Evidence for Book Collections and Libraries in the Roman Empire." Pages 233–67 in *Ancient Literacies: The Culture of Reading in Greece and Rome*. Edited by William A. Johnson and Holt N. Parker. Oxford: Oxford University Press, 2009.

Jellinek, Georg. *Allgemeine Staatslehre*. Edited by Walter Jellinek. 3rd ed. Berlin: Häring, 1914.

Jonge, Marinus de. "The Expectation of the Future in the *Psalms of Solomon*." Pages 3–27 in *Jewish Eschatology, Early Christian Christology and the Testaments of the Twelve Patriarchs: Collected Essays of Marinus de Jonge*. NovTSup 63. Leiden: Brill, 1991.

Joosten, Jan. "On Aramaising Renderings in the Septuagint." Pages 587–600 in *Hamlet on a Hill: Semitic and Greek Studies Presented to Professor T. Muraoka on the Occasion of His Sixty-Fifth Birthday*. Edited by M. F. J. Baasten and W. T. Van Peursen. OLA 118. Leuven: Peeters, 2003.

———. "The Impact of the Septuagint Pentateuch on the Greek Psalms." Pages 197–205 in *XIII Congress of the International Organization for Septuagint and Cognate Studies: Ljubljana 2007*. Edited by Melvin K. H. Peters. SCS 55. Atlanta: Society of Biblical Literature, 2008.

———. "The Original Language and Historical Milieu of the Book of Judith." Pages *159–76 in *Meghillot: Studies in the Dead Sea Scrolls 5–6: A Festschrift for Devorah Dimant*. Edited by Moshe Bar-Asher and Emanuel Tov. Jerusalem: The Bialik Institute, 2007. Repr. pages 195–209 in *Collected Studies on the Septuagint: From Language to Interpretation and Beyond*. FAT 83. Tübingen: Mohr Siebeck, 2012.

Kaibel, Georg, ed. *Epigrammata Graeca: Ex lapidibus conlecta*. Berlin: Reimer, 1878.

Kaiser, Otto. "Beobachtungen zur Komposition und Redaktion der Psalmen Salomos." Pages 362–78 in *Das Manna fällt auch heute noch: Beiträge zur Geschichte und Theologie des Alten, Ersten Testaments: Festschrift für Erich Zenger*. Edited by Frank-Lothar Hossfeld and Ludger Schwienhorst-Schönberger. HBS 44. Freiburg: Herder, 2004.

———. *Gott, Mensch und Geschichte: Studien zum Verständnis des Menschen und seiner Geschichte in der klassischen, biblischen und nachbiblischen Literatur*. BZAW 413. Berlin: de Gruyter, 2010.

———. "Tradition und Gegenwart in den Psalmen Salomos." Pages 315–57 in *Prayer from Tobit to Qumran*. Edited by Renate Egger-Wenzel and Jeremy Corley. DCLY 2004. Berlin: de Gruyter, 2004.

Karrer, Martin and Wolfgang Kraus, eds. *Septuaginta Deutsch: Das griechische Alte Testament in deutscher Übersetzung*. 2nd ed. Stuttgart: Deutsche Bibelgesellschaft, 2010.

———, eds. *Septuaginta Deutsch: Erläuterungen und Kommentare*. 2 vols. Stuttgart: Deutsche Bibelgesellschaft, 2011.

Keel, Othmar. "Psalm 127: Ein Lobpreis auf Den, der Schlaf und Kinder gibt." Pages 155–63 in *Ein Gott, eine Offenbarung: Beiträge zur biblischen Exegese, Theologie und Spiritualität: Festschrift für Notker Füglister OSB zum 60. Geburtstag*. Edited by Friedrich V. Reiterer. Würzburg: Echter, 1991.

Kim, Heerak Christian. *Psalms of Solomon: A New Translation and Introduction*. Highland Park, NJ: Hermit Kingdom Press, 2008.

Kim Harkins, Angela. *Reading with an "I" to the Heavens: Looking at the Qumran Hodayot through the Lens of Visionary Traditions*. Ekstasis 3. Berlin: de Gruyter, 2012.

Kittel, Gerhard, and Gerhard Friedrich, eds. *Theological Dictionary of the New Testament*. Translated by Geoffrey W. Bromiley. 10 vols. Grand Rapids: Eerdmans, 1964–1976.

Klausner, Joseph. *The Messianic Idea in Israel: From Its Beginning to the Completion of the Mishnah*. Translated by William F. Stinespring. New York: Macmillan, 1955.

Klawans, Jonathan. "Idolatry, Incest, and Impurity: Moral Defilement in Ancient Judaism." *JSJ* 29 (1998): 391–415.

———. *Josephus and the Theologies of Ancient Judaism*. Oxford: Oxford University Press, 2012.

Kraus, Thomas J. "'Der Herr wird deinen Eingang und deinen Ausgang bewahren': Über Herkunft und Fortleben von LXX Psalm CXX 8A." *VT* 56 (2006), 58–75.

Kugler, Robert A. "Rewriting Rubrics: Sacrifice and the Religion of Qumran." Pages 90–112 in *Religion in the Dead Sea Scrolls*. Edited by John J. Collins and Robert A. Kugler. Grand Rapids: Eerdmans, 2000.

Kuhn, Karl Georg. *Die älteste Textgestalt der Psalmen Salomos: Insbesondere auf Grund der syrischen Übersetzung neu untersucht*. BWANT 73. Stuttgart: Kohlhammer, 1937.

Lane, William L. "Paul's Legacy from Pharisaic Tradition: Light from the *Psalms of Solomon*." *Concordia Journal* 8 (1982): 130–38.

Lange, Armin and Matthias Weigold. *Biblical Quotations and Allusions in Second Temple Jewish Literature*. JAJSup 5. Göttingen: Vandenhoeck & Ruprecht, 2011.

Laqueur, Richard. *Der jüdische Historiker Flavius Josephus: Ein biographischer Versuch auf neuer quellenkritischer Grundlage*. Giessen: Münchow Verlagsbuchhandlung, 1920.

Lattke, Michael. *Odes of Solomon: A Commentary*. Translated by Marianne Ehrhardt. Hermeneia. Minneapolis: Fortress Press, 2009.

Lautenschlager, Markus. "Εἴτε γρηγορῶμεν εἴτε καθεύδωμεν: Zum Verhältnis von Heiligung und Heil in 1Thess 5,10." *ZNW* 81 (1990): 39–59.

Le Goff, Jacques. "Les mentalités. Une histoire ambiguë." Pages 76–94 in *Nouveaux objets*. Vol. 3 of *Faire de l'histoire*. Edited by Jacques Le Goff and Pierre Nora. Paris: Gallimard, 1974.

Lenz, Friedrich Walter, ed. *Ovid: Die Liebeselegien: lateinisch und deutsch*. 3rd ed. SQAW 15. Berlin: Akademie, 1976.

Leo, Heinrich. *Vorlesungen über die Geschichte des jüdischen Staates*. Berlin: Duncker & Humblot, 1828.

Levenson, Jon D. *The Death and Resurrection of the Beloved Son: The Transformation of Child Sacrifice in Judaism and Christianity*. New Haven: Yale University Press, 1993.

Lim, Timothy H. *Pesharim*. CQS 3. Sheffield: Sheffield Academic, 2002.

Loader, William. *The Dead Sea Scrolls on Sexuality: Attitudes Towards Sexuality in Sectarian and Related Literature at Qumran*. Grand Rapids: Eerdmans, 2009.

———. *The Pseudepigrapha on Sexuality: Attitudes Towards Sexuality in Apocalypses, Testaments, Legends, Wisdom, and Related Literature*. Grand Rapids: Eerdmans, 2011.

Long, Arthur A. and David N. Sedley. *The Hellenistic Philosophers*. 2 vols. Cambridge: Cambridge University Press, 1987.

Long, George. *The Discourses of Epictetus*. London: Bell, 1890.

Lövestam, Evald. *Spiritual Wakefulness in the New Testament*. Translated by W. Francis Salisbury. LUÅ NS 55/3. Lund: Gleerup, 1963.

Lührmann, Dieter. "Paul and the Pharisaic Tradition." *JSNT* 36 (1989): 75–94.

Lundbom, Jack R. *Jeremiah 21–36: A New Translation with Introduction and Commentary*. AB 21B. New York: Doubleday, 2004.

Mack, Burton L. "Wisdom Makes a Difference: Alternatives to 'Messianic' Configurations." Pages 15–48 in *Judaisms and Their Messiahs at the Turn of the Christian Era*. Edited by Jacob Neusner, William S. Green, and Erich S. Frerichs. Cambridge: Cambridge University Press, 1987.

Magness, Jodi. *Stone and Dung, Oil and Spit: Jewish Daily Life in the Time of Jesus*. Grand Rapids: Eerdmans, 2011.

Maier, Paul L., ed. *The New Complete Works of Josephus*. Translated by William Whiston. Grand Rapids: Kregel, 1999.

Mason, Steve. *Flavius Josephus Translation and Commentary, Volume 1B: Judean War 2*. Leiden: Brill, 2008.

Mattlock, Michael D. *Discovering the Traditions of Prose Prayer in Early Jewish Literature*. LSTS 81. London: T&T Clark, 2012.

McAlpine, Thomas H. *Sleep, Divine and Human, in the Old Testament*. JSOTSup 38. Sheffield: Sheffield Academic, 1987.

Merkelbach, Reinhold and Martin L. West, eds. *Fragmenta Hesiodea*. Oxford: Clarendon, 1999.

Metso, Sarianna. "Qumran Community Structure and Terminology as Theological Statement." *RevQ* 20 (2002): 429–44.

Meyer, Eduard. *Die Entwicklung des Judentums und Jesus von Nazaret*. Vol. 2 of *Ursprung und Anfänge des Christentums*. 4th and 5th ed. Stuttgart: Cotta, 1925.

Meyers, Carol. L. and Eric M. Meyers. *Haggai and Zechariah 1–8: A New Translation with Introduction and Commentary*. AB 25B. New York: Doubleday, 1987.

Meyer-Zwiffelhoffer, Eckhard. "Orientalismus? Die Rolle des Alten Orients in der deutschen Altertumswissenschaft und Altertumsgeschichte des 19. Jahrhunderts (ca. 1785–1910)." Pages 501–94 in *Getrennte Wege? Kommunikation, Raum und Wahrnehmung in der Alten Welt*. Edited by Robert Rollinger, Andreas Luther, and Josef Wiesehöfer.

Oikumene: Studien zur antiken Universalgeschichte 2. Frankfurt am Main: Verlag Antike, 2007.
Michel, Otto. "Zur Lehre vom Todesschlaf." *ZNW* 35 (1936): 285–90.
Mitchell, Nathan D. *Liturgy and the Social Sciences*. Collegeville, MN: Liturgical Press, 1999.
Moulton, James H. "New Testament Greek in the light of Modern Discovery." Pages 60–97 in *The Language of the New Testament: Classic Essays*. Edited by Stanley E. Porter. JSNTSup 60. Sheffield: Sheffield Academic, 1991.
Mowinckel, Sigmund. *The Psalms in Israel's Worship*. Translated by D. R. Ap-Thomas. New York: Abingdon Press, 1962. Repr. Grand Rapids: Eerdmans, 2004.
Murphy, Catherine M. *Wealth in the Dead Sea Scrolls and the Qumran Community*. STDJ 40. Leiden: Brill, 2002.
Mussies, Gerard. "Greek in Palestine and the Diaspora." Pages 1040–64 in vol. 2 of *The Jewish People in the First Century: Historical Geography, Political History, Social, Cultural and Religious Life and Institutions*. Edited by Shemuel Safrai and Menahem Stern. CRINT 2. Assen: Van Gorcum, 1976.
Newman, Judith H. *Praying by the Book: The Scripturalization of Prayer in Second Temple Judaism*. EJL 14. Atlanta: Scholars Press, 1999.
Newsom, Carol A. *The Self as Symbolic Space: Constructing Identity and Community at Qumran*. STDJ 52. Leiden: Brill, 2004.
Nickel, Rainer, ed. *Xenophon: Kyrupädie: Die Erziehung des Kyros, griechisch–deutsch*. Sammlung Tusculum. Munich: Artemis und Winkler, 1992.
Nickelsburg, George W. E. *Jewish Literature between the Bible and the Mishnah: A Historical and Literary Introduction*. 2nd ed. Minneapolis: Fortress Press, 2005.
Nöldeke, Theodor. *Orientalische Skizzen*. Berlin: Paetel, 1892.
Oepke, Albrecht. "ἀνίστημι κτλ." *TDNT* 1:368–72.
———. "καθεύδω." *TDNT* 3:431–7.
Ogle, Marbury B. "The Sleep of Death." *MAAR* 11 (1933): 81–117.
Park, Joseph S. *Conception of Afterlife in Jewish Inscriptions: With Special Reference to Pauline Literature*. WUNT 2/121. Tübingen: Mohr Siebeck, 2000.
Perles, Felix. *Zur Erklärung der Psalmen Salomos*. SOLZ 5. Berlin: Peiser, 1902.

Pietersma, Albert and Benjamin G. Wright, eds. *A New English Translation of the Septuagint and the Other Greek Translations Traditionally Included Under That Title.* Oxford: Oxford University Press, 2007.

Pohlenz, Max. *Die Stoa: Geschichte einer geistigen Bewegung.* 7th ed. Göttingen: Vandenhoeck & Ruprecht, 1992.

Popović, Mladen. "The Jewish Revolt Against Rome: History, Sources and Perspectives." Pages 1–25 in *The Jewish Revolt Against Rome: Interdisciplinary Perspectives.* Edited by Mladen Popović. JSJSup 154. Leiden: Brill, 2011.

Portier-Young, Anathea E. *Apocalypse against Empire: Theologies of Resistance in Early Judaism.* Grand Rapids: Eerdmans, 2011.

Pouchelle, Patrick. "Critique textuelle et traduction du treizième *Psaume de Salomon.*" *JSJ* 42 (2011): 508–30.

Prato, Gian Luigi. *Il problema della teodicea in Ben Sira: Composizione dei contrari e richiamo alle origini.* AnBib 65. Rome: Biblical Institute Press, 1975.

Rad, Gerhard von. *The Message of the Prophets.* Translated by D. M. G. Stalker. London: Oliver & Boyd, 1965. Repr. San Francisco: HarperSanFrancisco, 1972.

Rahlfs, Alfred. *Verzeichnis der griechischen Handschriften des Alten Testaments, für das Septuaginta-Unternehmen aufgestellt.* MSU 2. Berlin: Weidmann, 1914.

Rahlfs, Alfred and Robert Hanhart, eds. *Septuaginta: Id est Vetus Testamentum graece iuxta LXX interpretes.* Rev. ed. Stuttgart: Deutsche Bibelgesellschaft, 2006.

Rappaport, Roy A. *Ritual and Religion in the Making of Humanity.* CSSCA 110. Cambridge: Cambridge University Press, 1999.

Regev, Eyal. *The Hasmoneans: Ideology, Archaeology, Identity.* JAJSup 10. Göttingen: Vandenhoeck & Ruprecht, 2013.

Rising, Thilo. "Senatorial Opposition to Pompey's Eastern Settlement: A Storm in a Teacup?" *Historia* 62 (2013): 196–221.

Rocca, Samuel. "Josephus and the *Psalms of Solomon* on Herod's Messianic Aspirations: An Interpretation." Pages 313–33 in *Making History: Josephus and Historical Method.* Edited by Zuleika Rogers. JSJSup 110. Leiden: Brill, 2007.

Röhrer-Ertl, Olav, Ferdinand Rohrhirsch, and Dietbert Hahn. "Über die Gräberfelder von Khirbet Qumran, inbesondere die Funde der Campagne 1956 I: Anthropologische Datenvorlage und Erstauswertung aufgrund der Collectio Kurth." *RevQ* 19 (1999): 3–46.

Rosen, Debra and Alison Salvesen. "A Note on the Qumran Temple Scroll 56:15–18 and Psalm of Solomon 17:33." *Journal of Jewish Studies* 38 (1987): 99–101.
Rothschild, Clare K. and Trevor W. Thompson. "Galen: 'On the Avoidance of Grief.'" *Early Christianity* 2 (2011): 110–29.
Ryle, Herbert R. and Montague R. James. ΨΑΛΜΟΙ ΣΟΛΟΜΩΝΤΟΣ: *Psalms of the Pharisees, Commonly Called the Psalms of Solomon*. Cambridge: Cambridge University Press, 1891.
Sanders, Ed P. "Covenantal Nomism Revisited." *JSQ* 16 (2009): 23–55.
Schams, Christina. *Jewish Scribes in the Second-Temple Period*. JSOTSup 291. Sheffield: Sheffield Academic, 1998.
Schiffman, Lawrence H. "The Dead Sea Scrolls and the Early History of Jewish Liturgy." Pages 33–48 in *The Synagogue in Late Antiquity*. Edited by Lee I. Levine. Philadelphia: American Schools of Oriental Research, 1987.
Scholtissek, Klaus. *Vollmacht im Alten Testament und im Judentum: Begriffs- und motivgeschichtliche Studien zu einem bibeltheologischen Thema*. Paderborner theologische Studien 24. Paderborn: Schöningh, 1993.
Schorch, Stefan. "The Septuagint and the Vocalization of the Hebrew Text of the Torah." Pages 41–54 In *XII Congress of the International Organization for Septuagint and Cognate Studies, Leiden 2004*. SCS 54. Edited by Melvin K. H. Peters. Atlanta: Society of Biblical Literature, 2006.
Schreiber, Stefan. "Can Wisdom be Prayer? Form and Function of the *Psalms of Solomon*." Pages 89–106 in *Literature or Liturgy? Early Christian Hymns and Prayers in their Literary and Liturgical Context in Antiquity*. Edited by Clemens Leonhard and Hermut Löhr. WUNT 2/363. Tübingen: Mohr Siebeck, 2014.
Schröter, Jens. "Gerechtigkeit und Barmherzigkeit: das Gottesbild der Psalmen Salomos in seinem Verhältnis zu Qumran und Paulus." *NTS* 44 (198): 557–77.
Schüpphaus, Joachim. *Die Psalmen Salomos: Ein Zeugnis Jerusalemer Theologie und Frömmigkeit in der Mitte des Vorchristlichen Jahrhunderts*. ALGHJ 7. Leiden: Brill, 1977.
Schürer, Emil. *Geschichte des jüdischen Volkes im Zeitalter Jesu Christi*. 3rd and 4th ed. 4 vols. Leipzig: Hinrichs, 1898–1902.
———. *The History of the Jewish People in the Age of Jesus Christ (175 BC–AD 135)*. Revised and edited by Géza Vermès and Fergus Millar. 2 vols. Edinburgh: T&T Clark, 1973.

Schwankl, Otto. *Licht und Finsternis: Ein metaphorisches Paradigma in den johanneischen Schriften.* HBS 5. Freiburg: Herder, 1995.
Scott, James C. *Weapons of the Weak: Everyday Forms of Peasant Resistance.* New Haven: Yale University Press, 1985.
Seitz, Christopher. *Prophecy and Hermeneutics: Towards a New Introduction to the Prophets.* Grand Rapids: Baker Academic, 2007.
Shantz, Colleen "Emotion, Cognition, and Social Change: A Consideration of Galatians 3:28." Pages 251–70 in *Mind, Morality and Magic: Cognitive Science Approaches in Biblical Studies.* Edited by István Czachesz and Risto Uro. Durham: Acumen, 2013.
Sharon, Nadav. "Setting the Stage: The Effects of the Roman Conquest and the Loss of Sovereignty." Pages 415–45 in *Was 70 CE a Watershed in Jewish History? On Jews and Judaism before and after the Destruction of the Second Temple.* Edited by Daniel R. Schwartz and Zeev Weiss. AJEC 78. Leiden: Brill, 2012.
———. "The End of the Hasmonean State and the Beginning of Roman Rule in the Land of Israel (67–37 BCE): History, Historiography, and Impact on Jewish Society and Religion." PhD diss., Hebrew University, 2013.
Steins, Georg. "Psalmoi Solomontos/Die Psalmen Salomos." Pages 1900–40 in vol. 2 of *Septuaginta Deutsch: Erläuterungen und Kommentare zum griechischen Alten Testament.* Edited by Martin Karrer and Wolfgang Kraus. Stuttgart: Deutsche Bibelgesellschaft, 2011.
Stemberger, Günter. "Was There a 'Mainstream Judaism' in the Late Second Temple Period?" *RRJ* 4 (2001): 189–208.
Steudel, Annette. "אחרית הימים in the Texts from Qumran." *RevQ* 16 (1993): 225–46.
Stone, Michael E. *Ancient Judaism: New Visions and Views.* Grand Rapids: Eerdmans, 2011.
———. "The Parabolic Use of Natural Order in Judaism of the Second Temple Age." Pages 298–308 in *Gilgul: Essays on Transformation, Revolution and Permanence in the History of Religions, Dedicated to R. J. Zwi Werblowsky.* Edited by Shaul Shaked, David Shulman, and Guy G. Stroumsa. SHR 50. Leiden: Brill, 1987.
Thackeray, Henry St. John. *Josephus, the Man and the Historian.* New York: Jewish Institute of Religion, 1929.
Thomson, James G. S. S. "Sleep: An Aspect of Jewish Anthropology." *VT* 5 (1955): 421–33.

Tov, Emanuel, "The Impact of the Septuagint Translation of the Torah on the Translation of Other Books." Pages 183–94 in *The Greek and Hebrew Bible. Collected Essays on the Septuagint*. VTSup 72. Leiden: Brill, 1999.

Tov, Emanuel and Robert A. Kraft, eds. *The Greek Minor Prophets Scroll from Nahal Hever (8HevXIIgr) (The Seiyal Collection I)*. DJD VIII. 2nd ed. Oxford: Clarendon, 1995.

Trafton, Joseph L. "Commentary on Genesis (4Q252)." Pages 203–19 in *Pesharim, Other Commentaries, and Related Documents*. Vol. 6b of *The Dead Sea Scrolls*. Edited by James H. Charlesworth. PTSDSSP. Louisville: Westminster John Knox, 2002.

———. *Reading Revelation: A Literary and Theological Commentary*. Reading the New Testament 12. Macon, GA: Smyth & Helwys, 2005.

———. Review of *Sinners and the Righteous: A Comparative Study of the Psalms of Solomon and Paul's Letters*, by Mikael Winninge. *RBL* (2009). http://www.bookreviews.org/pdf/2815_1253.pdf.

———. "Solomon, Psalms of." *ABD* 6:115–117.

———. "The Bible, the *Psalms of Solomon*, and Qumran." Page 427–46 in *The Dead Sea Scrolls and the Qumran Community*. Vol. 2 of *The Bible and the Dead Sea Scrolls: The Second Princeton Symposium on Judaism and Christian Origins*. Edited by James H. Charlesworth. Waco, TX: Baylor University Press, 2006.

———. "The *Psalms of Solomon* in Recent Research." *JSP* 12 (1994): 3–19.

———. "The *Psalms of Solomon*: New Light From the Syriac Version?" *JBL* 105 (1986): 227–37.

———. *The Syriac Version of the Psalms of Solomon: A Critical Evaluation*. SCS 11. Atlanta: Scholars Press, 1985.

Trampedach, Kai. "Between Hellenistic Monarchy and Jewish Theocracy: The Contested Legitimacy of Hasmonean Rule." Pages 231–59 in *The Splendors and Miseries of Ruling Alone: Encounters with Monarchy from Archaic Greece to the Hellenistic Mediterranean*. Edited by Nino Luraghi. SAM 1. Stuttgart: Steiner, 2013.

Tromp, Johannes. "The Sinners and the Lawless in *Psalm of Solomon* 17." *NovT* 35 (1993): 344–61.

Uhlig, Siegbert. "Das äthiopische Henochbuch." *JSHRZ* 5:461–80.

Unnik, Willem Cornelis van. *Das Selbstverständnis der jüdischen Diaspora in der hellenistisch-römischen Zeit*. Edited and revised by Pieter W. van der Horst. AGJU 17. Leiden: Brill, 1993.

VanderKam, James C. *From Joshua to Caiaphas: High Priests after the Exile*. Minneapolis: Fortress, 2004.
Vaux, Roland de. *Ancient Israel: Its Life and Institutions*. 2 vols. New York: McGraw-Hill, 1961. Repr. Grand Rapids: Eerdmans, 1997. Translated from *Les institutions de l'Ancien Testament*. Paris: Cerf, 1958–1960.
Viteau, Joseph. *Les Psaumes de Salomon: Introduction, texte grec et traduction, avec les principales variantes de la version syriaque par François Martin*. Documents pour l'étude de la Bible. Paris: Letouzey et Ané, 1911.
Vovelle, Michel. *Piété baroque et déchristianisation en Provence au XVIIIe siècle: Les attitudes devant la mort d'après les clauses des testaments*. Paris: Plon, 1973.
Ward, Grant. "The *Psalms of Solomon*: A Philological Analysis of the Greek and the Syriac Texts." PhD diss., Temple University, 1996.
Weinfeld, Moshe. "The Charge of Hypocrisy in Matthew 23 and in Jewish Sources." *Immanuel* 24/25 (1990): 52–58.
Weitzman, Steven. "Sensory Reform in Deuteronomy." Pages 123–39 in *The Formation of the Self in Antiquity*. Edited by David Brakke, Michael L. Satlow, and Steven Weitzman. Bloomington, IN: University of Indiana Press, 2005.
Wellhausen, Julius. *Die Pharisäer und die Sadducäer: Eine Untersuchung zur inneren jüdischen Geschichte*. Greifswald: Bamberg, 1874.
Werline, Rodney A. *Penitential Prayer in Second Temple Judaism: The Development of a Religious Institution*. EJL 13. Atlanta: Scholars Press, 1998.
———. "Prayer, Power and Politics in the Hebrew Bible." *Interpretation* 68 (2014): 5–16.
———. Review of *The Psalms of Solomon: A Critical Edition of the Greek Text*, by Robert B. Wright. *RBL* (2009). http://www.bookreviews.org/pdf/6010_6398.pdf.
———. "The Experience of God's *Paideia* in the *Psalms of Solomon*." Pages 17–44 in *Experientia, Volume 2: Linking Text and Experience*. Edited by Colleen Shantz and Rodney A. Werline. EJL 35. Atlanta: Society of Biblical Literature, 2012.
———. "The *Psalms of Solomon* and the Ideology of Rule." Pages 69–87 in *Conflicted Boundaries in Wisdom and Apocalypticism*. Edited by Lawrence M. Wills and Benjamin G. Wright III. SymS 35. Atlanta: Society of Biblical Literature, 2005.

Westermann, Claus. *The Psalms: Structure, Content and Message*. Minneapolis: Augsburg, 1980.
Whybray, Norman. *Reading the Psalms as a Book*. JSOTSup 222. Sheffield: Sheffield Academic, 1996.
Wicke-Reuter, Ursel. *Göttliche Providenz und menschliche Verantwortung bei Ben Sira und in der frühen Stoa*. BZAW 298. Berlin: de Gruyter, 2000.
Willitts, Joel. "Matthew and *Psalms of Solomon*'s Messianism: A Comparative Study in First-Century Messianology." *BBR* 22 (2012): 27–50.
———. Review of *The Psalms of Solomon: A Critical Edition of the Greek Text*, by Robert. B. Wright. *RBL* (2009). http://www.bookreviews.org/pdf/6010_6722.pdf.
Winninge, Mikael. *Sinners and the Righteous: A Comparative Study of the Psalms of Solomon and Paul's Letters*. ConBNT 26. Stockholm: Almqvist & Wiksell, 1995.
Wöhrle, Georg. *Hypnos, der Allbezwinger: Eine Studie zum literarischen Bild des Schlafes in der griechischen Antike*. PMTKA 53. Stuttgart: Steiner, 1995.
Wright, Robert B. "*Psalms of Solomon*." *OTP* 2:636–70.
———. *The Psalms of Solomon: A Critical Edition of the Greek Text*. JCTC 1. London: T&T Clark, 2007.
———. "The *Psalms of Solomon*: The Pharisees and the Essenes." Pages 136–54 in *1972 Proceedings for the International Organization for Septuagint and Cognate Studies and the Society of Biblical Literature Pseudepigrapha Seminar*. Edited by Robert A. Kraft. SCS 2. Missoula, MT: Society of Biblical Literature, 1972.
Zahn, Theodor. *Geschichte des Neutestamentlichen Kanons*. Erlangen: Deichert, 1890.
Ziegler, Joseph. "Die hexaplarische Bearbeitung des griechischen Sirach." *BZ* NS 4 (1960): 174–85.
———, ed. *Isaias*. SVTG 14. 2nd ed. Göttingen: Vandenhoeck & Ruprecht, 1967.
———, ed. *Sapientia Iesu Filii Sirach*. SVTG 12/2. 2nd ed. Göttingen: Vandenhoeck & Ruprecht, 1965.
———, ed. *Sapientia Salomonis*. SVTG 12/1. 2nd ed. Göttingen: Vandenhoeck & Ruprecht, 1967.

CONTRIBUTORS

Kenneth Atkinson is Professor of History at the University of Northern Iowa. He holds degrees from the University of Chicago (MDiv) and Temple University (MA, PhD). His books include *I Cried to the Lord: A Study of the Psalms of Solomon's Historical Background and Social Setting* (Brill), *An Intertextual Study of the Psalms of Solomon* (Mellen), and, most recently, *Queen Salome: Jerusalem's Warrior Monarch of the First Century B.C.E.* (McFarland).

Sven Behnke, born in 1982, studied Protestant Theology in universities at Frankfurt (Main), Heidelberg, and Mainz. Since 2009 he has worked as a Research Assistant at the Department for Old Testament Studies at the Faculty of Theology at Humboldt-University, Berlin. His forthcoming dissertation focuses on Ps. Sol. 14 and its traditio-historical background.

Eberhard Bons has studied theology, philosophy, and Romance languages at universities in Mainz, Tübingen, Rome (Gregorian University), and Frankfurt (Faculty of Sankt Georgen). In 1988 he obtained a PhD from the University of Mainz. In 1993, he also obtained a doctoral degree in theology from the Philosophisch-Theologische Hochschule St. Georgen, Frankfurt am Main. He received his habilitation in 2000 from the University of Strasbourg (France), where he teaches as a Professor of Old Testament Exegesis. He is member of the editorial board of *Septuaginta Deutsch* (Deutsche Bibelgesellschaft) and co-editor of the *Historical and Theological Lexicon of the Septuagint*. Moreover, he has edited several books on Septuagint studies, Old Testament prophetism, and biblical monotheism, such as *Der eine Gott und die fremden Kulte: Exklusive und inklusive Tendenzen in den biblischen Gottesvorstellungen* (Neukirchener Verlag).

Benedikt Eckhardt, born 1983, is a postdoctoral researcher in ancient history at the University of Bremen, Germany. He has published on Second

Temple Judaism and on the history of the Greco-Roman world. He is the author of *Ethnos und Herrschaft: Politische Figurationen judäischer Identität von Antiochos III. bis Herodes I.* (de Gruyter).

Brad Embry is Associate Professor of Hebrew Bible/Old Testament at Regent University. In addition to research interests in the Psalms of Solomon, he is currently editing a collection of essays on the Megilloth and writing a book on Gen 1–11. Some of his recent publications include work on the books of Ruth and Judges.

Jan Joosten (born 1959 in Ekeren, Belgium) studied theology in Brussels and Princeton and Semitic languages in Jerusalem. He earned a PhD in Semitic languages at the Hebrew University in 1989, a ThD at the Protestant Faculty in Brussels in 1994, and a HDR (*Habilitation à diriger des recherches*) in Strasbourg in 1994. From 1994 to 2014 he taught at the Faculty of Protestant Theology of the University of Strasbourg, first as Professor of Biblical Languages, and from 2004 as Professor of Old Testament. Since 2014 he has been the Regius Professor of Hebrew at the University of Oxford. He has been editor-in-chief of *Vetus Testamentum* since 2010, president of the International Organization for Septuagint and Cognate Studies since 2012, and editor, together with Eberhard Bons, of the *Historical and Theological Lexicon of the Septuagint*, to be published by Mohr Siebeck.

Patrick Pouchelle is assistant professor at the Centre Sèvres (Jesuit Faculty in Paris). He graduated with an engineering Diploma in 1996 and has worked on train motion control in several companies. In the meantime he studied theology and exegesis at the University of Strasbourg and obtained a doctoral degree in 2013. His dissertation, "Dieu éducateur: Une nouvelle approche d'un concept de la théologie biblique entre Bible Hébraïque, Septante et littérature grecque classique," will be published by Mohr Siebeck the FAT series.

Joseph L. Trafton is Distinguished University Professor of Religion at Western Kentucky University. The author of *The Syriac Version of the Psalms of Solomon: A Critical Evaluation* and *Reading Revelation: A Literary and Theological Commentary*, he has published numerous articles in the area of Second Temple Judaism, with a particular focus on the Psalms of Solomon.

Rodney A. Werline is Professor and the Marie and Leman Barnhill Endowed Chair in Religious Studies, and Director of the Center for Religious Studies, at Barton College, Wilson, NC. He is the author of *Penitential Prayer in Second Temple Judaism: The Development of a Religious Institution* and is a co-editor of Experientia, Volumes 1 and 2: *Inquiry into Religious Experience in Early Judaism and Early Christianity* and *Linking Text and Experience*.

Index of Ancient Sources

Hebrew Bible/Old Testament
(Including LXX and Revisers)

Genesis
- 2–3 — 56
- 2:21 — 45
- 31:40 — 106
- 43:29 — 170
- 49:10 — 157, 173, 191

Exodus
- 4:31 — 128
- 6:9 — 128
- 13:18 — 122
- 16:9 — 128
- 17:17 — 127
- 33:19 — 170

Leviticus
- 13:6 — 122
- 13:7 — 122
- 13:13 — 122
- 13:17 — 122
- 13:23 — 122
- 16 — 92
- 16:29 — 92
- 16:31 — 92
- 19:10 — 172
- 19:34 — 172
- 23:11–19 — 92
- 23:22 — 172
- 23:27 — 92
- 23:27–32 — 80
- 23:33 — 92
- 26 — 70
- 26:18 — 169

Numbers
- 6:25 — 170
- 24:17 — 173
- 25:4 — 35
- 29:7 — 92
- 29:7–11 — 80
- 34:17 — 168

Deuteronomy
- 8:5 — 127, 128, 169
- 8:18 — 66
- 10:19 — 172
- 13:17 — 170
- 14:28–29 — 172
- 17 — 173
- 17:8–10 — 169
- 17:14–15 — 161, 187
- 17:16–17 — 170, 188
- 21:18–20 — 169
- 24:19–21 — 172
- 26:11–13 — 172
- 28 — 140
- 28–30 — 70
- 28:25 — 36–37, 38
- 30:15 — 56
- 30:19 — 56

Joshua
- 1:8 — 106
- 19:51 — 168

2 Samuel [2 Kingdoms]
- 3:25 — 50

2 Samuel [2 Kingdoms] (cont.)

5:6–9	166
7:8–29	160, 164
7:12	163
7:12–13	165
11:1–12:16	172
12:22	170
19:10	120

1 Kings [3 Kingdoms]

1:21	111
2:10	111
5:5	165
8	140
12:11	129, 169
12:14	129, 169
17:17–24	112

2 Kings [4 Kingdoms]

4:18–37	112
7:7	169
13:20–21	112
13:23	170
22:8–23:3	167

1 Chronicles

17:7–27	160, 164
17:11	163

2 Chronicles

10:11	129, 169
10:14	129, 169
20:12	120
29:5	166
29:6	167
29:15	166
29:18	166–167
34:3	167
34:3–7	167
34:5	167
34:8	167
34:14–32	167

Ezra

9:15	140

Job

5:17	122
14:12	111
19:25–27	112

Psalms

1:2	106
2	159, 161, 187
6:2	170
9:13	170
18[17]	160
18[17]:3	50
18[17]:7	32, 49
18[17]:31	50
25[24]:16	170
26[25]:11	170
28[27]:1	49
30[29]:9	49
32[33]:3	145
33[34]:13	40
35[34]:22	49
39[38]:13	49
40[39]:3	145
45[44]	161, 187
51[50]	172
51[50]:2	172
53[52]	35
53[52]:6	34–35
72[71]	161, 187
73[72]	112, 113
86[85]:3	49
86[85]:5	50
86[85]:12	178
89[88]	160
91[90]:12	124
94[93]:12	122, 169
96[95]:1	145
98[97]:1	145
101[100]	160, 165
101[100]:3–5	165
101[100]:7	165
104[103]:19–23	106
109[108]:1	49
109[108]:6	120
110[109]	160

INDEX OF ANCIENT SOURCES

111[110]:1	178	11:5	171
114[113]:2	57	11:10	169–170
114[113]:5	122	11:11–16	168
119[118]:2	178	11:13–15	170
119[118]:10	178	14:1	170
119[118]:34	178	16:4–5	160
119[118]:58	178	19:14	34
119[118]:62	106	26:19	112
119[118]:69	178	30:1	118
119[118]:148	106	37:28	50
119[118]:145	178	42:10	145
121[120]:3	106	43:25	127
121[120]:8	50	49:8	169
127[126]	106	49:8–13	168
132[131]	160	49:26	140
132[131]:4	106	50:6	122
138[137]:1	178	53	75
144[143]:9	145	53:4	123
145[144]:9	123	53:10	112, 122
149:1	145	60:1–3	169
		60:4	168

Proverbs

3:6	123	Jeremiah	
3:11	117	7:6	172
3:12	122, 169	10:24	169
3:24	113	12:15	170
6:4	106	17:23	121
6:9–11	106	23:3	168
6:22	106	23:5	163
13:1	129–130	23:5–6	160
25:12	129	30[37]:9	160
		31[38]:7–14	168
Ecclesiastes		31[38]:26	113
8:8	57	33:14–16	160
		34[41]:17	36–37
Isaiah		51[28]:39	111
2:1–4	169		
5:3	120	Lamentations	
9:6–7	160	3:25	123
11	75, 159		
11:1–5	171	Ezekiel	
11:1–12:3	160	7:20	72
11:2	171	7:21	72
11:3	171	7:23	72
11:4	170, 171	7:24	72

INDEX OF ANCIENT SOURCES

Ezekiel (cont.)		
21:30	72	
22:26	72	
22:29	172	
26:6	140	
26:9	140	
26:16	140	
26:21	140	
30:8	140	
30:19	140	
30:25	140	
30:26	140	
31:18	111	
34:13–14	168	
34:20–22	163	
34:20–31	160	
34:23	163	
37–48	62	
37:1–14	112	
37:21–22	168	
37:21–28	160	
39:25	170	
44:23	72	
47:13–48:29	168	
47:22–23	172	

Daniel		
3:2	51	
5:11	107	
5:14	107	
9:7	140	
11:32	45	
12:2	113, 184	

Hosea		
2:23	170	
3:4–5	160	
3:5	62	
5:2	121	
10:10	119, 169, 184	

Amos		
5:15	170	
6:5	62	
7:1–6	70	

9:11	62, 163	
9:11–15	160	

Micah		
5:2–4	160	

Nahum		
1:7	123	

Habakkuk		
2:8	185	

Haggai		
1:1	165	
1:12–15	165	
2:20–23	160	

Zechariah		
1:17	170	
3:8–10	160	
6:12–15	160	
8:7–8	168	
8:20–22	169	
9:6–12	168	
9:9–13	161, 187	
12–13	62	
12:7–13:1	160	
12:10	76–77	
13:1–4	76	

Malachi		
3:5	172	

Apocryphal/Deuterocanonical Books

Baruch		
1:15	141	
2:6	141	
2:15	140	

Prayer of Azariah		
4	140	
12–14	140	

INDEX OF ANCIENT SOURCES

1 Maccabees
  2:1 — 88
  6:10 — 106–107
  6:12 — 107

2 Maccabees
  6:12 — 131–132
  12:43–45 — 112

Sirach
  3:27 — 118
  5:5 — 118
  9:13 — 51
  10:1 — 129
  15:11–17 — 56–57
  23:2–3 — 125–126, 131
  51:26 — 120

Tobit
  3:2 — 140

Pseudepigrapha

2 Baruch
  30:1 — 112
  36:11 — 112

1 Enoch
  1:8 — 148
  5:5–9 — 148
  39:12–13 — 107
  40:2 — 107
  49:3 — 112
  61:12 — 107
  61:12–13 — 184
  91:10 — 112
  92:3 — 112
  100:5 — 112

Psalms of Solomon
  1 — 18, 20, 68, 142–143, 173
  1:1 — 32, 49
  1:1–3 — 73
  1:3–4 — 190
  1:6 — 84, 85, 86, 178
  1:7–8 — 88–89, 90
  1:8 — 83, 85, 90, 167, 178, 190
  2 — 14, 17, 18, 19, 68–72, 94, 104, 173
  2:1 — 49
  2:1–3 — 190
  2:1–5 — 73
  2:1–9 — 69–70
  2:2 — 72, 90, 167
  2:3 — 72, 85, 87, 89, 167
  2:3–4 — 90
  2:3–14 — 15
  2:6 — 87, 178
  2:7 — 143
  2:8 — 50, 72
  2:9 — 49
  2:9–10 — 178
  2:10 — 70
  2:11–13 — 90
  2:11–14 — 70, 71–72
  2:12 — 35
  2:13 — 72, 85, 87, 190
  2:15 — 70–71
  2:15–21 — 143
  2:17 — 89, 127
  2:19–23 — 73
  2:21 — 190
  2:22–36 — 83
  2:23 — 190
  2:25 — 72
  2:25–27 — 190
  2:26 — 18
  2:26–27 — 71
  2:28–31 — 83
  2:30 — 164
  2:30–31 — 103–104
  2:30–33 — 184
  2:31 — 97, 98, 110, 183, 184
  2:32 — 164
  2:33–37 — 143
  2:34 — 190
  2:36 — 123
  3 — 94, 104, 116–19, 121, 124, 145, 146
  3:1 — 98
  3:1–2 — 97, 101, 102, 107, 116, 145, 183
  3:2 — 98, 105, 107, 178, 190

Psalms of Solomon (cont.)

Reference	Pages
3:3	91, 116, 145, 146
3:4	84, 115, 116–117, 173
3:5	118
3:5–6	145, 190
3:5–11	118
3:6	145
3:6–8	186
3:7	164, 186
3:7–8	83, 91–92, 119, 178
3:8	92, 145
3:9	118, 145
3:10	98, 118
3:11	127, 145
3:12	98
4	11, 13, 18, 20, 35, 99, 104, 148, 183
4:1	83
4:2–3	190
4:3	51
4:4	85
4:5	90
4:6	45, 164
4:6–7	148
4:7	89
4:8	164
4:9–10	190
4:9–13	90
4:9–22	135
4:11	164
4:11–12	190
4:12	164
4:12–13	178
4:13	145
4:14	50
4:14–22	148–149
4:15	98, 183
4:15–16	97, 98–101, 183
4:15–17	190
4:19	34–35
4:20	40, 45
4:21	83
4:22	45, 164
4:22–23	190
4:23–26	83
4:24	164
5	94
5:1	91
5:2	49, 84, 85, 86
5:4	49
5:6	186
5:8	49
5:11	84, 85
5:12	50
5:16	51
5:18	73
6	104
6:1–2	91
6:1–6	145
6:3–4	94, 99–101, 183
6:3	178
6:4	98, 104, 105
6:5	190
6:5–6	178
7	18, 68, 119–20, 144
7:1–2	73
7:2	82, 90, 119, 184
7:3	84, 115, 173
7:6	120
7:6–7	91
7:7	50, 190
7:8	73, 81, 120, 127
7:8–10	186, 190
7:9	84, 115, 120
7:10	73
8	14, 17, 19, 68, 86–87, 90, 120–21, 143–44, 173
8:3	49, 164
8:3–6	144
8:4	73, 190
8:5	164
8:7–8	144
8:8	89
8:8–13	15
8:9	72
8:9–10	85
8:9–13	88, 90
8:10	190
8:10–12	88, 188
8:11	50
8:11–13	89

8:12	90, 167, 190	10:4	73
8:12–13	85	10:5–8	73
8:13	16 n. 29, 83	10:6	84, 85
8:14	34, 178	10:6–7	190
8:15	164	10:7	173
8:20	87	10:8	149
8:20–22	15	11	43, 73
8:21	87	11:1	73
8:21–22	190	11:4	190
8:22	167	11:5	190
8:23	43	11:6–9	73
8:23–26	144	11:7	81
8:24	120, 164	11:7–11	186
8:25	50	11:8	98
8:26	73, 84, 115, 120, 164	11:8–9	149
8:27–29	190	12:3	190
8:27–32	144	12:4	149
8:28	43, 73	12:4–6	83
8:29	84, 115, 121	12:6	73, 149
8:30	50	13	94, 124–27
9	38, 73	13:1–3	124
9:1	38	13:1–5	145
9:1–2	73, 186	13:3	32, 40
9:1–11	144	13:5	145
9:2	36–37, 186, 190	13:5–8	178
9:2–3	43	13:7	83, 84, 115, 129, 186
9:3	89	13:7–8	124–25
9:4	39, 51–58, 179–81, 190	13:7–9	129
9:5	190	13:8	115, 173
9:6	178	13:9	115, 127, 129
9:6–7	82, 186	13:10	83, 84, 115, 186, 190
9:8	73, 190	13:10–12	83
9:8–11	81, 144, 186	13:11	127, 186
9:9	73	14	94
9:9–11	81	14:1	115
9:10	73, 178, 190	14:1–5	145
9:11	73, 149	14:2–4	73
10	94, 121–24	14:2–5	186
10:1	186	14:3	190
10:1–2	121–122	14:5	39, 73, 81
10:1–3	124	14:7	83
10:1–4	84, 145	14:8	89
10:2	115	14:9–10	83
10:3	115, 123–24	15	94, 146
10:3–5	190	15:1–9	145

Psalms of Solomon (cont.)

15:1	39, 40, 49, 73, 84, 85, 86, 91
15:2–4	146, 186
15:5	164
15:12–13	83
16	94, 104, 128, 146
16:1	45, 98
16:1–4	97, 101–03, 110, 146–47, 183
16:3	73
16:4	84, 98, 105, 107
16:5–11	147
16:11	115, 173, 186
16:11–15	84
16:13	115, 128
16:14	164
16:18–19	90
17	5, 14, 18, 20, 24, 60, 62, 68, 74–75, 77, 94, 129, 155–74, 187–88, 191
17:3	14 n. 24, 169
17:4	73, 81, 163, 186
17:4–6	84–85, 87
17:5	162, 164, 168, 186
17:5–6	190
17:6	20–21 n. 46, 162, 175
17:6–9	178
17:7	18, 162, 169
17:9	165
17:11	162, 167
17:11–15	169
17:12	18, 168, 170
17:13	190
17:13–14	167
17:14	16 n. 29
17:14–15	15, 167
17:15	83
17:15–18	168
17:16	94, 173
17:16–18	43–44
17:19	40
17:19–20	167
17:20	168, 170
17:21	73, 98, 163, 164
17:21–25	82
17:22	164, 166, 169, 170, 171, 187
17:22–24	190
17:22–25	187
17:22–31	73
17:23	164, 170, 171
17:23–24	82
17:24	82, 164, 170
17:24–25	169
17:25	164, 170
17:26	163, 164, 168, 171
17:26–46	187
17:27	165, 166
17:28	168, 171–72
17:29	94, 163, 164, 171
17:30	166, 169, 187
17:30–31	82
17:31	168, 190
17:32	151, 160, 163, 171
17:33	170, 187
17:34	169, 171
17:35	164, 166, 171
17:36	164, 170, 172, 187
17:37	166, 171
17:38	166, 171
17:39	171
17:40	164, 171
17:41	164, 171
17:42	73, 98, 115, 129, 130, 164, 169, 171
17:43	40, 163, 164, 169, 171
17:44	168, 173
17:44–45	73
17:45	149
18	68, 129–130, 150–152, 163
18:1	73, 151
18:2	85, 86
18:2–3	151
18:3	73, 84
18:4	51, 83, 115, 129, 151
18:5	51, 73, 151
18:5–9	151
18:6–7	151
18:7	115, 130
18:9	94
18:10–12	151–152
18:11–12	152

INDEX OF ANCIENT SOURCES

Dead Sea Scrolls

CD (Cairo Damascus Document) 187
  IV, 15–18   88, 188

1QH (Thanksgiving Hymns)
  XXI, 4–7   184

1QH^a (Thanksgiving Hymns^a)
  XIV, 37   184

1QpHab (Pesher Habakkuk)
  VII, 9–14   185
  VIII, 8   86
  IX, 3–4   185
  IX, 4–7   20 n. 42
  XI, 4   86

1QS (Rule of the Community)
  I, 2b–11a   150
  I, 25b–26   141
  II, 1b–9   148

4Q161 (4QIsaiah Pesher^a)   187

4Q162 (4QIsaiah Pesher^b)
  II, 6–7   19 n. 41
  II, 9   19 n. 41
  II, 10   19 n. 41

4Q169 (4QNahum Pesher)   17, 20 n. 42

4Q174 (4QFlorilegium)   62, 187

4Q246 (4QAramaic Apocalypse)   157, 187, 191

4Q252 (4QCommentary on Genesis) 187

4Q285 (4QSefer ha-Milhamah)   187
  fr. 5   62

4Q333 (4QHistorical Text E)   18 n. 35

4Q504 (4Qwords of the Luminaries^a)
  fr. 1–2, V, 6b–11a   140
  fr. 1–2, VI, 3   141

4Q521 (4QMessianic Apocalypse)   187
11Q19 (11QTemple^a)   187
  LVI, 15   188

MMT (Miqṣat Maʿaśê ha-Torah)   22, 86–87, 186

Ancient Jewish Writers

Josephus, *Antiquitates Judaicae*
  13.171–173   180
  13.245   176
  13.288–292   21
  14.41–45   22, 175
  14.77   17

Josephus, *Bellum Judaicum*
  2.119   180
  2.164–165   54, 180

New Testament

Matthew
  24:42   110
  25:13   110
  26:41–46   109
  26:47–56   109

Mark
  1:35   109
  5:35–43   112
  5:39   112
  13:35   110
  13:37   110

Luke
  6:12   109

John
  11:11–14   112
  19:34   77

Romans
13:11–4   108

1 Corinthians
16:13   109

1 Thessalonians
5:1–11   108–109
5:6   109
5.10   109

Revelation
1:7   77
5:9   145
14:3   145
19:11   120

GRECO-ROMAN LITERATURE

Arrian, *Epicteti dissertations*
1.1.5   54
1.25.2–3   55
4.10.30   55

Cassius Dio, *Historia romana*
37.49.4–5   23

Diodorus Siculus, *Bibliotheca historica*
40.2   22, 175
40.3   24, 176
40.5–6   176

Diogenes Laërtius, *Vitae philosophorum*
7.105   53

Homer, *Ilias*
14.165   106
14.253   106
16.672

Ovid, *Amores*
2.9.41   111

Plutarch, *Lucullus*
42.6   23

Plutarch, *Pompeius*
46.3   23

Quintilian, *Institutio oratoria*
1.8–9   181

Stobaeus, *Eclogae*
2.7.7   53

Strabo, *Geographica*
12.3.34   176

Xenophon, *Cyropaedia*
8.7.21   110 n. 29

GREEK INSCRIPTIONS

IGUR 3
1310   110

RABBINIC WORKS

b. Berakot
5a   132

Index of Modern Authors

Aalen, Sverre 104, 108
Albrecht, Felix 2
Asad, Talal 136–38, 141, 142, 145, 150, 153
Atkinson, Kenneth 2–3, 4–5, 15–16, 17, 18, 21, 52, 61, 64, 65, 68, 79, 81, 82, 84, 86, 87, 90, 91, 92, 94, 115, 125, 133, 134, 148, 157, 159, 160, 177, 178, 181, 182, 186
Austin, John L. 147
Baars, Willem 20–21, 94
Bakhtin, Mikhail 138
Baltrusch, Ernst 26
Balz, Horst 105, 107, 112
Bar-Kochva, Bezalel 23
Barthélemy, Dominique 44
Baumgarten, Albert I. 80
Bautch, Richard 140
Beentjes, Pancratius C. 56
Begrich, Joachim 33, 174
Behnke, Sven 5, 131, 183–84
Bell, Catherine 147, 152
Ben-Dov, Jonathan 87
Berrin, Shani 17–18, 74, 78
Bevan, Edwyn R. 27
Blackburn, Rollin J. 3
Boda, Mark J. 140
Bonhöffer, Adolf 54
Bons, Eberhard 4, 39, 40, 41, 121, 179–81, 188
Bourdieu, Pierre 137, 138, 141
Brandt, Ahasver von 7
Braun, Herbert 83
Bringmann, Klaus 14
Brooke, George 61–62, 95
Brooks, Ernest W. 190
Brueggemann, Walter 63
Burr, Viktor 13–14
Collins, John J. 9, 21, 42, 65, 157, 158, 187
Crawford, Sidnie W. 93
Curtis, Michael 27
Davies, Philip R. 80
Davila, James R. 189
Delcor, Matthias 31
Denis, Albert-Marie 50, 53, 180
Dobbin, Robert 53, 55
Dupont-Sommer, André 134
Eckhardt, Benedikt 4, 16, 22, 23, 27, 156, 162, 175–77
Efron, Joshua 8–9, 23, 25–26, 29, 31
Embry, Bradley J. 4, 63, 65, 77, 181–83
Eshel, Hanan 18, 185
Fernández Marcos, Natalio 44
Fischer, Thomas 176
Fitzmyer, Joseph A. 157, 158, 159, 160, 161
Foucault, Michel 138
Frankenberg, Wilhelm 32, 39, 117
Franklyn, Paul N. 92, 134, 150–51, 153
Frede, Dorothea 52
Fritzsche, Otto Fridolin 122
Fuentes González, Pedro Pablo 54
García Martínez, Florentino 94
Gawantka, Wilfried 27
Gebhardt, Oscar von 52, 98, 126
Geertz, Clifford 143
Geiger, Eduard Ephraem 57, 99, 102, 125
Gillingham, Susan E. 60

INDEX OF MODERN AUTHORS

Gold, Barbara K.	24	Laqueur, Richard	176
Goodblatt, David	23	Lattke, Michael	183
Gray, George B.	117, 125, 158	Lautenschlager, Markus	109
Gunkel, Hermann	63	Le Goff, Jacques	8
Haelewyck, Jean-Claude	50, 53	Lenz, Friedrich Walter	111
Hahn, Dietbert	86	Leo, Heinrich	13, 14
Hann, Robert R.	3, 52, 85, 92, 93, 95, 134, 189	Levenson, Jon D.	73
		Lim, Timothy H.	94
Hanson, Paul D.	65	Loader, William	89
Harl, Marguerite	123	Long, Arthur A.	53
Harrington, Hannah K.	80	Long, George	55
Harris, Rendel	33	Lövestam, Evald	108, 109
Heil, John Paul	108–9	Lührmann, Dieter	92, 118, 133
Hengel, Martin	13, 53	Lundbom, Jack R.	160
Hilgenfeld, Adolf	31, 177	Mack, Burton L.	94–95
Hitzig, Ferdinand	51	Magness, Jodi	80, 92
Hoffmann, Christhard	10, 28	Maier, Paul	54
Holladay, Carl R.	180	Mason, Steve	180, 190
Holland, Dorothy	138	Mattlock, Michael D.	140
Holm-Nielsen, Svend	90, 95, 122, 123, 125	Mauss, Marcel	137, 141, 145
		McAlpine, Thomas H.	105, 106
Holz, Traugott	109	Merkelbach, Reinhold	110
Horbury, William	66–67, 77	Metso, Sarianna	19
Horsley, Richard	134–135	Meyer, Eduard	9, 10–12, 13, 14, 24, 26, 28
Horst, Pieter W. van der	180		
Houston, George	179	Meyers, Carol L.	160
James, Montague R.	3, 32, 45, 51, 56, 92, 115, 117–18, 122–23, 125, 133, 134, 143, 155, 156, 158, 160, 177	Meyers, Eric M.	160
		Meyer-Zwiffelhoffer, Eckhard	27
		Michel, Otto	112
Jellinek, Georg	27	Mingana, Alphonse	33
Jonge, Marinus de	59–60	Mitchell, Nathan D.	147
Joosten, Jan	4, 34, 41, 50, 57, 117, 177–79, 188, 189	Moulton, James H.	41–42
		Mowinckel, Sigmund	63
Kaiser, Otto	16, 19, 20, 21, 115–16	Murphy, Catherine M.	86
Keel, Othmar	106	Mussies, Gerard	50
Kim Harkins, Angela	153	Newman, Judith H.	140
Kim, Christian Heerak	31	Newsom, Carol A.	138
Klausner, Joseph	160	Nickelsburg, George W. E.	64, 68, 136
Klawans, Jonathan	81, 89	Nöldeke, Theodor	28
Kraft, Robert A.	44	Oepke, Albrecht	109, 112
Kraus, Thomas J.	50	Ogle, Marbury B.	111
Kugler, Robert A.	91	Park, Joseph S.	113
Kuhn, Karl Georg	14, 21	Perles, Felix	53, 57
Lane, William L.	133, 155–56	Pohlenz, Max	53
Lange, Armin	49	Popović, Mladen	177

INDEX OF MODERN AUTHORS

Portier-Young, Anathea E. 135
Pouchelle, Patrick 5, 66, 125, 184–85
Prato, Gian Luigi 56
Rad, Gerhard von 60–61, 75
Rahlfs, Alfred 181
Rappaport, Roy 141–42, 150
Regev, Eyal 16, 23, 86, 177
Rising, Thilo 23
Rocca, Samuel 22
Röhrer-Ertl, Orlav 86
Rohrhirsch, Ferdinand 86
Rosen, Debra and Alison Salvesen 188
Rothschild, Clare K. 179
Ryle, Herbert R. 3, 32, 45, 51, 56, 92, 115, 117–18, 122–23, 125, 133, 134, 143, 155, 156, 158, 160, 177
Sanders, Ed P. 96
Saulnier, Stéphane 87
Schams, Christina 135
Schiffman, Lawrence H. 91
Scholtisssek, Klaus 54
Schorch, Stefan 189
Schreiber, Stefan 17
Schrenk, Gottlob 57
Schröter, Jens 2
Schüpphaus, Joachim 51, 52, 82, 143, 151
Schürer, Emil 14
Schwankel, Otto 108
Scott, James C. 134, 135
Sedley, David N. 53
Seitz, Christopher 60–61
Shantz, Colleen 153
Sharon, Nadav 16, 23
Steins, Georg 99–100, 125
Stemberger, Günter 17
Steudel, Annette 19
Stone, Michael E. 152, 183
Thackeray, Henry St. John 180
Thompson, Trevor W. 179
Thomson, James G. S. S. 112
Tov, Emanuel 44, 51
Trafton Joseph L. 1–2, 5, 16, 31, 32, 54, 117, 122, 129, 156, 157, 159, 162, 163, 164, 166, 168, 170, 171, 174, 187–88, 189, 190, 191
Trampedach, Kai 14–15
Tromp, Johannes 87
Uhlig, Siegbert 107
Unnik, Willem Cornelis van 37, 43
VanderKam, James C. 21
Vaux, Roland de 80, 92
Viteau, Joseph 16, 18, 49, 50, 51, 92, 93, 124, 125, 180
Vovelle, Michel 8
Ward, Grant 32, 33
Weigold, Matthias 49
Weinfeld, Moshe 45
Weitzmann, Steven 139
Wellhausen, Julius 9, 10, 12–13, 14, 22, 24–26, 28, 31, 50
Werline, Rodney A. 2, 3, 5, 64–65, 66–67, 77, 87–88, 93, 115–16, 134–36, 140, 145, 147, 183, 185–87
West, Martin L. 110
Westermann, Claus 63
Whybray, Norman 63
Wicke-Reuter, Ursel 56
Willits, Joel 2, 77, 78
Winninge, Mikael 2, 3, 51, 52, 83, 84, 92, 116, 118, 119, 121, 123, 125, 156–57, 159, 162
Wöhrle, Georg 105, 106, 110
Wright, Robert B. 1–2, 3, 31, 52, 53, 61, 65–66, 68, 69, 70, 72, 88, 102, 125, 139, 147, 151, 157, 168, 182
Zahn, Theodor 182
Ziegler, Joseph 182

www.ingramcontent.com/pod-product-compliance
Lightning Source LLC
Chambersburg PA
CBHW031709230426
43668CB00006B/163